Hedge Funds

A Resource for Investors

Wiley Finance Series

Hedge Funds

A Resource for Investors

Simone Borla
and
Denis Masetti

WILEY

Copyright © 2003   John Wiley & Sons Ltd, The Atrium, Southern Gate, Chichester,
West Sussex PO19 8SQ, England

Telephone   (+44) 1243 779777

Email (for orders and customer service enquiries): cs-books@wiley.co.uk
Visit our Home Page on www.wileyeurope.com or www.wiley.com

This publication is designed to provide accurate and authoritative information in regard to the
subject matter covered. It is sold on the understanding that the Publisher is not engaged in
rendering professional services. If professional advice or other expert assistance is required, the
services of a competent professional should be sought.

Other Wiley Editorial Offices

John Wiley & Sons Inc., 111 River Street, Hoboken, NJ 07030, USA

Jossey-Bass, 989 Market Street, San Francisco, CA 94103-1741, USA

Wiley-VCH Verlag GmbH, Boschstr. 12, D-69469 Weinheim, Germany

John Wiley & Sons Australia Ltd, 33 Park Road, Milton, Queensland 4064, Australia

John Wiley & Sons (Asia) Pte Ltd, 2 Clementi Loop #02-01, Jin Xing Distripark, Singapore 129809

John Wiley & Sons Canada Ltd, 22 Worcester Road, Etobicoke, Ontario, Canada M9W 1L1

Wiley also publishes its books in a variety of electronic formats. Some content that appears in print
may not be available in electronic books.

Library of Congress Cataloging-in-Publication Data

Borla, Simone.
     Hedge funds : a resource for investors/Simone Borla and Denis Masetti.
        p. cm.—(Wiley finance series)
     Includes index.
     ISBN 0-470-85095-7 (paper : alk. paper)
        1. Hedge funds.   2. Hedge funds—European Union countries.   I. Masetti, Denis.   II. Title.
III. Series.
     HG4530 B666   2003
     332.64′5—dc21   2002038053

British Library Cataloguing in Publication Data

A catalogue record for this book is available from the British Library

ISBN 0-470-85095-7

Typeset in 10/12pt Times by TechBooks, New Delhi, India
Printed and bound in Great Britain by Antony Rowe Ltd, Chippenham, Wiltshire
This book is printed on acid-free paper responsibly manufactured from sustainable forestry
in which at least two trees are planted for each one used for paper production.

In every phase of the market cycle
even the most difficult
when everything is about to crash
when pessimism pervades all
and of opportunities, there appear to be none

but opportunities do exist
and space for development
of new financial services
which enable us
to conquer new frontiers

there is always
a product
for each moment
now is the time
of hedge funds

thanks to visionaries
who through genius and courage
transform these opportunities
into concrete advantages
for the market and for the public

Contents

About the Authors

SIMONE BORLA is Managing Director of JD Farrods Securities Ltd., a company that has developed a global network for the distribution of innovative financial products and services to institutions. In Italy he created the distribution network of Lombard International Assurance and launched the first Unit Linked product on the market. In the past he worked for companies like Lombard International Assurance, JP Morgan and Philip Morris.

DENIS MASETTI has been working in the financial services industry for over twenty years with companies such as Dival, ING, Flemings and more recently GIA JD Farrods, a company specialising in the distribution of alternative investments. In 1995 Masetti founded Bluerating.com, a company providing rating to investment products and in 2001 Bluehedge.com, a website offering state-of-the-art information on hedge funds. He is the Editor of Hedge, the first Italian magazine on alternative investments.

A Word of Thanks

A warm thank you to all our partners who work with us on a daily basis to develop ideas and implement innovative projects. Many thanks to Rahel Tumzghi and Enrico Ferrari for helping us to put together the English version of this book.

We would also like to thank a number of friends and opinion leaders who each day help us grow more knowledgeable. In particular, we extend our gratitude to:

Bobby Aguirre, Chairman of Banco Filipino for introducing us to the game of kings, polo, and his generosity.

Emanuel Arbib, CEO of IAM plc, a pioneer in London's hedge fund market.

Giovanni Beliossi, advisor at AIMA, for his excellence as a promoter of alternative investments.

Samuele Camellini, Managing Director of Bluerating.com, a true expert in fund analysis.

Emanuele Carluccio, President of Benchmark & Style, a true expert in the world of asset management.

Paolo Catafalmo, Managing Director of Invesclub SGR, a leader in the Italian marketplace for alternative investments.

Max Clapham, publisher of *Portfolio International* and *Hedge Funds International* for his dynamism and support.

Jose Manuel Espirito Santo, President of Espirito Santo Financial Consultants, for his extensive international experience in private banking.

Ricardo Espirito Santo Silva Salgado, President of Banco Espirito Santo for his grand vision of distribution channels in the world of banking.

Martin Gilbert, CEO of Aberdeen Asset Management plc. For having taught us how quickly company growth can be achieved.

Roberto Giuffrida, Director of Permal.

Simon Hopkins, CEO of Global Fund Analysis, for his skill and professionalism.

Sohail Jaffer, Managing Director of Premium Select Lux, leader in the application of multi-manager funds of funds.

Bedros Kazandjan, who helped us penetrate the Middle East market.

Olivier Le Grand, CEO of Banque Cortal, for having succeeded in becoming the European leader in online fund distribution.

Francesco Micheli, President of e.biscom, market expert and innovator.

Massimo Monti, partner at Rasini & Co., who has been active for many years in the areas of consultancy and information.

Michael Nessim, Managing Director of Michael Nessim Associates plc.

Tushar Patel, institutional advisor for the Middle East for GIA JD Farrods Ltd.

Todd Robinson, CEO of LPL Financial Services, for having shown that with technology and innovative systems, you can dominate the distribution of financial services.

Jeremy Soames, Managing Director of Marsh Private Client Services.

John Stone, Chairman of Lombard International Assurance, for his great European vision.

Giorgio Strini, President of BSI Monaco who has comprehensively demonstrated that coupling experience and dynamism leads to success.

Alberto Van Der Mye, institutional advisor for Latin America and Emerging Markets for GIA JD Farrods Ltd for the enthusiasm that he can transmit in selling hedge funds.

Thanks to our families for patiently supporting us in our business commitments. Thank you also to all optimists who in being positive and proactive inspire us to grow, convince us to take new ideas and projects forward and become active participants in the imminent boom.

Denis Masetti and Simon Borla

Introduction

Finding a universally accepted definition of what a hedge fund is has proved somewhat difficult over the years. Lore has it that the first hedge fund was created in 1949 by Alfred Jones. Some 20 years later George Soros launched his Quantum Fund and the first fund of hedge funds, Leveraged Capital Holdings, was launched at roughly the same time. What is a hedge fund? The original definition, utilised *inter alia* by Alfred Jones, is of a fund that by taking both long and short positions in a given sector or market neutralises the market risk and effectively "bets" only on the spread between one security, sector or market vis-à-vis the other. While this investment technique is still utilised today by many hedge funds, it does not apply to all of them. The unique characteristic exhibited by substantially all hedge funds is the propensity, or at least the ability, to "go short".

The ability to go short is one of the constraints that mutual fund managers have to contend with, and according to a recently published essay by Clarke *et al.*,[1] portfolio constraints may reduce by up to one-half expected portfolio returns. Just like anything in life, it seems that performance is affected by the imposition of constraints. While it is beyond the scope of this introduction to go into technical explanations, we hold that the inability to go short is a fundamental constraint imposed on the mutual fund manager, both at a macro and at a micro level.

Over the last two years, probably with the assistance of a pervasive bear market in equities, investors world-wide are beginning to realise that the question is not, "should I invest in hedge funds?" but rather, "can I afford not to invest in hedge funds?". Especially in difficult markets, investors look to their portfolio managers for expertise that will help to protect the portfolio from excessive market fluctuations. Judging from the relative performance during the bear market of 2000–2001, hedge fund managers seem to have achieved this result. And, as the saying goes, investors are voting with their feet. Investment in hedge funds is at a historic high.

We maintain that this trend is not a temporary phenomenon but the beginning of a sustained historical move to hedge fund investments that will grow from the current roughly 5% of the global mutual fund net aggregated capital to a proportion in the middle teens. The effect of this shift to hedge funds is twofold. To the extent that investing in securities is a zero sum game, most analysts are forecasting a general flattening out of hedge fund returns. Hedge funds are outperforming mutual funds by being many times on the other side of the trade. As hedge fund assets grow, and as the proportion hedge fund to mutual fund grows, it follows that the scope

---

[1] R. Clarke, H. DeSilva and S. Thorley, 2001, "Portfolio constraints and the fundamental law of active management".

to take advantage of this phenomenon will decrease. In addition, certain hedge fund strategies are scarce. This is due to the fact that, unlike long-only investing (and long/short investing), certain hedge fund strategies (such as for example merger arbitrage and market neutral) have limited capacities. If there are no IPOs it is simply not possible to put on merger arbitrage trades!

The seasoned investor can and must take advantage of the outperformance of hedge funds even though this outperformance may in future years be less dramatic than in the present circumstances. When investing in hedge funds, diversification across strategies and single funds is very important. Funds of hedge funds are investment vehicles that typically invest in a broad portfolio of hedge funds aiming to enhance risk-adjusted returns by diversification. By investing in a selection of strategies and funds, a well managed fund of hedge funds can enhance Sharpe ratios and reduce risk, while "tailor-making" expected risk/return profiles that suit the particular target investor of that fund. In practical terms this means that, for example, investors with a low risk appetite can invest in funds of hedge funds that can lower volatility, and for a certain measure of volatility, maximise the return. On the other hand, a common critique of funds of hedge funds is that they add another layer of cost for the investor. Judging from the near explosive growth that these particular hedge funds have enjoyed, investors seem to be more interested in what risk-adjusted returns they get, rather than on the load factors. Nevertheless, one of the likely results of the spread of hedge fund investing will be the lowering of the fees paid to hedge fund managers.

Just as it took many years to convince stock market regulators in the United States that selling covered calls against equity portfolios was a conservative investment strategy, it may take time for regulators to understand that investing in a properly managed portfolio of hedge funds offers a lower risk profile than investing in an average equity mutual fund. There are signs that this change in perception is beginning to happen, perhaps catalysed by the poor performance of the world's equity market indices in the recent period. The authors of this book describe the current trends and key recent events in this shift to alternative investments from a European viewpoint.

Emanuel Arbib
CEO, Integrated Asset Management plc

1
Hedge Funds and Alternative Investments in Europe

In recent years, hedge funds have once again returned to the limelight and are becoming increasingly popular with both private and institutional investors. Whilst the alternative investment industry has already existed for more than 50 years, this form of investment has never been the preserve of the wider investing public. Investors as a whole have always associated hedge funds with the spectacular raids made by certain individuals. Perhaps the most famous of these was George Soros's attack on sterling in 1992 and the collapse of Long Term Capital Management (LTCM) in 1998.

The objective of this chapter is to explain hedge funds simply and clearly, to find common characteristics amongst these particularly versatile instruments, to explain the different investment strategies that hedge fund managers pursue and to highlight advantages, risks and opportunities linked to different hedge funds.

Firstly, it is important to make the distinction between the investment structure and the investment method. The term hedge fund indicates that the investment structure is in the form of a limited partnership. The legal structure of the fund allows the manager to receive and therefore invest capital, whilst subject to certain conditions. The investment structure defines the number and type of investors, the method of remuneration for the manager, the rights and responsibilities of the underlying investors relating to returns, rebates, taxes and finally legal responsibilities relating to third parties. The investment strategy refers to the investment method chosen by the manager, the definition of the markets in which the fund is active, the instruments to be used and the fund objectives in terms of returns and volatility.

Above all, the objective of this chapter is to present hedge funds as an asset class (i.e. an investment instrument) different from the conventional categories to which investors are more used. In perceiving hedge funds as instruments with their own particular characteristics, we can evaluate the benefits that hedge funds offer when inserted in traditional portfolios. Indeed, when inserted in a portfolio made up of equity and bond investments, hedge funds can improve overall returns while at the same time reducing the level of risk in that portfolio.

Many investors are of the opinion (not unfounded) that hedge funds are imprecise products, which come to the fore on the back of a few spectacular trades, or when they register performance figures far in excess of those achieved by other financial instruments. Others consider these products to be excessively risky, to be explored only by a knowledgeable and elite private client base. Whilst all envy the returns achieved during negative market conditions, many feel such returns are unsustainable over time. These are some of the criticisms most often directed at hedge funds.

The next section, on the history of hedge funds, is not intended as a defence of the alternative investment industry but rather to bring a little clarity to hedge funds, explain why they came into being as well as how they have evolved and adapted to financial markets. It is our intention to go beyond labelling an industry with a name, and instead provide the reader with a greater understanding of the subject and its implications today.

1.1   THE BIRTH OF HEDGE FUNDS

It is generally acknowledged that hedge funds came into being on 1st January 1949, when Alfred Winlow Jones established his fund. This fund was conceived as a portfolio benefiting from maximum flexibility in terms of the range of sectors in which it could invest and of the trading approaches it adopted. The company formed by Alfred Jones and four partners was named A. W. Jones & Co. and was a partnership with limited liability. The fund's capital initially totalled $100,000, $40,000 of which was contributed by Mr. Jones. The innovative idea which characterised the fund consisted of the fund's capital being both hedged and leveraged. They took advantage of leverage in order to make acquisitions with the minimum margin deposited whilst they would short sell to hedge the portfolio's long positions.

An important aspect of the investment philosophy which henceforth gave its name to this type of fund was demonstrated by the fact that the fund always took short positions with the view of protecting the portfolio from market risk.

In general, a portfolio runs a long position on any given security when the manager, through his own analysis, purchases the security estimating that the security's price will rise in the future. A position is defined as being short when the manager makes an uncovered sale of a given security, estimating that the security will fall in price. If the manager's calculations prove to be correct, the security can be bought at a lower price and therefore deliver a profit on this price differential.

From 1949 and for almost 15 years, Alfred managed his fund outside of the limelight. His activities only became widely known in 1966 following an article which appeared in *Fortune* under the heading "The Jones nobody keeps up with", written by Carol J. Loomis. The article eulogised this unknown money manager who had beaten all the most famous managers of the era. The article cited the extraordinary performance that the fund had achieved in the five years from 1960 to 1965. Indeed, during this period, the fund had registered a 325% gain whilst The Fidelity Trend fund, which had the best performance of any mutual fund at the time, had only managed 225% growth. In the 10 years from 1955 to 1965, Mr. Jones's fund had achieved 670% whilst the best of the mutual funds was the Dreyfuss fund which had managed 358%. Following this article, Alfred Jones joined the ranks of legendary Wall Street figures. The second effect of this article was the proliferation of managers seeking to copy the investment style of Alfred Jones. The Jones model was conceived so that the performance of the fund depended almost exclusively on stock picking, i.e. the activity of stock selection, whilst relying little on the direction taken by the market.

During the moments in which the market was experiencing growth, good stock selection (and by extension, investment) results in much higher returns than the market average, whilst good stock selection in terms of short selling will most likely result in returns lower than the market average. In negative market conditions, a portfolio with well-selected long positions will in theory fall less than the market and the short positions will ideally fall further than is average for the market. In this way, the Jones model succeeded in obtaining returns in all market conditions, whether bull or bear. The Jones fund became the model to imitate by the emerging hedge fund industry. The success of hedge funds following the publication of the article was notable. Indeed in 1968, the number of hedge funds reached 200. Among these new hedge fund managers, the names of George Soros and Michael Steinhardt appear for the first time.

The sixties were a bullish time for the market and many hedge fund managers took advantage of this rising trend, obtaining excellent results. However, the euphoria surrounding these new hedge funds disappeared when the long period of favourable market conditions ended at the start of the seventies. The market contractions of 1969–1970 and 1973–1974 caught many managers unprepared to deal adequately with the market's fall. In the early years, the bull market led hedge fund managers to use financial leverage to increase their returns, paying little attention to the short constituent of their portfolio. But the innovation of the Jones model resided in the fact that both leverage and hedging were used to manage the portfolio. The Jones hedge fund demonstrated its superiority in relation to mutual fund investments, precisely during falling markets, thanks to uncovered selling of securities. Jones was able to profit notwithstanding the negative market trend.

Following the exit from the market of many managers, hedge funds returned to obscurity, far from the attention of the press. In the eighties, only a modest number of hedge funds were launched. In 1984, according to Tremont data, only 68 funds existed and investors were almost exclusively high net worth individuals. The relationship between the manager and the investor was personal and through word of mouth, the assets controlled by these funds rose.

In general, however, it was still difficult to establish the exact number of hedge funds in operation. The majority of managers traded on international financial markets and as such, were not registered under the SEC (Securities and Exchange Commission). In those years, the American authorities forbade managers to advertise, limited the number of investors to 99, and this forced managers to demand elevated minimum investments. These factors resulted in hedge fund managers basing their operations in offshore markets where such restrictions did not exist. For this reason, it was difficult to establish the extent of the hedge phenomenon.

In the United States, the financial community is bound by three separate pieces of legislation.

1. Legislation intended to protect the novice investor who does not fully understand the transactions, strategies and instruments used by the hedge fund manager, be that because of the individual's limitations, or because of the limited information available on these instruments.
2. Legislation intended to protect the integrity of the market in such a way that prices are formed correctly, in accordance with the principle of competition. This principle aims to guarantee absolute transparency relating to transactions, thereby preventing any form of collusion, price and information manipulation (insider trading and any form of market rigging).
3. Legislation relating to risk: representing legislation relating to financial markets within different countries (capital requirements, margins and limits on open positions) in order to ensure the robustness of the markets, rendering them more immune from speculation and arbitrage. This legislation affects all financial activities conducted by traders based in the USA, such as mutual funds, pension funds, insurance funds, etc. To escape the confines of such legislation, to avoid the strict supervision of the SEC, the hedge fund industry devised a system based on two distinct types of company, the "Limited Partnership" for companies based in the USA and the "Offshore Investment Corporation" for those companies headquartered in offshore locations. In 1986, a new article entitled "The Red Hot World of Julian Robertson" once again brought hedge funds back into the limelight. The article presented Julian Robertson's Tiger Fund which, in its first six years, had achieved 43% growth (net of commissions) contrasting with the 18.7% registered by the S&P 500 index. In this article, Robertson explained that he had adopted "a new working method". The innovation gave rise to a new type of hedge fund called *global macro* or simply *macro*. The name global macro derived from the investment philosophy of the fund: a global macro fund is characterised by its high risk/return profile, global approach and

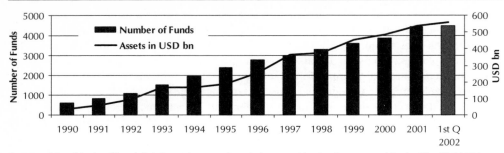

Source: Van Hedge Fund Advisors International, Inc. and/or its licensors, Nashville, TN,USA as of 2002, reproduced with permission.

Figure 1.1   Growth of the number of hedge funds 1988–2000

absence of limits in terms of investment instruments and sector diversity. Financial leverage was used aggressively and the fund's assets reached $20–30 billion which, compared with the average levels of other hedge funds ($60–100 million), was extremely high. The hedge fund industry became dominated by global macro funds, which had captured the wider press's imagination during this period. The managers leading this trend were Julian Robertson, George Soros and Michael Steinhardt, personalities who became known even to the man in the street. Their funds achieved returns during this period of around 40% per year. In 1990 for example, George Soros's Quantum Fund gained 30%, Julian Robertson's Jaguar Fund registered +20% whilst the S&P 500 had contracted by 3%. In the same year, the MSCI World index lost a staggering 16%. The sudden clamour awoke the interest of European investors, attracted by the advantages offered by this new breed of manager, both in terms of returns and the beneficial tax regimes of the offshore centres in which they were domiciled.

As demonstrated in Figure 1.1, the second half of the nineties saw a rapid increase in the numbers of hedge funds. Where hedge funds had in the past been rare exceptions, it is certainly true that the cult of major hedge players such as Robertson, Soros and Steinhardt had contributed to the exceptional growth of this industry.

During the early nineties, two interesting phenomena emerged: the first was that many money managers working for major institutions were suddenly tempted to defect to the world of hedge funds. This phenomenon began around 1994 but the role of the hedge fund manager was to be transformed. Whilst obtaining high returns was obviously important, the real objective was definable more in terms of the pursuit of this new "ostentatious" lifestyle. This is important in that the managers contributed a large proportion of their own assets to their funds' capital. Whilst this tendency could be described as a return to the Jones model, the second phenomenon was completely new. The second factor refers to the fact that a growing number of money managers introduced limits to the growth of their funds' capital. They defined a threshold beyond which new client monies and increases in the stakes of existing clients would not be accepted.

With the possibility that the fund manager would close the fund, the size of hedge funds fell, thereby imitating the Alfred Jones model. The guiding philosophy was that the manager should find a niche, where his ability and discipline would result in absolute returns whilst at the same time limiting portfolio risk. In 1992, as you can see in Figure 1.2 based on TASS data, global macro hedge funds were responsible for 74% of assets within the hedge fund industry.

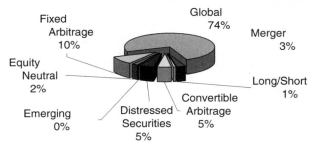

Source: TASS, 2001, reproduced by permission of Tremont (TASS) Europe, Ltd.

Figure 1.2 Hedge fund market in 1992

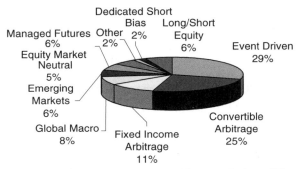

Source: TASS, 2002, reproduced by permission of Tremont (TASS) Europe, Ltd.

Figure 1.3 Hedge fund market in Q1 2002

Fixed income arbitrage accounted for 10% of industry assets whilst 5% each was taken up by the assets of funds focused on convertible arbitrage and distressed securities.

Figure 1.3 on the other hand shows the radical change which transformed the entire hedge fund industry. Comparing the market breakdowns from 1992 to 2001, global macro funds accounted for only 8% of the total in 2001. At the same time, funds adopting a long/short equity strategy became the predominant market constituent and currently account for 48% of hedge fund assets. This change was due to various reasons, but mainly because macro funds succeeded in riding America's bull market.

A period such as that seen from the mid-eighties to the mid-nineties was ideal for the development of macro funds; within the diverse strategies of hedge funds, global macro is best adapted to growing economies such as America's. In betting on the direction, be that positive or negative, of any trend or macroeconomic cycle, macro funds are ideally positioned to benefit. As the American economy began to falter, long/short hedge funds came to the fore.

With the collapse of equity markets and subsequent negative performance of mutual funds, both private and institutional investors turned to alternative investment methods in order not to suffer passively the adverse swings in financial markets. Hedge funds therefore came to the fore for their ability to take long or short positions in order to better protect the invested capital.

The strong rise in the take-up of hedge funds is down to the fact that these funds can effectively hedge themselves from the risk inherent in today's equity markets. When we add the skill of individual hedge fund managers into the equation, and the possibility of achieving positive returns during a contracting market, the return to prominence of the hedge fund is inevitable.

1.2   HEDGE FUNDS

After presenting the evolution of hedge funds over the last 50 years, we arrive at an important if difficult stage: the precise definition of hedge funds. The difficulty stems from the fact that the reality of hedge funds is very elusive, the investment methods employed by hedge fund managers are not only diverse but also subject to extreme flexibility. For this reason, hedge funds are often associated with the category of alternative or non-traditional investments. This is true in that compared to traditional equity or bond investments, hedge funds represent nothing if not an alternative approach.

In Figure 1.4, all activities generally placed in the category of alternative investments are presented. This category is constituted of very diverse investments including private equity, strategies based on the managers' skills, i.e. hedge funds, packaged products and real estate investments. Private equity in its turn can be divided into specific activities such as venture capital, leveraged buyout transactions, mezzanine financing and unusual financing operations such as restructuring.

In this book, we have chosen to classify hedge funds based on their involvement in equity markets; in this way, we can identify three classes.

- Relative Value or Market Neutral: offer low or zero correlation with equity markets. Convertible arbitrage, fixed income arbitrage and equity market neutral strategies all belong to this class.
- Event Driven: offer low correlation. Merger arbitrage and distressed securities belong to this category.
- Opportunistic: offer different levels of correlation to financial markets. Global macro, short sellers, emerging markets and long/short equity strategies belong to this category.

In the following paragraphs, all of the above strategies will be explained in further depth.

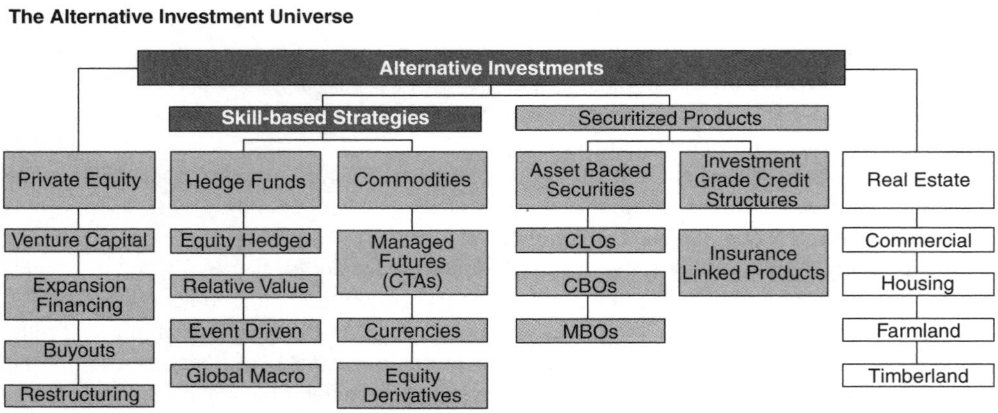

The Alternative Investment Universe

Source: RMF Research, reproduced by permission of RMF Investment Consultants.

Figure 1.4   Alternative investments

Packaged products have witnessed a large take-up in the USA whilst in Europe the same can only be said when such products are linked to unit and index-linked insurance contracts. Finally, the real estate sector is split between residential and commercial property, to which we also add investment programmes relating to natural resources such as agriculture, forestry, oil and gas. All of these investments offer advantages in terms of absolute returns, low volatility and low correlation with traditional investments. Disadvantages take the form of low liquidity, long investment horizons, an absence of regulation and high commission levels.

The term alternative investments, when related to hedge funds, does not mean the opposite, but rather refers to the fact that legislation (based on the principle that the wider investing public must be adequately informed) governs and restricts the activity of money managers. For example, mutual funds are subject to a series of laws that establish precisely which activities are permitted and which are not, amounting to a range of parameters within which the funds can operate.

In general, hedge fund managers must subscribe to only two legally imposed limits.

1. The limit in investor numbers (maximum 100 investors).
2. The law relating to privacy (hedge fund managers cannot contravene the laws governing the soliciting of private clients).

The trade-off is clear – in imposing these two conditions on hedge funds, legislation allows the hedge fund manager to operate without observing all regulations governing mutual funds. Such freedom of action enables hedge funds to use investment instruments that the manager deems necessary to achieve his objectives in terms of returns. For this reason, it is very difficult to find a definition that allows us to precisely identify the multiple characteristics of hedge funds and by extension to understand the diverse strategies adopted by those hedge funds.

Whilst a hot topic of discussion, there is still no suitable definition of hedge funds in so much as we are still confronted by the absence of a legal definition for these financial instruments. Many an educated person, in attempting to define the distinctive aspects of such instruments, has highlighted certain characteristics at the expense of others.

Amongst the many definitions, there are two major interpretations: the first tends mainly to examine the possibilities open to the hedge fund manager. The second underlines the legal/operational considerations linked to these instruments. For example, the limited numbers of participants and the possibility of short selling securities.

> Hedge Funds are private partnership contracts in which the manager or general partner has a significant personal interest in the fund and is free to operate in a variety of markets and use investments and strategies with long and short exposure and with varied leverage.
>
> William Crerend (1995)

1.3   MAIN CHARACTERISTICS OF THE INDUSTRY

1.3.1   Size and Growth of the Hedge Fund Industry

In the previous section regarding the history of hedge funds, we alluded to the size of the industry and the growth experienced by these funds. The total assets controlled by the industry have changed profoundly. Indeed, if we compare data from 1992 with that of 2001, we see just how the reality of hedge funds at the beginning of this new millennium has changed over the past 10 years.

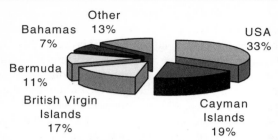

Other
Bahamas   13%   USA
7%   33%

Bermuda
11%

British Virgin   Cayman
Islands   Islands
17%   19%

Source: TASS, 2001, reproduced by permission of Tremont (TASS) Europe, Ltd.

Figure 1.5   Hedge fund domiciles

To understand the role and weight of hedge funds in the global financial market is complex. It is nevertheless useful to make a comparison of assets managed by hedge funds in relation to those managed by other financial institutions. The US financial market, as it appears in research from 1999, gives an extremely precise snapshot of the subdivisions of the major sectors.

"The report of The President's Working Group on Financial Markets" estimated that the hedge fund universe at the end of 1998 was made up of 2500–3500 funds; that these funds controlled assets of $200–300 billion, effectively constituting a portfolio of between $800 billion and $1 trillion. At the end of 1998, hedge funds represented 4.5% of the market, commercial banks had portfolios worth $4 trillion corresponding to 20.2% of the market, mutual funds managed around $5 trillion, representing almost a quarter of the market, private pension funds controlled 21.8% and public and regional pension funds together accounted for 11.3%. Finally, insurance companies, with $3.7 trillion accounted for 18.2%.

The American hedge fund industry therefore represented a niche market competing with far bigger players. Hedge funds first emerged in the United States and for many years remained linked to the American financial market. As you can see in Figure 1.5, based on Tremont-TASS data, 33% of all funds are domiciled in the United States. If we consider however the countries in which the manager is registered, we see that more than 90% of managers operate under the supervision of the American authorities. Looking again at the data, we point to another interesting fact. More than 50% of hedge funds are domiciled in tax havens, whilst Europe's market weighting is approximately 9% (for a closer analysis of the European marketplace and an overview of individual states, please refer to successive chapters).

Between the eighties and nineties, the market was dominated by global macro funds that administered more than 75% of total assets in the industry. In those years, hedge funds were justly associated with the global macro funds and the names of Soros and Robertson. With their new methods of tackling financial markets, they forced hedge funds out of the cloud of mystery under which they had always resided, onto the front pages of daily newspapers. This helped the investing public to associate hedge funds with these personalities, and made them the industry spokespeople for over a decade.

As a result, the world of hedge funds has experienced a profound transformation. Global macro funds have seen their weighting within the hedge fund market fall drastically for several reasons, including the collapse of LTCM; having seen the closure of George Soros's Quantum Fund and Julian Robertson's Tiger Fund other global macro funds also began to reduce their activities.

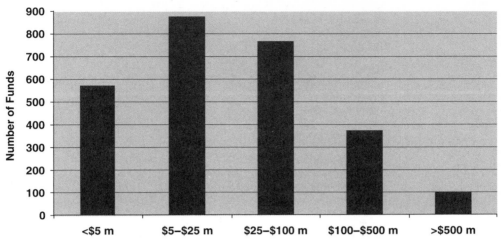

Source: Van Hedge Fund Advisors International, Inc. and/or its licensors, Nashville, TN, USA as of 2001, reproduced with permission.

Figure 1.6   Size of hedge funds in millions of dollars

The nineties witnessed a gradual tendency towards the reduction of assets under management. As you can see from Figure 1.6, based on data from Van Hedge Fund Advisors, the number of funds with capital in excess of $500 million represent only 6% of the total number of hedge funds. More than 50% of the number of hedge funds have less than $25 million in capital, this figure being important for two reasons: the first implies that the size of the average fund is falling, the second that many new funds were launched during the last few years.

Concerning the first trend, we can confirm that the industry no longer identifies itself with global macro funds but more with the role of the manager as a niche player, using his specific competence to achieve interesting returns. The second consideration relates to the fact that 20% of hedge funds have capital totalling less than $5 million, the result of so many new funds being launched during the last year.

Despite having limited funds, managers who believe in their own ability are coming onto the market, looking to build up a track record (the historical performance of the fund) which will in turn attract new investment.

The changes experienced by the hedge fund industry are summarised in Table 1.1 showing a comparison between 1990 and 1997 of assets managed by the various hedge fund classes.

From the comparison, we clearly see the reduction (of almost 30%) in the capital of the global macro funds. This negative trend continued in the following years as is shown in Figure 1.7. For example, according to Tremont data, macro funds accounted for only 4% of the total number of funds in 1999. Whilst macro funds experienced this negative trend, the industry leader was assumed by equity market funds pursuing a philosophy of long/short investment.

The data in Table 1.1, originating from Hedge Fund Research, Chicago, reflect the same message as that of TASS (Figure 1.7), although the different categories applied by the two companies can be deceptive. Indeed, in adding the equity non-hedge and equity hedge classes from Table 1.1, we arrive at a total of approximately 30%, similar to that reported by TASS for

Table 1.1   Variations in assets under management between 1990 and 1997

%	1990	1997	Change
Macro	50.6	22.4	−28.2
Equity non-hedge	14.1	15.8	1.7
Equity hedge	9.8	14.8	5
Emerging markets	2.8	12.7	9.9
Event driven	4.5	7.9	3.4
Equity market neutral	1	4.7	3.7
Sector	0.5	3.5	3
Distressed securities	1.7	2.5	0.8
Fixed income arbitrage	0.6	2	1.4
Convertible arbitrage	1.9	1.8	−0.1
Risk arbitrage	0.2	0.9	0.7
Short selling	2.7	0.2	−2.5
Other	9.6	10.8	1.2

Source: Bluehedge News, reproduced with permission.

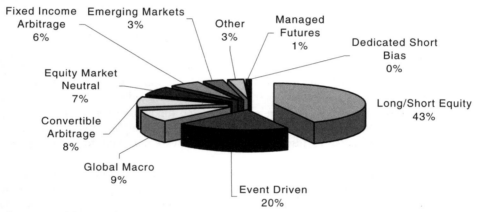

Source: TASS Research, 2002, reproduced by permission of Tremont (TASS) Europe, Ltd.

Figure 1.7   Assets per strategy March 2002

those years. The long/short equity class is today the most significant class within the industry, with 48% of total assets.

Within the world of asset management, hedge funds represent one of the sectors with the highest growth. Indeed, in the last 10 years, the number of new funds has risen by 25.74% per year, with overall growth of 648% (according to TASS data). According to Tremont Partners, the reason for this incredible growth is simple. Money finds its way to talented people.

The managers who had previously gained experience and wealth as fund managers or traders tend to abandon the institutions for which they had worked to set up on their own and manage their own capital. Their company structure is very straightforward, with a limited number of partners and the sole objective of achieving absolute returns, not linked to any particular benchmark.

Hedge funds can operate without observing the principal laws governing mutual investment funds, including the obligation to publish the fund's value, whilst they are subject to certain limitations where conducting any marketing activity is concerned, thus restricting their relationship with the outside world. This fact has contributed to the low profile of hedge funds when compared with other investment instruments. The absence of any obligation for hedge funds to publish their results, that hedge funds can operate out of the limelight and in so doing, escape the market's attempts to track or copy their activity, their limited communication to the outside world, the fact that many funds are domiciled in tax havens all contribute to the substantial difficulties in obtaining accurate information on the reality of the hedge fund universe.

A report by the RMF Investment Group estimates that the number of hedge funds should today be between 6000 and 7000. The data from this source may differ vastly from other sources. For example, Tremont estimates that the entire industry consisted of more than 5000 funds at the end of 2000.

This discrepancy in the estimates can confuse anyone unfamiliar with the world of hedge funds. This can be explained by different reasons:

- The hedge fund industry has evolved under a somewhat secretive culture due to legal requirements, because some traders short sell securities, or because some funds invest in unquoted companies. However, once the market finds out about a position taken by a hedge fund manager, it often provokes a reaction.
- In the United States, hedge funds are structured as private limited partnerships. In the past, these instruments were aimed at private investors desiring the utmost secrecy. It is therefore very likely that certain offshore fund managers are not especially keen to find their funds in any database.
- There exists no single definition of hedge funds. There may therefore be some variation in the funds recognised by different databases.

Data on the growth of hedge funds demonstrates the extent to which these funds have become the focus of attention during these last three years. It is useful to show just how this attention has translated into actual investment in these instruments.

In Figure 1.8, we see data on the in-flow/out-flow of capital into this industry. Since January 1994, the hedge fund industry has grown 400% from the initial $50 billion invested. This growth can be subdivided in the following way:

- 120%, equal to $65 billion is accounted for by new investment.
- 280% is attributable to the managers' performance during these years. Following the debacle of LTCM in the second half of 1998, new investment in the industry was clearly going to be affected and this is reflected in the negative capital flow during the final two quarters of that year. Indeed, capital in-flows proved particularly unsatisfactory also for the following two years.

In 2000, out-flows of approximately $5 billion were registered. This can be attributed to the liquidation of the global macro Tiger Fund and the major restructuring of Soros's funds. The collapse in stock prices which signalled the end of the nineties bull run in the American markets coincided in a re-invigorated hedge fund industry.

The first quarter of 2001 demonstrated these gains with in-flows totalling $6.9 billion. This represented the highest figure since 1986 and is almost equal to the amount invested in the whole of 2000. But the really good news for hedge fund managers did not stop here. Indeed, the second quarter of 2001 proved even better with $8.5 billion of new funds being invested.

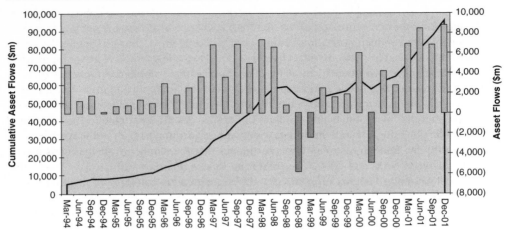

Source: TASS Research, 2001, reproduced by permission of Tremont (TASS) Europe, Ltd.

Figure 1.8   Hedge fund flows

Therefore, a staggering $15 billion was invested during the first two quarters of the year, more than double that achieved in the whole of 2000.

"The numbers speak for themselves. Investors throughout the world are diversifying their investments in favour of strategies which add value to portfolios, particularly during extremely difficult market conditions." Nicola Meaden, CEO of Tremont-TASS in Europe. Long/short equity and convertible arbitrage lead the field during the first quarter of 2001, registering in-flows of $2.5 billion. Conversely, the short seller class registered out-flows of $38 million and global macro funds $1.51 billion. The TASS research centre conservatively estimated the hedge fund industry to be worth $400–450 billion. To this figure, we can add the $50 billion in segregated private accounts and $100 billion representing those managers not wishing to be included in TASS's statistics.

1.3.2   The Characteristics of a Typical Hedge Fund

We would now like to highlight the characteristics of a typical hedge fund. In a hedge fund, the manager is known as the general partner. They can either be an individual or a legal entity (in the first case, the manager will work through a separate company in order to avoid being held responsible for the unlimited liability assumed).

Investors in a hedge fund assume the title of limited partners and their liability is limited in proportion to their stake in the fund. Their stakes may neither be traded nor given to other potential investors but only re-sold to other fund members or rebated by the fund. 65% of these investors must be accredited. This type of investment is restricted only to citizens living in the United States.

There are therefore two key figures in a limited partnership; the general partner has unlimited liability for the obligations assumed in the name of the company and limited partners are liable to third parties only to the tune of their stake in the company. Consequently, they cannot act in any administrative role nor conduct any business on behalf of the company; if they do, they assume the same level of responsibility as the general partner.

In being legally configured in this way, hedge funds are not obliged to be registered with the SEC as investment companies, as defined by the Investment Company Act of 1940 and by the successive National Securities Markets Improvement Act of 1996. This last piece of legislation refers to "qualified purchasers", which permits a consortium of such persons to be excluded from the obligation of registration with the SEC as an Investment Company.

More often than not, the limited partnership reaches a size where it becomes necessary to diversify the activity of the fund. This is impossible to effect because of the 100-investor restriction. Indeed, the fund manager cannot establish a new limited partnership to run alongside the first, in that it would contravene the limits imposed by American legislation. The only solution available to the general partner is to form an offshore investment corporation.

The characteristics of these offshore hedge funds are as follows:

• They are targeted mainly at foreign investors and not limited to 100 investors.
• They may not solicit business in America.
• American investors must be accredited.
• The fund manager must ensure that the majority of the monies invested are from non-Americans and that the American investors number fewer than 100.
• The fund enjoys the freedom and flexibility guaranteed by the host countries whose laws are inevitably less restrictive than those of America.
• The fund enjoys beneficial tax regimes.
• In some cases, stakes can be sold to American institutional investors.

The company type of an offshore fund is "Corporation", which allows the fund's capital to be divided into shares. Shareholder liability is restricted to the amount of capital invested; if the shareholders wish to contribute to the management of the company, they may participate in the election of the board or actually become board members. In short, the company possesses a judicial capacity.

Table 1.2 clearly summarises the particular characteristics of a hedge fund and is a useful source of information in studying the world of alternative investments for the first time. It will moreover be useful to show how these investment instruments have utterly different characteristics. The freedom enjoyed by the manager in choosing the investment strategy, i.e. the way in which the manager intends to execute his objectives in terms of markets and instruments used, makes hedge funds unique. One can compare a hedge fund to medium/small

Table 1.2   Characteristics of a typical hedge fund as of Q4 2000

	Mean	Median	Mode
Fund size	$90 million	$22 million	$10 million
Fund age	5.0 years	3.9 years	2.9 years
Minimum investment required	$630,729	$250,000	$250,000
Management fee	1.30%	1.00%	1.00%
Performance allocation ("fee")	16.70%	20.00%	20.00%
Manager's experience:			
1) in securities industry	17 years	15 years	10 years
2) in portfolio management	12 years	10 years	10 years

Source: Van Hedge Fund Advisors International, Inc. and/or its licensors, Nashville, TN, USA as of November 2001, reproduced with permission.

businesses, highly identifiable with the owner/artisan, specialised in a specific niche and with the ability to easily adapt to changing circumstances.

As with small businesses, the manager invests a large part of their capital, he is the fulcrum of all decisions and the future of the fund is highly dependent on him. Just as two artisans can adopt different approaches to the same sector, so can hedge funds differ in that some might use complex statistical analysis and software to invest in futures contracts on commodities and others focus exclusively on profiting from company mergers and acquisitions.

In Table 1.2, the mean, median and mode values are shown. The mode represents the most common class, the median represents the midpoint value above and below which fall the same number of funds and the mean is the average value of hedge funds. In a normal range, these values match but if the range of values is particularly wide, i.e. some funds register values quite outside the norm, the mean is quite different from the median.

According to data from Van Hedge Fund Advisors International of Nashville, TN, the mean and median values are quite different.

The variety in hedge funds is demonstrated effectively by these statistical indicators, with the mean value at $90 million and the median value at $22 million. The difference amounts to $68 million and is caused by the size of global macro funds which have an average value of $10–15 billion, which massively inflates the mean value.

If the mean value is inflated by the effect of global macro funds, the median value shows how at $22 million the capital managed by hedge funds is tiny in comparison with conventional mutual funds. It is also interesting to note that the mode value of $10 million confirms that today's hedge funds are in the main, made up of niche players.

Hedge funds are by and large very young: the median age is 3.9 years and the average age is 5 years. Over the last four years, the number of hedge funds has grown by 30% and this trend is expected to continue in the coming years.

The minimum investment required, indicated by the median and mode values, is the same at $250,000, whilst the average is higher ($630,000). The higher average value is linked to the fact that certain managers, particularly those currently in vogue because of impressive track records, can demand a higher minimum investment.

One of the accusations levelled at the hedge fund industry is that the minimum investment is extremely high when compared to investment in mutual funds. The minimum threshold stated by the Italian authorities is much higher than that applied in other European countries. However, in general the minimum demanded by hedge fund managers is far higher than that expected by mutual funds. Canada is a notable exception to this rule.

The Canadian authorities allow individual provinces autonomy in defining the minimum investment levels. In this way, the province of British Columbia has set a minimum of only 25,000 Canadian dollars, whilst Ontario has imposed a minimum investment of 150,000 Canadian dollars. This is because in Canada, funds that invest in hedge funds are viewed differently to single manager funds. Therefore, in Canada a fund of hedge funds can accept investment from as little as 5000 Canadian dollars, equal to about 2000 USD. As in Canada then, we can see the possibility for hedge fund managers to raise capital from a wider public than has been the case in the past.

In Italy, funds of hedge funds are viewed no differently to single manager funds, both for the minimum invested and for the obligations implicit on speculative SGRs.

Annual management fees are 1% and performance fees are fixed at 20%. These two commissions are a characteristic of hedge funds in that the management fee should cover the costs of managing the fund, whilst the manager is remunerated by the performance fee. This fee is set at a high level with the view of incentivising the manager. Indeed, only if the fund registers a positive performance may the manager receive an attractive payout. To some commentators, such incentives may lead managers to take riskier investment decisions. However, we must consider two elements:

- The manager has contributed a large part of his wealth to the fund.
- Certain clauses such as the hurdle rate and the high water mark reduce the likelihood of such behaviour.

The term *hurdle rate* represents the minimum return under which the manager receives no performance fee. A risk-free interest rate such as LIBOR is often used as the guide for the hurdle rate. Performance fees are therefore calculated on returns achieved above this level.

If we hypothesise that the hurdle rate is set at (for simplicity) 10%, and the fund achieves returns of 25%, the performance fee will only be calculated on the 15% return above the hurdle rate.

The term *high water mark* represents the guarantee for the investor that the fund only applies a commission on the management of the fund once a year.

The following example will help to better understand this clause: hypothesising that a fund is launched with capital of 1000. The first year of the fund sees performance of −50% and the fund's capital is reduced to 500. The second year however sees the fund grow by 100% with capital returning to 1000. For this year, notwithstanding the positive performance of the fund, the manager does not apply a performance fee. The manager will only apply a performance fee if the value of the fund is higher than the level of the fund at its launch.

Table 1.3 shows a comparison between the situation as recorded in 1995 and 2000. The majority of the managers working in the hedge fund industry are registered in the role of investment advisor. The number of funds applying a hurdle rate is relatively small and this proportion changed little in subsequent years. However, the number of funds applying a high water mark rose from 64% to 87%. The percentage of funds choosing to have the value of their funds certified by third parties is extremely high. This represents an important element of security for investors, who in this way are certain of the state of their investments. Unlike

Table 1.3 Trend of characteristics of a typical hedge fund

Manager is a US registered investment advisor	68%			
Fund has hurdle rate	18%			
Fund has high water mark	87%			
Fund has audited financial statements or audited performance	96%			
Manager has $500,000 of own money in fund	79%			
Fund is diversified	52%			
Fund can short sell	84%			
Fund can use leverage	72%			
Fund uses derivatives for hedging only, or none	71%			
Level of turnover	Low 21%	Medium 25%	High 54%	
Capitalisation of underlying investments	Small 13%	Medium 5%	Large 10%	Mixed 72%

Source: Van Hedge Fund Advisors International, Inc. and its licensors, Nashville, TN, USA, reproduced with permission.

the mutual fund industry, which requires funds to report the value of the fund on a daily basis, hedge funds communicate performance figures either monthly or quarterly. Whilst this varies from fund to fund, the tendency in the market is to report figures more frequently, i.e. from quarterly to monthly reporting.

As discussed previously, characteristic of this industry is the fact that the manager invests a significant proportion of his own capital in the fund. At the launch of the fund, the manager is therefore taking the same bet as the other investors. He acts therefore in both the roles of investor and fund manager.

In general, it is believed that the ample freedoms enjoyed by the hedge fund manager are counterbalanced by the fact that he has an equal interest (to other investors) in the fund's wellbeing. To continue, we assume that in the quest for high returns, he will not expose the fund to excessive risk.

Indeed, losses would clearly not favour the manager both for the fact that his remuneration is dependent on achieving positive performance and because any reduction in the fund's capital would be reflected in the loss of capital which he invested in the fund. Table 1.3 shows how 4/5 of managers invest more than $500,000 in the fund.

The data relating to derivative instruments is particularly interesting. More than 70% of managers state that they only use such instruments to cover positions or don't use them at all, whilst 72% use financial leverage. This is often used because the fund's capital is not vast and leverage can be used to achieve superior returns. As expected the level of turnover, i.e. the amount of securities transactions made on behalf of the fund, is high. Almost half of hedge fund managers trade with over 75% of the fund's capital. This indicates that hedge fund managers are very active on the markets.

A good quality of hedge fund managers is their sense of timing; to intervene in a market before that market has formed a determined opinion. This quality shows their knowledge and skill.

Referring to the question of leverage by hedge funds, Table 1.4 shows the situation in 2000. The use of financial leverage depends on the strategy pursued by the manager. In that 30%

Table 1.4   Use of leverage by the different hedge fund styles as of December 2001

Hedge Fund Style	Don't Use Leverage	Use Leverage Low (<2.0:1)	Use Leverage High (≥2.0:1)	Total
Aggressive growth	27.70%	55.10%	17.20%	72.30%
Distressed securities	49.40%	48.10%	2.50%	50.60%
Emerging markets	35.00%	50.00%	15.00%	65.00%
Fund of funds	30.90%	52.20%	16.90%	69.10%
Income	42.90%	31.90%	25.30%	57.20%
Macro	10.70%	44.00%	45.30%	89.30%
Market neutral – arbitrage	19.40%	22.00%	58.70%	80.70%
Market neutral – securities hedging	28.50%	31.30%	40.20%	71.50%
Market timing	39.10%	22.60%	38.30%	60.90%
Opportunistic	24.50%	44.00%	31.50%	75.50%
Several strategies	32.10%	46.90%	21.00%	67.90%
Short selling	38.60%	40.90%	20.50%	61.40%
Special situations	23.00%	60.90%	16.10%	77.00%
Value	32.20%	53.60%	14.20%	67.80%
Total sample	25.40%	45.30%	29.30%	74.60%

Source: Van Hedge Fund Advisors International, Inc. and/or its licensors, Nashville, TN, USA, reproduced with permission.

Table 1.5   Leverage levels in Wall Street

Banks	Assets in USD m	Leverage Coefficient
Merril Lynch	365.45	18.9
Morgan Stanley Dean Witter	359.58	14.8
Lehman Brothers	179.07	19.8
Donaldson, Lufkin and Jenrette	79.56	12.3
Paine Webber Group	63.97	10

Source: Bluehedge News, reproduced with permission.

state that they do not use financial leverage, we must highlight that different strategies require a different approach. Strategies such as distressed securities, value and emerging markets find it difficult to use leverage at a rate of more than 2 to 1. Other strategies such as macro, market neutral arbitrage make frequent use of high levels of leverage. Taken in isolation, the extensive use of leverage does not indicate whether a strategy is particularly risky or not. Indeed, funds making arbitrage trades using an investment policy aiming to achieve exposure to neutral market risk are no more risky than funds which make no use of financial leverage.

As will be explained in greater depth in the subsequent section, several hedge fund strategies (fixed income arbitrage) imply significant use of financial leverage to support the investment policy (20–30 times capital). This is because the profitability of certain transactions such as arbitrages is only significant if those transactions are on a very large scale. Otherwise, interest in such trades would fade. Other strategies such as long/short equity, distressed securities, short selling and emerging markets make little use of financial leverage (1 to 2 times capital). For example, hedge funds that specialise in emerging markets make little use of leverage mainly because in such markets, stock lending and derivative facilities are often underdeveloped.

Hedge funds are not the only market participants to use financial leverage. Indeed, even the main investment banks use leverage to manage their own investments. According to a survey conducted by Salomon Smith Barney in 1998, the total exposure of the largest investment banks equaled 25–35 times capital (Table 1.5).

These figures hide a worrying situation: the credit and investment sectors are so closely interconnected that the collapse of any of the pieces could result in the collapse of the entire system, as happened in the case of LTCM. On that occasion, Alan Greenspan, President of the FED, had to come to the rescue of the fund in so much as its collapse and resulting liquidation would have inflicted severe damage on the entire credit system.

1.4   HEDGE FUND STRATEGIES

In this section, we will present the different hedge fund strategies as used by the hedge fund managers to achieve their investment objectives. Hedge funds, as was also stated in previous sections, are comprised of a wide range of investment styles.

The differences in terms of investment styles are far greater than those seen in the mutual fund industry; indeed, the fund manager can define his investment policy by geographic area, sector and the size of companies in which to invest. For example, the fund may aim to invest in any size of company, could choose to trade only in European markets, only in the banking sector or large caps or even perhaps invest in all of the above. For example, a fund may invest in European small caps in the technology sector.

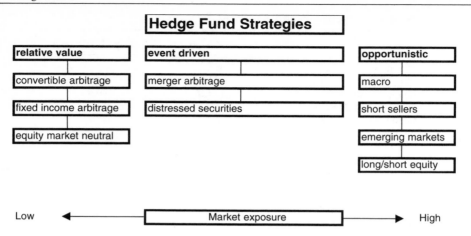

Figure 1.9   Hedge fund strategies

Compared to all other types of investment, hedge fund strategies offer investors far greater diversity. This is due to the specific characteristics of the alternative investment industry which, composed of a wide range of activities, is not subject to a great deal of regulation. As explained earlier, hedge funds belong to the main class of these alternative investments, which comprises activities from real estate, venture capital, the entertainment industry to hedge funds.

The lack of regulation, or better, the lack of limits in terms of leverage, short selling, shareholdings in other companies and investment instruments has enabled hedge funds to avoid becoming a monolithic class. Indeed, the opposite is the case. Therefore, there are difficulties when seeking to classify the different strategies employed by hedge fund managers. The different classifications nevertheless seek to define the behaviour of the hedge fund manager and the environments in which they work.

Every hedge fund classification must also take into account that many funds are hybrids by nature, i.e. they employ methods belonging to different investment styles. Having done this, the most commonly used approach is to categorise hedge funds by analysing their relationship with equity markets.

In Figure 1.9, the hedge fund universe is divided into three major investment classes: relative value, event driven and opportunistic. The different strategies are allocated to the three classes depending on their exposure to market risk. Funds belonging to the relative value class tend to have a very low exposure or correlation to market direction. The event driven category has low exposure to markets whilst the opportunistic class comprises all investment styles which imply variable levels of correlation with market direction.

1.4.1   Relative Value Strategies

The strategies belonging to this class seek to extract profit from the price inefficiencies of certain financial instruments. In general, the managers of these funds avoid betting on the direction of a specific sector or market as a whole. Relative value strategies therefore represent an attractive prospect for investors seeking high returns which are stable over time and have low correlation with the direction of the equity markets.

Table 1.6   Characteristics of the relative value strategy

	Convertible Arbitrage	Fixed Income Arbitrage	Equity Market Neutral
Returns	average	low	average
Volatility	low	low	low
Downside risk	low	average	low
Sharpe ratio	average	low	high
Shares correlation	average	low	low
Market exposure	low	low	low
Leverage (degree of)	average	high	average
Time horizon	average	average	average

Source: Bluehedge News, reproduced with permission.

We generally associate three characteristics with this investment class: leverage, complexity and derivatives. This class achieved certain fame, firstly because of the potentially high returns but also because of the problems (e.g. LTCM) and the risks associated with market neutral strategies. Within relative value strategies, we can differentiate the funds that use:

- Arbitrage trades on convertible securities;
- Arbitrage trades on fixed income securities;
- Strategies which invest in equity markets, seeking to maintain zero exposure to market direction.

The skill of these managers is to identify inefficiencies in financial markets, i.e. to understand when financial instruments (equities, bonds, convertible securities) deviate for whatever reason from their historical value. The managers who apply these strategies employ many formulae as well as statistical and fundamental analysis. It seems therefore that the objective of the manager is to identify a discrepancy in the price of a security, take on a position relative to this discrepancy, simultaneously eliminating all external risk so that a return can be achieved as the price of the security converges on its theoretical value.

In general, relative value strategies achieve returns even when the market is falling. This is mainly due to two reasons: the first derives from the decision of the manager to assume zero market risk by protecting his position; the second relates to the fact that in falling markets, panic results in significant pricing inefficiencies and therefore profit opportunities for the manager.

Table 1.6 shows the characteristics of relative value strategies by comparing eight indicators. The three possible levels, low, medium and high, are based on historical data for each of the strategies.

The term *downside risk* represents the negative volatility of an investment. It measures negative price discrepancies relative to the average or theoretical value.

The Sharpe ratio is the most commonly used risk/return indicator in the world; it is determined by taking the difference in the returns achieved by the fund and those achieved by activities with zero risk, and dividing it by the standard deviation of excess returns.

Convertible Arbitrage (Figure 1.10)

Typically, arbitrageurs of convertible securities (be they equities or bonds) extract profits by buying the convertible security and short selling the underlying equity. Managers who apply this strategy seek to identify undervalued securities, which can be converted into ordinary shares.

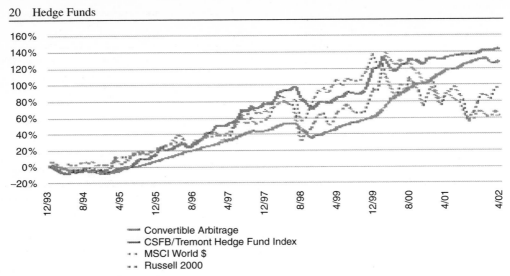

Source: www.hedgeindex.com

Figure 1.10   Convertible arbitrage. Reproduced by permission of CSFB, MSCI and Frank Russell Company

Once they have identified an arbitrage opportunity, they decide what is the most appropriate way to cover the position. Usually, the manager takes a neutral position in relation to delta, which measures the correlation level between the convertible security and the underlying equity.

Convertible securities are hybrids in that they provide downside protection for the investor as with fixed income securities but with the upside potential of equity capital. However, the manager must confront both equity market and interest rate risk thanks to the instrument's bond characteristics.

Such strategies rely heavily on complex models and statistical formulae that aim to measure the theoretical value of a given convertible security. In applying such models, the manager can establish whether the market has correctly valued the security. It is now important to calculate the hedge ratio which indicates the number of shares to be short sold in order to counterbalance the fluctuations in the price of the convertible bond, with the view of eliminating all volatility attributable to the equity component.

If executed properly, covering the convertible bond by short selling the underlying offers several advantages: the underlying security has a high correlation with the convertible and provides an additional source of revenue because of the short interest rebate. That not all securities may be short sold is a disadvantage.

Another alternative for hedging consists of using equity options, which provide greater flexibility than short selling; however, options are not available on all equities. Other variations include buying warrants covered by futures.

In general, the fund manager will choose convertible securities which offer the greatest upside potential (the positive volatility of an equity) whilst at the same time minimising the impact of downside risk of the underlying on the convertible.

Notwithstanding the fact that convertible arbitrage requires certain mathematical formulae, the experience and skill of the fund manager are fundamental. The amount of leverage used varies greatly depending on the composition of the portfolio but generally is from 2 to 10 times the fund's capital.

Amongst the strategies most commonly used by managers of convertible arbitrage, we find:

- Taking a long position in convertible securities and short selling the underlying equity. Since convertible bonds move inversely to changes in interest rates, the manager must take account of this risk. Managers often cover themselves by short selling the underlying security and to manage interest rate risk, use futures contracts on government bonds or interest rate swaps.
- Executing arbitrages, whilst seeking to eliminate volatility by taking on a long position in the convertible bond and a short position in an index option.
- Taking on a long position in convertible bonds and short selling the underlying equity, thereby eliminating credit risk. In this case, the manager is taking advantage of the privileged status of the convertible bond (during company restructuring or closure) with respect to the ordinary share.

As for target returns, convertible arbitrage funds aim for 15–20% net of commissions. The volatility of equity markets has a positive influence on returns; on the other hand, volatility in the bond market has a negative effect. In general, convertible managers concentrate on one of the following areas: American convertible securities, Japanese warrants and high-quality international convertibles.

Fixed Income Arbitrage (Figure 1.11)

Fund managers who concentrate on fixed income arbitrage generally take on long or short positions in fixed income securities and derivatives, to profit from market fluctuations and general trends. The majority of managers take on neutral positions relative to the security's maturity, using financial leverage as an integral part of the investment strategy. Moreover, managers do not generally seek to profit from expected changes in the interest rates of a

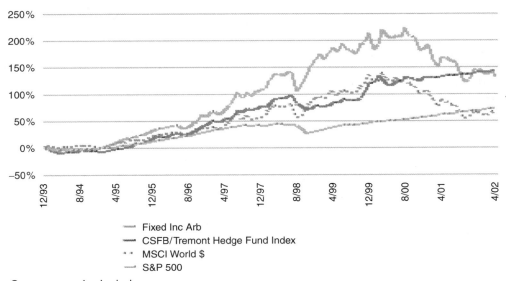

Source: www.hedgeindex.com

Figure 1.11   Fixed income arbitrage. Reproduced by permission of CSFB and MSCI. Also reproduced by permission of Standard & Poor's, a division of The McGraw-Hill Companies, Inc. Copyright © 1993–2002 The McGraw-Hill Companies, Inc. Reproduction of the S&P 500 Index Values in any form is prohibited without S&P's prior written permission

specific country. Managers may use a wide range of arbitrage techniques. The spreads which permit the implementation of these strategies are however very small (around a couple of tenths of a point), making profits dependent on the use of financial leverage (often as much as 20–30 times capital).

The manager may choose government bonds for arbitrages by studying the yield curve and the differences between the yields for different country debt (yield curve spreads arbitrage); the manager is betting on the convergence or divergence in the prices of selected securities within a given time. Other types of arbitrage use options to take advantage of the different volatility levels in government debt and in doing so adopt a neutral position relative to interest rates. Arbitrage in corporate debt profits from the spread between a long position in undervalued securities and a short position in government bonds or derivatives. This is also possible on mortgage-backed securities (constructed by a process of securitisation where returns are guaranteed by house loans). Mortgage bonds are characterised by their higher level of complexity and risk.

In general, the risk management philosophy for this strategy takes into account the maturity, convexity, liquidity and leverage. The manager seeks pricing anomalies, using mathematical analysis, fundamentals and historical data. These price distortions may be caused by investor opinion, events affecting the market, exogenic shocks or structural characteristics of the fixed income market. Given the sophistication of the models used and the fact that spreads are particularly compressed, the level of transparency is far lower compared to other strategies. This negative aspect is compensated by the fact that fixed income arbitrage succeeds in generating constant returns with very low volatility.

Equity Market Neutral (Figure 1.12)

The majority of market neutral funds consist of a portfolio of long positions covered by a diversified portfolio of short positions. These strategies are used to extract profit from anomalies

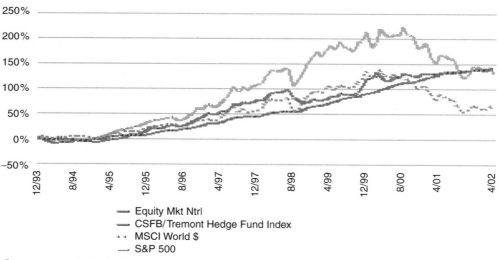

Source: www.hedgeindex.com

Figure 1.12 Equity market neutral. Reproduced by permission of CSFB and MSCI. Also reproduced by permission of Standard & Poor's, a division of The McGraw-Hill Companies, Inc. Copyright © 1993–2002 The McGraw-Hill Companies, Inc. Reproduction of the S&P 500 Index Values in any form is prohibited without S&P's prior written permission

between securities and/or derivatives directly or indirectly correlated; therefore, market direction plays no role in their successful implementation. The market neutral strategy comprises a wide variety of arbitrage techniques and requires the use of sophisticated statistical models. However, the skill of the manager in identifying where there is value and constructing coverage remains a fundamental element.

Using a market neutral strategy does not automatically imply neutral risk. In general, the techniques used do not eliminate the positive relationship between risk and returns but seek to concentrate attention on stocks which promise added value, at the same time seeking to eliminate undesired risk and enabling more efficient use of capital in comparison to traditional strategies.

The base strategy for market neutral funds is known as the equal dollar balance and corresponds to a portfolio with long and short positions with the same value in a given currency at all times. This investment philosophy begins with capital of one dollar, a long and a short position. The proceeds of the short sale of the security are invested providing returns close to those obtainable with zero risk bonds (called the short interest rate).

If the alpha is positive, the fund manager will have two alphas: one derived from the long position, the other from the short portfolio. Long portfolios which assume a level of market risk only receive one alpha plus the market return, corresponding to the sum of the risk premium derived from the investment in a given security and the zero risk interest rate.

Once the securities with pricing distortions have been identified, the manager can adopt one of the following positions:

- Buy undervalued securities and protect from market risk by shorting correctly valued securities.
- Short sell overvalued securities and protect from market risk by buying correctly valued stocks.
- Buy undervalued stocks and short sell overvalued stocks.

When we previously referred to the possibility of obtaining two alphas from the same portfolio, we were alluding to this final possibility. The equity market neutral strategy can also be defined as a statistical arbitrage technique or long/short equity investment strategy with the objective of achieving zero market risk.

From the Figure 1.12, we can assess how this strategy can be employed to positive and constant returns over time. Such returns are correlated with equity market indicators. We can see that as the S&P 500 began its negative trend (in the second half of 1999), equity market neutral funds continued to generate value by protecting invested capital with low volatility.

1.4.2 Event Driven Strategies

Event driven strategies are important in the world of hedge funds. This strategy is also known as risk arbitrage and focuses on the shares of companies going through structural changes such as mergers, acquisitions and restructuring.

Risk arbitrage is a bet on a specific event. In a typical situation, the manager buys shares in a company undergoing restructuring in the hope of exchanging them at a later date for cash or securities with a greater value. When successful, such operations deliver satisfactory returns for the arbitrageur. Above all, these trades have little correlation with the performance of equity or bond markets. Even if market risk is not to be ignored, the key to success for this strategy is to manage deal risk, i.e. the risk that any merger, acquisition or restructuring might not go ahead.

Table 1.7   Characteristics of event driven strategies

	Merger Arbitrage	Distressed Securities
Returns	high	average
Volatility	average	average
Downside risk	average	average
Sharpe ratio	high	average
Shares correlation	average	average
Market exposure	average	average
Leverage (degree of)	average	low
Time horizon	average	long

Source: Bluehedge News, reproduced with permission.

Typically, these strategies are based on in-depth analysis of the companies prior to investment. This might include legal and economic evaluations of the situation faced by the company, which is the subject of speculation.

Legal factors affect the profits of these funds but also impose restrictions on investors that can be dangerous if not respected. Indeed, in the majority of industrialised countries, anti-trust laws, laws specific to certain sectors (as for radio and television, transport and banking), regulations on financial conditions or other regulations affecting buyers (as in the banking and insurance sectors which are highly regulated), are all factors that limit what deals are possible.

At the moment at which the authorities intervene or otherwise in a particular deal, uncertainty abounds, with the possibility of falls in the prices of the securities concerned. Equally, this uncertainty generates opportunities. In general, the influence exerted by the authorities does not necessarily affect the outcome of the deal but rather, the time taken to achieve closure.

The fund manager who pursues this strategy achieves diversification by limiting the capital committed to each deal, by investing in transactions which offer different levels of risk and by carefully managing financial leverage. To maximise the returns of the portfolio, it is important that the riskiest trades have a low-level reciprocal correlation so that whilst a deal might fail, there should be no knock-on effect on other deals. In general, risk arbitrage strategies can be divided into two distinctive subgroups (Table 1.7):

- Merger arbitrage, which relates to arbitrage on companies in the process of merging.
- Distressed securities, which concentrates on shares in companies in the process of restructuring or liquidation.

This strategy has obtained excellent returns (Figure 1.13) apart from 1998 when total assets contracted by approximately 5%. After this negative performance, the event driven class reacted very well and in 1999 registered 22% growth. As shown by the 2000 and 2001 (partial) figures, returns have levelled off at around 7–8% per annum.

Event driven strategies are generally more volatile when compared to relative value styles. However, managers succeed in restricting this indicator to approximately 6–7% per annum. On average, the funds in this class register a Sharpe ratio value of around 1 and fairly low correlation with equity markets (approximately 0.20).

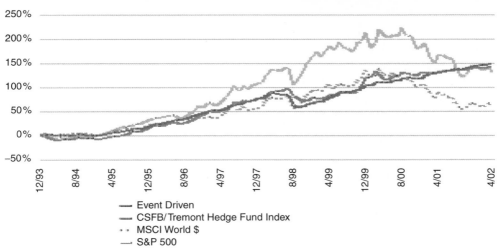

Event Driven
CSFB/Tremont Hedge Fund Index
MSCI World $
S&P 500

Source: www.hedgeindex.com

Figure 1.13 Event driven strategies. Reproduced by permission of CSFB and MSCI. Also reproduced by permission of Standard & Poor's, a division of The McGraw-Hill Companies, Inc. Copyright © 1993–2002 The McGraw-Hill Companies, Inc. Reproduction of the S&P 500 Index Values in any form is prohibited without S&P's prior written permission

Merger Arbitrage

The merger arbitrage strategy focuses on companies that have announced mergers or acquisitions. The objective is to achieve returns regardless of market direction. The strategy works as follows: when a company announces its intention to purchase another, the price of the target company rises, but not to the level of the bid. Indeed, because of the risk specific to the deal, i.e. that the deal will not be concluded in the expected time or that the deal falls through, the shares in the target company will be traded at a lower price than that offered through the acquisition. This difference will increase relative to the time taken to achieve closure and therefore the perceived deal risk. The merger arbitrageur seeks to profit on this spread. In the case of cash being offered for the target company, the arbitrageur need only buy shares in the target company. However when, as in the majority of cases, the offer includes shares in the company making the offer, the manager must also take into account the likelihood of this company's shares falling. He does this by short selling the shares of the company making the offer.

As discussed, the major risk with this kind of strategy is that the merger or acquisition might not go ahead. This may be due to anti-trust legislation, such as was applied in the recent case of GE–Honeywell, or because of management indecision in the face of negative market reaction.

We must highlight two aspects that help to reduce the risk of these strategies: many managers ignore rumours, investing only in deals which have been officially announced. Moreover, the majority of non-hostile take-overs are successful with only a 3% fail rate.

In general, returns from this type of strategy are consistent. Due diligence on and screening of the companies in question is performed by the manager, thereby simplifying the whole process of reviewing the merits of any given deal. In the case of hostile take-overs, careful analysis can establish the legal and strategic defence of the target company, the ability of the buyer to finance the deal and the possibility of regulatory authorities impeding or blocking the deal.

Distressed Securities

By distressed securities, we mean equities, bonds and in general, the rights to companies which are either unstable, close to collapse or indeed emerging from such situations. The prices of these securities fall in anticipation of this period of instability, the negative direction fuelled by shareholders preferring to sell their holdings in companies with financial problems. Often, however, this reaction is motivated by a fear that the company in question might collapse. This leads them to ignore the actual value and potential of the company. In such cases, managers specialised in distressed securities understand the real risks and value, buying the shares at a discount to sell them later at a profit.

The strategy consists of capitalising on the knowledge, flexibility and patience of the distressed securities fund manager, characteristics which creditors often lack. The activities of many institutional investors, such as pension funds, are governed by precise regulations which prevent them from buying or holding bonds under a certain rating (BBB or under), whether or not the underlying company is sound. They can therefore find themselves in the unenviable position of having to sell at unfavourable prices, simultaneously contributing to the fall in price. Even banking institutions often prefer to sell their worst loans to remove them from their balance sheets and free up capital for other uses. Moreover, it is quite possible that the bank's actions are either erroneous or that they lack the skill to investigate the restructuring process which may take as long as several years. It is clearly important to investigate whether or not it is really worth investing in an unstable company, to understand if the company, having over-expanded and diversified, still has a valid core business. It is fundamental to understand if the buy price is more or less than the potential value or value at liquidation. To conduct such analysis effectively, you must fully understand the various types of financial debt and their order of priority regarding repayment.

Shares issued during periods of reorganisation usually have a low correlation with equity and bond markets in that the prices are already so depressed. With their low price and the number of available shares being so reduced, they are seldom influenced by market fluctuations.

In conclusion, distressed securities represent an interesting investment strategy with low correlation with the markets. Success depends mainly on the depth of analysis and distressed securities managers sometimes take on significant positions in the companies in question so that they can positively influence the time taken to conclude the process and the method of distributing the companies' assets.

1.4.3   Opportunistic Strategies

As highlighted previously, we chose to define hedge fund strategies by their correlation with equity markets. This class is in effect a residual class in that it comprises those strategies that have variable levels of correlation with equity markets. In this class, the strategies are very diverse. Macro funds, which invest in equity markets using a long/short approach, have variable exposure to market direction. Indeed, the objective of the investment philosophy of these equity funds is often not to achieve neutral risk, but to maintain a long net exposure to these markets (usually around 30%). This demonstrates how these funds do not fully protect their long positions but rather seek to bet on market direction. Where the trend is positive, the performance of these funds beats that of other investment strategies. In addition to relative value and event driven funds, we will also examine funds which focus on short selling as a main source of profits and funds, investing in emerging markets. Opportunistic funds, in the period

Table 1.8   The characteristics of opportunistic strategies

	Macro	Short Sellers	Long/Short Equity	Emerging Markets
Returns	high	average	high	high
Volatility	high	high	high	high
Downside risk	average	high	high	high
Sharpe ratio	average	low	low	low
Shares correlation	average	negative	high	high
Market exposure	high	high	high	high
Leverage (degree of)	average	low	low	low
Time horizon	short	average	short	average

Source: Bluehedge News, reproduced with permission.

between January 1990 and March 2000, achieved far higher volatility than relative value and event driven strategies.

Table 1.8 shows the reasons for grouping these four strategies under one class. Indeed, the strategies provide the same level of volatility (high) and equal exposure to the markets (high) whilst relative value and event driven funds are characterised by their low volatility and low market exposure. Moreover, as a result of their high volatility, the Sharpe ratio shows that the appropriate returns (relative to risk) are lower than for relative value and event driven strategies. The spread of returns is on average higher for the four strategies than for the two classes previously studied.

The differences in the other criteria show that the generic term "opportunistic strategies" can be applied to macro, long/short equity, emerging markets and short selling funds.

We must also highlight how these strategies are primarily focused on achieving high returns and how the time horizon is short for both macro funds and short sellers. Somewhat predictably, the correlation particularly between short sellers and equity markets is negative.

Global Macro

Global macro funds (also known more simply as macro funds) enjoy a great deal of flexibility in terms of both investment philosophy and the investment strategies used. Macro funds are by far the largest funds in the hedge fund industry. For this and a number of reasons they are also the funds which attract the most attention from the press.

Their fame is attributable to the spectacular trades that punctuate their history. Many are convinced that because of the size of these funds and their use of leverage, they are capable of influencing or rather manipulating financial markets. Everyone remembers that in 1992, macro funds were credited with the crash in British sterling which as a result of their intervention, had to exit the European Monetary System. This fact brought a great deal of attention from the press and put macro funds in the dock.

A study conducted by the International Monetary Fund confirmed that macro funds took on huge short positions on sterling in 1992 but that it was difficult to ascertain if their action caused the devaluation in the currency since at the same time it was also true that large amounts of capital were flowing out of the UK.

Tremont distinguishes two types of macro fund manager, those that have a background in equity markets and those who come from derivative trading:

- Macro funds such as Tiger Investment Management and Soros Fund Management originally invested in the US equity markets. The success they achieved through their skill as stock pickers enabled them to vastly increase the capital of their funds. When funds increase in size, it becomes increasingly difficult for them to take on positions in small and medium-sized companies. Instead, they are forced to take larger bets on more liquid companies and markets.
- Funds such as Moore Capital, Caxton & Tunder Investment arose from trading activities in futures contracts. Their true nature is therefore much more in line with a global and macroeconomic viewpoint. The greater freedom offered by the world's currency markets and the strong development of futures exchanges outside the United States, which came about in the eighties, suddenly provided investors with a greater range of investment opportunities.

Therefore, macro funds use long/short equity strategies and futures trading techniques to take bets on a global scale. These funds seek to take advantage of opportunities and trends in financial markets, using their extreme flexibility to obtain maximum returns by applying strategies which best fit the moment. It is important to highlight two elements. The first is that such funds bet on trends, seeking to anticipate the market, the second is that these funds operate in highly liquid and efficient markets in which it would be very difficult for them to cause any trend by their actions.

As discussed previously, macro funds analyse certain events and if profit opportunities exist, choose which positions to assume. It is very problematic for these funds to reveal these strategic decisions since their actions would be copied by a myriad of smaller funds, thereby reducing the fund's profit margins. Macro funds often trade in the fixed income, currency and derivative markets. These markets are highly liquid and liquidity goes hand in hand with efficiency. Indeed, it is said that the more liquid a market, the more efficient it is. However, high levels of liquidity and efficiency also imply perfect information and a high degree of competition, which also translates into fewer opportunities. It is for this reason that macro funds offer low levels of transparency. The fact that these funds trade in such markets makes it difficult for us to believe they are capable, by their actions, of inducing a trend. It seems more realistic that macro funds employ in-depth analysis and as soon as they discover inefficiencies, assume positions in the same way as other hedge funds. The skill of the manager is to know at exactly what moment he should intervene in the market. It is not important to know the conditions necessary to interrupt a trend but rather to understand when the market will perceive that the conditions no longer exist for the continuation of this trend. It is at this time that the hedge fund manager takes advantage of his relative freedom to make trading decisions. He assumes positions seconds before the market changes its mind (and price).

The end of the nineties saw a reduction in terms of assets and number of macro funds, a slow decline leading to their ultimate end. Certainly, the collapse of LTCM contributed to the problems faced by all macro fund managers. Moreover, that personalities such as Robertson and Soros have decided to give up the game because of their age has added to the fact that macro funds are losing their influence in the world of hedge funds.

It is one thing to face a period of crisis but another to declare the imminent extinction of a strategy such as that employed by macro funds. This strategy assigns the mandate to invest in any activity from which the manager believes he can generate high profits. As an investment philosophy, it is not particularly appropriate for pension funds seeking stable performance, low volatility and above all, low correlation with other asset classes. However, there are always parties interested in obtaining high returns, such as are possible with this strategy.

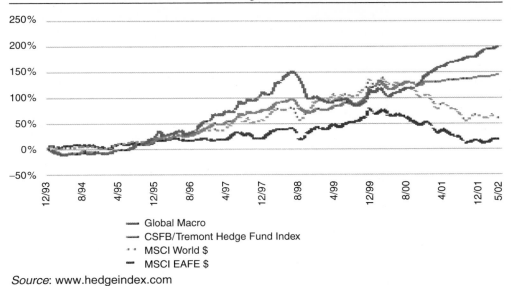

Source: www.hedgeindex.com

Figure 1.14   Macro. Reproduced by permission of CSFB and MSCI

In Figure 1.14, we compare historical data on macro funds with that of the major equity markets. One's attention is immediately drawn to the strong fall suffered by macro funds in 1998, caused by the collapse of LTCM and the negative repercussions this event had on other macro funds. These fund managers took a year to get over this event but as the graph shows from the second half of 1999 onwards, macro funds again started to post impressive figures. In March 2001, macro funds succeeded in beating the S&P 500. Average annual returns from 1994 onwards are 14% whilst the level of standard deviation is around 14%. Together, these two figures result in a risk/return figure of 0.66, much less than event driven funds (Sharpe ratio of around 1) and equity market neutral (Sharpe ratio of around 2).

Short Sellers

Short selling is the main technique that separates the hedge fund industry from that of traditional funds. Traditional funds may only sell short under extremely restrictive conditions. Short selling means to sell securities, which the manager does not currently possess. Securities are borrowed from a credit institution, insurance company or one of the major brokerage houses, which hold the securities in clients' portfolios and buy as collateral securities or liquid funds for an amount equivalent to the market price of the borrowed securities.

After having borrowed the securities, the manager sells them on the equity market, buys them back at a lower price and delivers them back to the borrower. If the price of the stock which the manager has short sold falls, as expected by the manager, the profit will equal the price at which he sold them less the price at which he bought them back. On the other hand, if the price were to rise, the manager would register a loss equal to the difference in the two prices. Once the shares have been sold on the market, the proceeds of the sale are allocated to a brokerage account yielding an interest rate. The fund manager must respect the restrictive conditions imposed by the FED (Reg. T) and open a margin account, i.e. deposit a margin of guarantee to protect himself from possible fluctuations in the price of the security (the margin is 50% of the value of the securities borrowed and can be in the form of cash or securities owned by the fund manager). The brokerage house calculates the gain or loss on the client's position on a weekly basis. If the security in question is highly volatile, the position will be checked daily.

The manager who sells short faces two risks:

- The price of the shares rises as opposed to falling. The fund is obliged to pay the margin. In the worst case where the coverage has failed, the manager will face high costs as he finds himself with a long position in those securities falling in price and a short position in securities which have risen in value. It is for this reason that the success of the hedge between the long and short positions depends on the stock picking abilities of the manager.
- The broker requests that the securities be returned. The broker is able to demand that (some or all of) the loaned securities be returned at any time. This generally creates significant problems for the manager and often leads to losses. Usually, the less liquid the stock, the greater the risk.

Public opinion and market-related press have always viewed this as a purely speculative technique and as such, a threat to market stability. In the United States, they have tried to make this more transparent by only allowing short selling after the price of the share has risen: it is therefore not possible to take advantage of a downward trend.

Managers following a short selling strategy after the attack on the WTC were praised for their funds' excellent performance. Nevertheless, these managers have been widely criticised for having been responsible, more than any other parties, for causing the fall in financial markets.

The short bet at times of high volatility is generally a winner in that these are often followed by several months of market contraction. As you can see from Figure 1.15, which is based on CSFB/Tremont data, short seller funds began a strong upward trend as of last September onwards, whilst the S&P 500 and MSCI World indices began their falling trends which are as yet unfinished. Short selling funds managed to achieve a beta of −0.93, i.e. registered a strong negative correlation with the equity market (for this analysis, we chose the S&P 500 index). A beta of +1 would indicate a perfect positive correlation with the equity markets whilst a perfect negative correlation would be indicated by a beta of −1. The beta value of short seller funds is also negative when compared to the MSCI World (−0.75), whilst against the JP Morgan Government Bond index the beta is almost neutral (+0.02). We must not ignore however that short sellers had to suffer 10 years of American market growth.

Emerging Markets

This strategy focuses on equity and bond investment in emerging markets. These funds are far more volatile in relation to all other hedge fund strategies not only because emerging markets are more volatile than developed markets but also because the possibilities to short sell are more limited and the futures markets are not so developed as to offer valid risk control. The lack of adequate instruments to control risk makes these hedge funds more inclined to take on long positions.

Investing in emerging markets can be an opportunity or a trap, depending on one's point of view. What is true is that in being less developed from a financial perspective, they are less efficient and offer opportunities to hedge fund managers. The risk in these markets is reflected

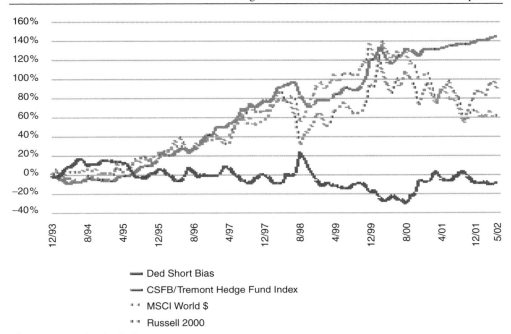

Ded Short Bias

CSFB/Tremont Hedge Fund Index

MSCI World $

Russell 2000

Source: www.hedgeindex.com

Figure 1.15   Dedicated short bias. Reproduced by permission of CSFB, MSCI and Frank Russell Company

by the difficulty in obtaining information, legal systems that are not adequately developed, unsophisticated local investors, a potentially unstable political and economic environment and local companies run by managers with less experience. All these factors create opportunities that hedge fund managers seek to exploit.

Long/Short Equity

The long/short equity strategy has become the in-vogue strategy of the last few years. Indeed, the capital managed by managers of these funds represents 48% of the total assets of the industry. The main difference between long/short managers and long only managers (i.e. mutual fund managers) consists of the fact that the former enjoy greater freedom to use financial leverage, sell short and cover the positions in the portfolio.

The main objective of these managers is to achieve absolute returns and not necessarily take on positions which enable them to beat the benchmark market. The portfolios of long/short funds are generally long by 30%. They also tend to be constructed with fewer securities than traditional portfolios. Long/short strategies enable the manager to adapt to market conditions, constructing a combination of long and short positions with various levels of exposure to the markets.

In general, a short portfolio can be constructed with three aims:

- To obtain a return (generate an alpha). This represents the main difference with traditional funds in so much as the selection of securities in which to invest can enable the manager to achieve two alphas. One alpha derives from the long portfolio (if the manager has bought

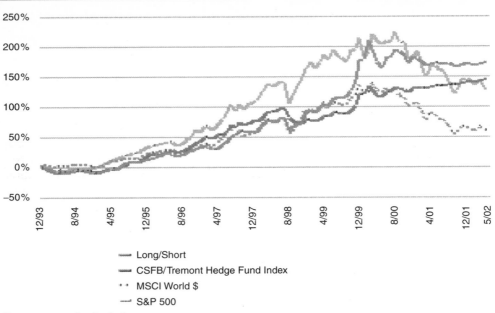

Source: www.hedgeindex.com

Figure 1.16 Long/short equity. Reproduced by permission of CSFB and MSCI. Also reproduced by permission of Standard & Poor's, a division of The McGraw-Hill Companies, Inc. Copyright © 1993–2002 The McGraw-Hill Companies, Inc. Reproduction of the S&P 500 Index Values in any form is prohibited without S&P's prior written permission

securities that increase in value) and the second stems from the short portfolio (if he has sold securities whose value falls).

• The short portfolio can be used to protect the fund from market risk.
• The manager earns interest generated by the account in which the proceeds from the short sale of securities are kept.

The ability to short sell enables hedge fund managers to capitalise on all opportunities in the market of which traditional fund managers cannot take advantage.

From 1994 onwards, returns for long/short equity funds have registered annual growth of 14% (Figure 1.16), with cumulative growth of 169%. The managers of these strategies achieved excellent results, particularly in 1999 when the long/short equity index achieved 47% annual returns. Compared to other investment styles, the long/short strategy has a greater correlation with equity markets (0.48 when compared to the S&P 500 and 0.65 in relation to the MSCI World). This is due to the fact that these fund managers look to take advantage of upward market trends. These managers, thanks to the short constituent of the portfolios, succeed in protecting capital from strongly negative trends in equity markets. For example, in 2000, the S&P 500 and MSCI World contracted by 10% and 14% respectively, whilst the managers of long/short equity funds succeeded in obtaining positive performance of approximately 2%. In 2001, both equity indexes lost 20% whilst managers employing this strategy succeeded in limiting their losses.

2
Hedge Fund Advantages and Opportunities

The success that the hedge fund industry is currently experiencing in Europe obviously stems from the low correlation between such funds and the underlying equity and bond markets. Also, the fact that hedge funds pursue absolute returns makes these products ever more attractive.

Hedge funds, like other alternative financial instruments (commodities, works of art, etc.) are characterised by their low correlation with equity markets. The performance of a hedge fund is much more closely linked with the ability and experience of the fund manager than for the manager of a traditional fund. The process of asset allocation, be that for a manager of a hedge or a traditional fund, is based on the portfolio theory devised by Harry Markowitz. This model shows the close relationship among return, risk and correlation and illustrates how by correctly analysing these three elements, the manager can construct an effective portfolio. Moreover, Markowitz was the first to formulate the concepts of "systematic risk" and "non-systematic risk".

To quantify systematic risk or beta, the measure of risk of an equity security is defined as the relationship between the variation in return of the equity as compared to the variation in the equity market, of which it is a constituent. The Markowitz theory defines β (systematic risk) as a measure of market risk. We quickly deduce that shares with $\beta>1$ are characterised by their greater variability in relation to the market. These shares can be classed as aggressive. On the other hand, stocks with $\beta<1$ are characterised by their low sensitivity when compared to the market and can therefore be seen as defensive stocks. The beta coefficient is a means of measuring the volatility of a security or portfolio of securities in comparison with the market as a whole.

The objective of a hedge fund is to minimise market risk; the fund manager aims to construct portfolios with β as close to zero as possible, in order to free the performance of the fund from the effect of market volatility. Hedge fund returns are therefore mostly attributable to the skill of the manager to pick stocks and construct a portfolio based on alpha, which expresses the non-systematic risk, i.e. the risk associated with specific stocks. The fact that the hedge fund manager can sell short enables the alpha values of a specific stock to be combined to achieve higher returns. The objective of speculative portfolios is to isolate assets from market movements and control factors such as sector risk, credit risk, the p/e ratio in such a way that returns generated by the portfolio are almost exclusively dependent on the α parameter. Minimised market risk, control of specific risk and absolute performance mean that hedge funds are an excellent instrument in which to diversify, providing a valid alternative to traditional financial instruments.

We can summarise the benefits of these investments and highlight which of these are essential reference points for potential investors. We will examine each in greater detail in the subsequent sections.

- High absolute and relative returns (in comparison to other financial instruments): extremely interesting for a private clientele, e.g. for discretionary asset management, trusts, private banking and "high net worth individuals".

- Extremely interesting and competitive performance and risk indicators (low volatility, good Sharpe ratio): attractive elements to both institutional and sophisticated private clients.
- Negative or zero correlation with traditional forms of investment: this characteristic allows institutional portfolios to obtain higher performance with the same level of risk, as we later analyse; credit institutions, surplus funds from insurance companies, and also pension funds could clearly exploit this important characteristic of hedge funds.
- Negative or zero correlation among the subcategories of alternative investment instruments: this represents the principal advantage sought by the new alternative investment managers.
- Fiscal advantages: structured products linked to hedge funds (bond instruments), the most attractive method for private clients to access the hedge fund market.

Also implicit in the alternative investment market are certain disadvantages. With increased demand for these products and growth in the industry, these issues are gradually being addressed.

- The lack of liquidity for hedge funds is gradually being overcome by the continual development of a more efficient secondary market.
- The elevated minimum investment thresholds no longer represent an obstacle. The minimum stakes in speculative funds of funds are available to almost everyone (participation begins at around Euro 10,000).
- A lack of transparency and limited reporting does not affect funds of funds or structured bonds where returns/capital protection is guaranteed by the asset allocator or issuer (usually banks or asset management companies with very high credit ratings).
- Elevated costs for investors remain a strong barrier to entry. Whilst on one side fees are being reduced, a greater dependency on management and performance fees reflects little in the way of substantial change.

2.1   ADVANTAGES OF HEDGE FUNDS FOR INSTITUTIONAL CLIENTS: ELEMENTS OF PORTFOLIO SELECTION

The universe of alternative instruments and particularly the hedge fund industry has seen substantial growth in recent years. Traditionally, this market was characterised by investors prepared to suffer the disadvantages of low liquidity and a lack of transparency in return for performance unrelated to the market of reference. In recent years, the rise in demand for these products on the part of institutions has changed the fundamental behavioural characteristics of hedge funds. In the place of a relationship based on trust, fund managers are now providing their customers with far greater transparency regarding portfolio composition, strategy, performance, commissions, liquidity, risk management and the use of financial leverage.

Institutional investors tend to view these products as long-term investments, they have a high aversion to risk and require stable returns, characteristics which make hedge funds ideal instruments for inclusion in institutional portfolios. The hedge fund industry represents, therefore, an important opportunity in terms of portfolio efficiency.

The purpose of this section is to assess the benefits, in terms of the trade off between risk/returns that hedge funds investment can bring to the construction of an efficient portfolio for the institutional investor. The reasons for institutional managers inserting hedge funds (or speculative funds) into portfolios begin with the analysis of the performance and risk indices of hedge funds, comparing these figures with the figures achieved by traditional investments. The second stage consists in the calculation of the correlation between these two different investment categories: the zero or sometimes negative correlation of hedge funds enables the investor to achieve higher returns with no increase in risk for the portfolio.

The last point shows the different benefits that hedge funds can bring in terms of efficiency when constructing portfolios for banks (comparative to a traditional investment without the use of hedge funds).

2.1.1 Hedge Funds and Traditional Investments

The principal characteristic of hedge funds is to seek absolute returns independent of market direction. In reality, this characteristic represents the principal distinctive element that differentiates them from other financial instruments. To obtain absolute returns means to guarantee a constant positive economic return from your investments regardless of the market cycle. To always obtain a return, however small in times of crisis, is an important objective for reasons of stability and risk management. Indeed, hedge funds offer an interesting risk/return profile, not only comparative to that of traditional investments but also in absolute terms.

This study comprised the analysis of four hedge fund strategies: global macro, equity market neutral, long/short equity and event driven and two representative stock market indexes: S&P 500 and MSCI World. The two factors taken into consideration when appraising the profitability of an investment in hedge funds are returns and risk. Amongst the indicators used to show the appropriate return/risk, we have selected the Sharpe ratio: it compares the value of an investment using measures of relative risk and returns to that of an investment with zero risk.

Tables 2.1 and 2.2 show the results of the analysis. The first shows performance. What immediately emerges from this, besides the profitable returns recorded during the last seven years, are the returns (mostly positive) achieved in the period 2000 and 2001. These were delivered in a time of strong contraction in the world's stock markets. In the face of a decrease of over 20% in the value of stock indexes, hedge funds recorded by comparison strongly positive returns with global macro strategies achieving over 10% annual growth. The second table shows some statistics but most importantly, risk indicators and the Sharpe ratio.

The risk/return profile of the various hedge funds is generally consistent. In the period considered the global macro and long/short equity funds achieved the highest returns (14.01% and 12.76% respectively). With such high average returns, these classes have a higher standard deviation (3.92% and 3.51%) than that of other strategies, but lower than that of stock market indexes. This data is confirmed by the Sharpe ratio: in both cases, higher results are achieved than by both the S&P and the MSCI World.

Equity market neutral fund strategies result in completely different characteristics and statistical data. The objective of fund managers that use this strategy is to achieve consistent returns whilst minimising correlation to equity markets. Indeed, the analysis shows an extremely positive risk/return profile: with average annual returns of 11%, the risk indicator is less than 3%. At the same time, the Sharpe ratio shows an extremely high figure for this type of strategy (2%).

We can conclude that all four strategies of the hedge funds analysed offer risk/return profiles which are much more efficient than the stock indices used in this comparison. That said, the most important piece of data that emerges is the 2% Sharpe ratio value for the market neutral strategy.

2.1.2 Elements of Portfolio Selection and Correlation Coefficient: The Competitive Advantage for Institutional Portfolios

The innovation upon which modern portfolio theory is based can be attributed to Harry Markowitz who in 1950 inserted the concept of the trade-off in the risk/return relationship

Table 2.1   Hedge funds performance

	Global Macro (%)	Market Neutral (%)	Event Driven (%)	Long/Short Equity (%)	S&P 500 (%)	MSCI World (%)
2001*	14.6	7.73	7.93	−5.12	−21.22	−24.17
2000	11.67	14.99	7.26	2.08	−10.14	−14.05
1999	5.81	15.33	22.26	47.23	19.53	23.56
1998	−3.64	13.31	−4.87	17.18	26.67	22.78
1997	37.11	14.83	19.96	21.46	31.01	14.17
1996	25.58	16.60	23.06	17.12	20.26	11.72
1995	30.67	11.04	18.34	23.03	34.11	18.70
1994**	−5.72	−2.00	0.75	−8.10	−1.54	3.36

Source: www.hedgeindex.com
* Data updated to September 2001. ** Data updated to January 1994.
Reproduced by permission of CSFB and MSCI. Also reproduced by permission of Standard & Poor's, a division of The McGraw-Hill Companies, Inc. Copyright © 1993–2002 The McGraw-Hill Companies, Inc. Reproduction of the S&P 500 Index Values in any form is prohibited without S&P's prior written permission

Table 2.2   Hedge funds statistics

Statistics	Global Macro	Market Neutral	Long/Short Equity	Event Driven	S&P 500	MSCI World
Monthly average	1.17%	0.90%	1.06%	0.94%	0.97%	0.55%
Best month	10.60%	3.26%	13.01%	3.68%	9.67%	8.91%
Worst month	−11.55%	−1.15%	−11.43%	−11.77%	−14.56%	−13.45%
Yearly average	14.01%	11.28%	12.76%	11.60%	10.33%	6.87%
Standard deviation	3.77%	3.24%	3.39%	1.77%	4.52%	4.06%
Sharpe ratio*	0.71	2.00	0.68	1.11	0.37	0.05

Source: www.hedgeindex.com
*Calculated using the rolling 90-day T-bill rate.
Reproduced by permission of CSFB and MSCI. Also reproduced by permission of Standard & Poor's, a division of The McGraw-Hill Companies, Inc. Copyright © 1993–2002 The McGraw-Hill Companies, Inc. Reproduction of the S&P 500 Index Values in any form is prohibited without S&P's prior written permission

of a financial investment. Through the contributions of Sharpe (1964), Lintner (1965) and Mossin (1966), this approach evolved into the Capital Asset Pricing Model.

Modern portfolio theory studies the process which generates the demand and supply of a financial activity as a function of the relationship between risk and return. Indeed, one of the fundamental stages in the construction of an efficient portfolio consists in identifying an appropriate combination of securities to reduce risk and optimise overall performance.

According to this theory, the choice of securities in an efficient portfolio is not only a function of the characteristics (risk, returns, etc.) of a single security but of these characteristics when combined with the other instruments inside the same portfolio. It becomes, therefore, interesting to calculate the correlation coefficient with the returns obtained by hedge and traditional funds. As the correlation is either a negative or in any case a very low figure, significant benefits accompany the insertion of this investment class into institutional portfolios.

Our analysis centres on the calculation of the correlation coefficient for the returns achieved by the representative indices of four hedge fund strategies (global macro, equity market neutral, long/short equity and event driven), two representative stock indexes (MSCI World and Dow Jones) and the JPM GovBond index. The results we obtained through this analysis of correlation (Table 2.3) are very interesting: when compared to the bond index, the different classes of hedge funds have either a negative correlation, or at least very close to zero (global macro). When on

Table 2.3 Correlation coefficients

	Global Macro	Market Neutral	Event Driven	Long/Short Equity
MSCI World	0.23	0.45	0.59	0.65
JPM GovBond	0.06	−0.14	−0.34	−0.18
Dow Jones	0.25	−0.34	−0.18	0.48

Source: www.hedgeindex.com. Reproduced by permission of CSFB, MSCI, J.P. Morgan Chase and Dow Jones & Co., Inc.

the other hand compared to the stock indexes the correlation is higher. The results are higher for the global macro and long/short equity strategies, whilst they are much lower and at times negative for the other two categories of funds. With these results and considerations we are able to correctly assess the benefits of including hedge funds in an institutional portfolio.

Our analysis on the risk/return profile and correlation coefficients has clearly shown the benefits of hedge funds forming part of an institutional portfolio. Figure 2.1 shows the advantages that are obtained in terms of portfolio efficiency with and without hedge fund investment.

The study began with the construction of an efficient frontier of a portfolio composed solely of equity securities and bonds, using the JPM GovBond index for the bond component and Standard & Poor's for the equity component. The result shows an equity portfolio that goes from a 5.72% risk level with almost 5% returns to a portfolio with around 15% standard deviation and annual returns just above 10%. In contrast, all four different classes of hedge fund strategies have decidedly better risk/return profiles than portfolios investing solely in equities or bonds. The new efficient frontier is positioned above the previous one, providing a better risk/return profile: the least risky strategy (equity market neutral) has a 3.32% standard deviation and returns of a little more than 11% and the riskiest (global macro) has nevertheless a more efficient risk/return relationship than the S&P (standard deviation 13.65%, average returns 14.03%).

In conclusion, we can say with certainty that by inserting hedge funds into a traditional portfolio, benefits can be obtained in terms of risk/returns. Those good performances analysed over the last seven years, the relative indicators of risk and the lower if not negative correlation coefficients with traditional activities compel the institutional manager to use these instruments to increase the efficiency of their portfolio. The last stage consists of constructing two portfolios with and without hedge funds to assess the benefits in terms of risk and returns.

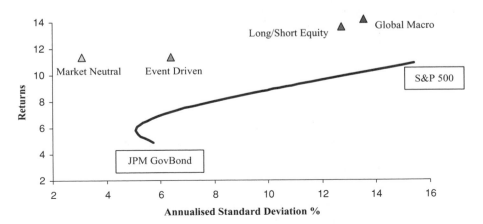

Figure 2.1 The efficient frontier

Table 2.4   Statistics of simulated portfolios

	Traditional Portfolio	Portfolio with Hedge Funds
Expected return	7.33%	8.76%
Standard deviation	6.61%	5.37%

This last analysis is a comparison between a traditional portfolio and one with hedge funds. For the analysis, we have used the MSCI World index (for equities), the JPM GovBond (for bonds) and the CSFB/Tremont index (for hedge funds – this is a representative index of around 400 hedge funds divided by strategy). We first considered a traditional portfolio comprising 60% bonds and 40% equities (Figure 2.2). Our figures show a 6.6% standard deviation and returns of over 7% (Table 2.4). By replacing part of the bond and equity investments with hedge funds, it is possible to see the advantages of diversification (Figure 2.3). The new portfolio with 30% invested in hedge funds, in turn diversified by strategy, results in returns of approximately 1% more than the traditional portfolio but with a lower standard deviation (approximately −1%).

Figure 2.4 shows how a portfolio containing hedge funds compares to the efficient frontier of a traditional portfolio. It also shows the benefits of diversification and the low correlation of hedge funds with traditional asset classes.

2.1.3   Conclusions

The benefits highlighted in the statistical analysis can be summarised as follows:

- **Excellent risk/return profile** – all the main risk indicators (standard deviation) and performances as analysed, confirm the safety and profitability of this investment category. The same Sharpe ratio (which measures the validity of an investment and the skill of the manager) shows that this investment category achieves superior figures to traditional investments.

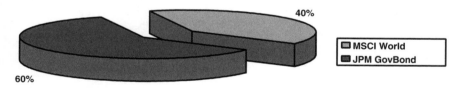

Figure 2.2   Traditional portfolio

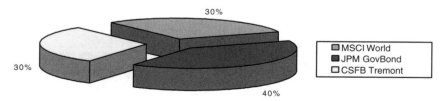

Figure 2.3   Portfolio with 30% invested in hedge funds

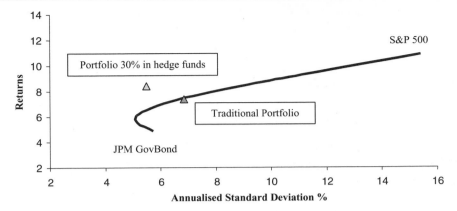

Figure 2.4   The efficient frontier

- **Low correlation with traditional investments** – all four of the studied strategies provide negative correlation with bond investments and extremely low correlation with equity investments. In this way, we see opportunities to diversify through hedge fund investment.
- **Convenience for institutional portfolios** – the insertion, therefore, of hedge funds in a portfolio otherwise composed of traditional asset classes results in certain advantages: it allows the manager to reduce the level of risk in the portfolio (standard deviation) and to increase at the same time the anticipated returns, positioning the portfolio above the efficient frontier achieved with traditional asset classes.

2.2   ADVANTAGES OF HEDGE FUNDS FOR PRIVATE CLIENTS: SECOND GENERATION FUNDS OF FUNDS AND STRUCTURED PRODUCTS

Hedge funds, particularly those domiciled in the United States, were always distinguished by their high barriers to entry in the form of elevated minimum investment thresholds. This contributed to the limited distribution of these instruments. The legal structure (limited partnership) of speculative funds and the subsequent success of global macro funds, the most complex in the hedge fund industry, also served to distance the majority of private investors from these products. Investing in hedge funds was the reserve of high net worth individuals whose portfolios were so large as to require them to seek products in which to diversify. Even now, high net worth individuals account for greater investment in hedge funds than institutions.

Therefore, if as previously discussed, the next stage in the growth of hedge funds is to come about through their acquisition by institutional portfolios, it will also be true that the role of private clients and discretionary asset management will also be significant. High net worth clients will remain one of the preferred sources of capital for these speculative funds but as a consequence of ever decreasing minimum investment thresholds, savers with less money will also be able to purchase stakes in these funds.

Fewer barriers to entry and increasingly accessible minimum participation levels are countered by a greater aversion to risk, characteristic of this type of investor. To fulfil the needs of this new but potentially limitless client base, we are seeing the launch of increasing numbers of alternative instruments that seek to limit volatility and risk in order to entice private investors. Such instruments include funds of hedge funds and bonds whose performance is linked to hedge fund growth.

2.2.1   Funds of Hedge Funds

Amongst the various possibilities for private investors to access the alternative investment market, one of the most commonly used methods has recently been to buy into funds of hedge funds or multi-manager hedge funds. The investment manager or asset allocator of a fund of hedge funds selects and invests directly in a series of hedge funds (usually in a minimum of five to six funds and a maximum of 40), reflecting the diversification strategy adopted. Returns are achieved through the performance of the underlying funds net of the commissions applied by each of these funds.

Through the use of financial engineering techniques and different management strategies, the asset allocator creates a new product that seeks to maximise the advantages of the underlying hedge funds but minimising volatility and exposure to risk. As with traditional funds of funds, the objective of these products is to reduce risk through diversification – by taking advantage of the varied correlation of the underlying activities. Through funds of hedge funds, investors can participate in the performance of a number of managers. For example, by combining the market neutral component of certain funds with the more aggressive global/macro strategy, investors can achieve high returns with high stability.

The advantages of funds of hedge funds can be summarised as follows:

- The possibility of directly accessing the most important hedge funds with minimal investment.
- The possibility of taking advantage of the know-how and experience of the asset allocator whose role is to analyse the various underlying funds, decide which strategy to implement, select the best funds by sector and construct the portfolio. One of the most important services provided by the fund of funds manager is the constant checking and monitoring of the portfolio.
- The possibility of reducing the risk of direct investment through diversification.

The aforementioned advantages of funds of hedge funds become much more important when these funds of funds are capable of investing in the most important funds on the market. These are often closed to new investment and equally, the major funds (Soros, Robertson, Steinhardt) do not allow the investment of small amounts of money. Therefore, a fund of funds seems much more interesting when we consider that its composition will include those funds with the largest assets under management. An excellent example of this is the GAIM fund of funds.

The GAIM fund, managed by Global Investment Advisers Ltd (a London-based company with the objective of developing alternative investment instruments), is one of the first passive strategy funds (strategy tracker) available on the market. It invests in 20 to 30 of the major funds as defined by the CSFB/Tremont Hedge Fund index. The assets of the fund will initially be divided between the five largest hedge funds of the four major equity strategies (20 funds in total):

- Global macro
- Market neutral
- Long/short equity
- Event driven

This particular strategy as pursued by the GAIM fund enables investors to participate in the most important hedge funds in every strategy, in this way guaranteeing transparency and security for the small investor.

The recourse to funds of funds also offers savings in terms of costs for investors as well as the analysis, selection and continuous monitoring of the best funds on the market, and the implementation of risk management mechanisms. All of which would otherwise have to be done by the investor at significant expense and time spent. The laborious work of performing due diligence on the hedge fund market is in this way assumed by the manager. Sometimes, as in the case of GAIM, this is limited by the implementation of a passive strategy.

The possibility for investors to obtain exposure to the world of hedge funds with minimal investment, to profit from greater diversification and the ability to access information on the level of exposure and positions taken by the fund online represent important selling points for private clients with little or no experience in alternative investments, which it must be repeated are highly complex products.

The transparency of the asset allocation of the GAIM fund that follows at least initially the CSFB/Tremont index is shown in Table 2.5. The data on the allocation of this fund of funds starts from July 2001.

The recent launch of GAIM came on the back of a wave of exponential growth in this sector in Great Britain which, according to research by the Tower Group, expanded by 56% to 39 billion dollars over the last 12 months (as large as the US market in 1990). It is predicted that in the coming years, the growth trend will confirm the success of this category.

As discussed previously, when constructing funds of funds, asset allocators must overcome the problem of funds that are closed ended, sometimes to new investors, sometimes even to those already holding stakes in the fund. An analysis conducted by Martin Fothergill and Carolyn Coke from the Global Equity Derivatives department of Deutsche Bank AG London identified and defined various hedge fund categories.

The majority of the funds analysed were "open ended", guaranteeing investors the facility of buying and selling shares directly with the company which represents the hedge fund in the same way as mutual investment funds.

A few of the funds under review belong to the "closed ended" category, and are quoted and regularly exchanged on the secondary market which guarantees them a reference market. A third category of hedge funds is defined as "quasi open" and consists of funds dealt on the secondary market or directly with the issuing company. Other funds result as being closed to new investors. Let us look at these categories in detail:

- "Closed end secondary market traded only": a small number of hedge funds quoted in Zurich (for example Altin and CreInvest) and in London (Xavex HedgeFirst and Alternative Investment Strategies) which can only be exchanged on the major European bourses.
- "Open end with a secondary market": offer investors the highest degree of flexibility and liquidity. This is the most "shareholder friendly" category guaranteeing a quarterly or even monthly option to liquidate positions. Moreover, these funds are dealt on the secondary market of a recognised exchange or on the OTC market. An example of these funds is Leveraged Capital Holdings, which offers daily subscriptions and monthly maturities, traded on the Amsterdam Stock Exchange and dealt OTC in London.
- "Open end, no secondary market": this category represents the most common structure for funds of hedge funds. Certain factors such as the fund's domicile may differ, but the structure remains the same and is very similar to that of mutual funds. Dealing activity is periodical

Table 2.5   GAIM asset allocation – April 2002

The Managers	Weight	Strategy
EUREKA USD FUND LTD SHARES	2.77%	
MAVERICK FUND LTD CLASS A	2.19%	
MAVERICK FUND LTD CLASS B	1.00%	
ORBIS OPTIMAL US$ FUND LTD ORD	2.19%	
P.A.W. OFFSHORE FUND CLASS A (USD)	1.95%	
PEQUOT INTL FD INC CLASS A	3.13%	
RAPTOR GLOBAL FUND LTD (THE) CLASS B	3.81%	Long/Short 28.37%
STANDARD PACIFIC CAP OFFSHORE CLASS A SHARES	0.83%	
STANDARD PACIFIC CAP OFFSHORE CLASS B SHARES	4.08%	
WG TRADING COMPANY LP SHARES	0.98%	
WGTC LTD CLASS B PARTICIPATING SHARES	2.35%	
ZWEIG-DIMENNA INTL CLASS A (USD)	3.10%	
ARBITRAGE ASSOCIATES LTD CLASS A SERIES 1	2.76%	
ARBITRAGE ASSOCIATES LTD CLASS A SERIES 4	0.81%	
CANYON VALUE REALIZATION FUND CLASS A	3.04%	
CERBERUS INTERNATIONAL LTD CLASS B RESTRICTED	4.80%	
DAVIDSON KEMPER INTL LTD CLASS B	4.26%	Event Driven 25.32%
FIRST EAGLE FUND N.V. CLASS A	4.35%	
KING STREET CAPITAL FUND LTD CLASS A	1.15%	
YORK INVESTMENT LTD CLASS A SERIES 1	1.26%	
YORK INVESTMENT LTD CLASS A SERIES 4	0.83%	
YORK INVESTMENT LTD CLASS A11-2001	2.06%	
ADVISORY US EQUITY MKT NEUTRAL OVERSEAS CLASS B SERIES 1	2.62%	
BALBOA FUND LTD CLASS B SERIES 2	4.09%	
FLETCHER INCOME ARBITRAGE FUND SERIES 1	3.97%	
KINGATE EURO FUND LTD REGISTERED SHARES	0.35%	Market Neutral 23.17%
KINGATE GLOBAL FUND LTD USD SHARES	4.50%	
NEW CASTLE MKT NEUTRAL OFFSHORE CLASS B	3.93%	
SABRE MARKET NEUTRAL FUND LTD SHARES	3.71%	
GROSSMAN CURRENCY FUND LTD INDIVIDUAL SERIES # 127	3.82%	
OMEGA OVERSEAS PARTNERS LTD CLASS A	1.18%	
QUANTUM ENDOWMENT FUND CL "A" (USD) – NETH. ANTILLES	5.00%	
TROUT TRADING FUND LTD REDEEMABLE PART INVEST SHS	5.66%	Global Macro 23.14%
TUDOR BVI GLOBAL FUND LTD CLASS A	2.59%	
UBS CURRENCY PORTFOLIO LTD CLASS B SERIES 3 (CAYMAN)	2.78%	
WIMBLEDON FUND LTD (THE) CLASS TT	2.11%	

and generally subject to commissions. A characteristic of some of these funds is the limit on the amount traded monthly (usually around 5–10% of capital).

The division of the categories defined by the Deutsche Bank analysis, shown graphically in Figure 2.5, highlights how "open ended" funds continue to increase in number.

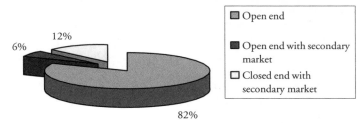

Source: Bluehedge News, reproduced with permission.

Figure 2.5   Open and closed structures

2.2.2 Second Generation Structured Products

Innovations in financial markets have opened hedge funds to a new category of investor, attracted both by capital guarantees and the returns achievable with hedge funds investments. The development of products linked to alternative investments began at the start of 2000, when several banks began to offer capital guaranteed structured products using techniques similar to those used for notes linked to equities or equity indexes. The opportunity of guaranteed capital provided by these products has had a notable positive effect on the uptake by investors, particularly in continental Europe, Japan and the Far East. Offered primarily through private bankers, these products offer a real protection against the loss of capital and provide fund of hedge fund managers with a source of capital for the medium to long term.

The first structured product linked to alternative investments was created in 1980. These rudimentary structures comprised the purchase of zero-coupon government bonds (two-thirds to three-quarters of the capital to be invested) to guarantee the capital and an investment in CTAs (Commodity Trading Advisors) and hedge funds. The history of returns achieved by these products was somewhat dictated by the fact that they offered no leverage: only a fraction of the capital was invested in alternative investments. The high commissions for this type of product applied by the bank in return for little added value certainly did not aid the popularity of these products.

A variation on the structure of these products that is still sometimes used is the "Letter of Credit" and an agent who acts as asset allocator. The letter of credit guarantees the capital while the asset allocator divides the capital between bonds and hedge funds as a function of the underlying funds. If the fund performs well, then the asset allocator invests larger tranches of the capital in the fund. Should the fund underperform, the asset allocator will move the capital into bonds in order to ensure that the initial capital plus commissions can be returned at maturity. The first disadvantage for investors in this type of product is the fact that even during brief periods of negative hedge fund returns, the amount of money actively managed will automatically be reduced.

A sudden fall in speculative investments can lead to 100% of the capital being invested in bonds, thus eliminating the particular characteristics of the product. In the meantime, investors must wait until the maturity of the structured product to receive the capital they invested. This structure has limited use because of the lack of transparency of both the leverage (and de-leverage) operations and the commissions charged by the bank issuing the letter of credit.

As a note can be constructed with rebates, for example, linked to the rise in the S&P, so can rebates be linked to the rise in the NAV of hedge funds, futures funds or funds of funds, and second generation structured products have arisen from this simple consideration.

This type of structured operation has always been arranged by private operators so it is not possible to know the total capital invested. However, it is generally assumed that a standard operation totals from $30 to $50 million with only a few trades of over $200 million. Those banks active in this market make profit from the margin built into the price of the "embedded option", from the sale of structured notes and from trades on the secondary market. These structures can be constructed using call options that run alongside the capital protected notes or through a form of closed end guaranteed funds. In the latter case, the performance of the fund is achieved by combining zero-coupon bonds with call options. Even if the majority of the assets are invested in bonds, the use of options (therefore leverage) enables high returns to be achieved.

In its simplest form, a typical capital guaranteed product will calculate rebates using the following formula:

$$100\%R \text{ of capital invested} + P \times \text{performance}$$

where p is the level of participation rate, also called "gearing"; for hedge funds, the amount rebated to the investor depends in the main on the structure of the note and the characteristics of the underlying hedge fund. A note structured with a 5-year maturity linked to a fund of hedge funds will generally offer a participation of 85%. Therefore, a rise of 120% in the underlying fund after 5 years (17.5% annualised) will result in returns of:

$$(100\% + 85 \times 120\%) = 202\% \text{ of the nominal}$$

i.e. annual returns of 15.1%. To evaluate the price of an option on a series of funds, the banks which offer them have developed a pricing model which takes into consideration, amongst other parameters, the historic performance and volatility of the funds, their correlation to equities, the currency and interest rate market, the level of diversification of their positions and the relative system of regulation. The banks face the difficult job of covering the risk inherent in these positions. The absence of an interbank market for options on funds and a communal pricing model means that positions are held to maturity, notwithstanding the future behaviour of the underlying fund. Different from "letter of credit based structure" products, the buyer of a second generation structured bond knows from the start what will be their level of participation in the performance of the underlying hedge fund.

From the point of view of the issuing bank, these new capital guaranteed notes linked to hedge funds present a further problem in the shape of the necessary delay in obtaining accurate valuations of certain hedge funds.

In the case of structured products which offer returns linked to the performance of a fund of funds, this problem may be amplified by the length of time taken by the administrators to value each fund included in the portfolio. Several special agreements relating to reporting valuations may be established between the bank and the fund manager to improve the visibility of the fund's performance: a fund which can be traded monthly can provide weekly estimates or reduce the monthly trading window to every few days. During times of high volatility as in August 1998, fund managers can keep the bank informed on a daily basis, thereby limiting the discrepancies in the information available to both parties and favouring the activity of dynamic leverage on the part of the issuer.

Certain investors upon considering the returns of structured products in recent years have rejected the capital guarantee, viewing it as an unnecessary expense. However, capital protected notes offer investors a series of advantages which easily make up for the added cost of using such instruments. These are as follows:

• The certainty of capital at maturity represents an important consideration for the small investor and sometimes is "conditio sine qua non" when choosing a financial instrument.
• The price of the bonds is guaranteed by the principal protection agreement with the issuer who agrees to act as market maker during the entire life of the note.
• The individual investor can, through this type of instrument, associate the returns typical of hedge funds with the favourable fiscal conditions (12.5% tax rate) as these instruments are in effect bond instruments.
• The bonds are often marketable to a wider investor base thanks to a more favourable regulatory status.

An example of a capital guaranteed structured product linked to a fund of hedge funds which has enjoyed particular success in the European markets is the note issued by Union Bancaire Privée called the UBP Multi-strategy Alpha Principal Protected Note. The bond, with a maturity of five years, enjoyed strong success in September 2001 on international financial markets which turned to the Swiss franc as a safe currency after the attack on the World Trade Centre. Unlike competing notes, UBP's offers the particular characteristic of being denominated in Swiss francs (the differences in the structured notes are insignificant in that the underlying fund of funds is the truly distinctive element of such products).

BNP Paribas is the issuer of the bond constructed on the fund of hedge funds managed directly by UBP. It is therefore BNP Paribas that guarantees the return of capital at maturity. The "Principal Protection Agreement" is therefore arranged between BNP Paribas and the investor who takes advantage of the high credit rating of the issuer. The note therefore has a rating capable of attracting a large proportion of potential investors (AA— as assigned by S&P).

This structured note, as well as providing a capital guarantee, offers 70% participation in the performance of the underlying fund of funds, the UBP Multi-strategy Alpha Fund. The level of participation as we have previously explained in detail guarantees returns if we compare these alternative instruments with traditional financial products. However, in terms of the returns this note is capable of generating (around 7–9%) this note does not sparkle. Nevertheless, it can generate better returns than numerous solutions which are often more risky.

2.3   NEW PROSPECTS FOR HEDGE FUNDS: INSURANCE POLICIES AND PENSION FUNDS

2.3.1   The Insurance Market

The continuous evolution of the hedge fund industry and the creation of structured products linked to the returns of a specific speculative fund also opens new doors for the insurance market. The inevitable proliferation of innovative insurance policies and the occasional search for more interesting indexing instruments, even for the small and conservative investor means that there exists a strong incentive for increased synergies between the insurance sector and the hedge funds market.

Nevertheless, problems emerge from a legal and supervisory perspective. The increasing complexity of financial instruments used by companies as "reference values" to index performance and as a consequence, the increased complexity of risk profiling for insurance companies leads to the need for intervention in order to protect insurance companies both in terms of limiting investment risk and facilitating greater transparency regarding the presentation of prospective returns and risks associated with such policies.

The difficulties and relative complexity which characterise the approach of the European market to the world of alternative investments are overcome by certain instruments which more or less facilitate direct entry into the hedge fund market.

Insurance policies authorised and distributed in some European countries can also be sold in other markets thanks to the EU passporting procedure. In this way, unit-linked policies linking returns to funds that invest in a certificate indexed to the performance of funds of hedge funds have been sold in Italy, Austria, etc.

Buyers of such products currently pay quite a high price that tends to drop in line with greater uptake of these products. Costs include the price of the policy, the management commission of the underlying fund and finally, the costs associated with the underlying bond whose returns are linked to the fund of hedge funds (the performance of which is net of commissions applied by the individual constituent funds).

The convenience of these products becomes more apparent when we look at the performance, that is far superior to more traditional investment methods and guaranteed for a medium to long time horizon. Average annual returns can easily reach 15% using not particularly aggressive strategies during times of falling markets: a truly excellent performance for an insurance product. Some samples of these products can be found in Italy, Ireland and Luxembourg.

For instance, up until 30th July 2001, Banco di Sicilia invested in the BdS Index Hedge Evolution index-linked insurance policy, a product with strong financial characteristics and issued by the insurance company Roma Vita. The policy is distinguished by its medium to long time horizon (7-year maturity) and the returns are linked to the performance of the Equinox Series Fund, a fund managed by Société Générale, specialised in alternative investment strategies and able to generate positive returns independently of market direction. Société Générale selected 20 hedge funds, each specialised in a specific sector (currencies, commodities, equity, arbitrage, etc.) with the objective of achieving absolute returns, even during falling markets. Minimum investment € 2500. At maturity, 100% capital is guaranteed as well as providing 100% participation in the performance of the Equinox Series Fund, payable at the contractual maturity date. The policy may be redeemed after one year.

Insurance products such as that offered by the Banco di Sicilia, constructed on structured bonds "linked to hedge funds" with capital protection, represent one of the competitive arenas in which the main protagonists of the European insurance market will soon go head to head. The unit-linked policy distributed by Nascent Sim is another recent example of an insurance policy which has as its underlying activity a capital protected structured bond, the returns of which are linked to a fund of hedge funds.

At the same time as the Banco di Sicilia, Nascent Sim began the exclusive distribution for the Italian market of Tudor, the new unit-linked single premium life insurance policy from J. Rothschild European Assurance, an Irish based and regulated insurance company.

Tudor is an insurance policy which, as well as providing a return should the insured party pass away, is also linked to the internal investment fund JRIA Absolute Return Fund, set up and managed by J. Rothschild European Assurance and investing 100% of assets in a 5-year capital protected dollar note.

The two insurance products we have referred to share many characteristics, particularly regarding the objectives of each of the issuers. The attempt to associate a secure financial instrument such as an insurance policy with the performance of speculative funds allows on the one hand for risk to be spread over the medium to long term, thereby eliminating the significant costs implicit in exiting from structured bonds. On the other hand, it proposes to traditional investors, sceptical of alternative investments, an indirect participation in a fascinating market such as hedge funds.

A more recent example of life policies linked to alternative investments is the Lombard GMI product which invests in a 5-year capital protected note issued by Barclays. The policy offers a return of 70% of the growth of a basket of hedge funds managed by Barclays Global Investors.

2.3.2 Pension Funds

The characteristics in terms of performance that distinguish hedge funds are particularly attractive for pension funds in that investors' current passivity must be compensated in the future from investment returns. Even a prolonged period of consistent outperformance might not be sufficient to cover the funds' obligations to investors. This consideration is particularly important when we take into account the rising volatility in financial markets following the positive period in the eighties and nineties. For pension funds and institutional investors in general, the lower correlation between hedge funds and traditional financial products enables fund managers to improve the performance of their portfolios' allocation.

Though mainly due to financial motives, changes in legislation (such as those coming into effect in the UK) seek to provide incentives for the inclusion of alternative investments within pension funds. The changes proposed by the British Accounting Standards Board will have the effect of making the actual performance of these funds more transparent. The consequence of this could well be the shift of assets under management towards hedge funds as such products offer protection against market volatility.

The many (if uncertain) prospects for the development of pension funds in the Italian marketplace could lead to the large-scale adoption of speculative funds. There remain however numerous concerns and problems, mainly of a legal and regulatory nature regarding the information and transparency that these funds must provide in accordance with the strict guidelines applied by the supervisory authorities, who, it can be said, do not openly embrace new frontiers.

The relationship between pension funds and alternative investment instruments is doubtless more harmonious in those European countries where there is a greater dependence on pension funds than on state provisions. The Swiss confederation represents the first European nation both for pension funds and for the allocation of managed assets into alternative instruments. We must remember that in Switzerland, state provisions are based around three pillars. Firstly, there are obligatory contributions to the state. Secondly, the existence of a complementary but nonetheless obligatory social security structure through life insurance subscriptions (which provides a lump sum or regular income at the end of citizens' working lives. Finally, those on higher incomes (above 28,000 Swiss francs per annum) may also invest in pension funds.

After Switzerland come the UK, Denmark, Holland and Sweden representing the countries with the greatest synergies between pension funds and alternative investment instruments. A study conducted in October 2001 by Watson Wyatt Partners and Indocam Asset Management (Credit Agricole group) analysed the propensity of 150 pension funds of several European countries to invest in alternative instruments:

Pension funds analysed:
154

Pension funds that
invest in instruments:
36

The laws of the above-mentioned countries and the social security culture which make pension funds an indispensable element for the futures of individual investors provide incentives for the inclusion of hedge funds within portfolios.

The UK is an even more particular case in that it boasts the highest proportion of pension fund assets invested in alternative instruments: 3% of the entire portfolio of British pension funds is invested in alternative instruments. In Europe, only 2% of assets managed by pension funds are allocated to hedge funds. Overall, it is clear that today there is little to suggest a strong push towards these types of financial products.

The reasons for British and Swiss pension funds using alternative financial instruments are the same as for all other categories of investor: low correlation and "outperformance" in relation to equity markets rather than "outperformance" in relation to bond markets and immunity from inflationary trends.

In countries like Italy, the expectation that hedge funds and products linked to them will be increasingly adopted within pension funds first requires the greater uptake of such pension funds. If, when these products become more mainstream, hedge funds and alternative instruments have already won the battle against private investor diffidence, pension funds will become a major target audience for the speculative fund industry.

2.4   HEDGE FUNDS AND MUTUAL FUNDS

Whilst similar in denomination, the two financial instruments are completely different and are aimed at satisfying different investment requirements. We will analyse in detail the principal structural and operational differences, which exist today between hedge funds and mutual funds. There are four main differences:

- *Returns*. Mutual funds are judged against a relative activity, i.e. a benchmark index or against funds within the same category. The objective of hedge funds is to guarantee absolute returns, in all circumstances, even when the traditional equity and bond indices are falling.
- *Regulation*. Mutual funds are highly regulated products. In particular, there are restrictions on short selling. These limitations prevent mutual funds from protecting their investments from market contractions. Financial leverage for mutual funds is also subject to strict limitations, making such operations of little use. Hedge funds on the other hand have no such restrictions. Indeed, they are characterised by their ability to take advantage of every opportunity offered by the market and to use every conceivable instrument to do so. They are allowed to sell short and use other strategies to accelerate the growth of their investments and reduce volatility. The only limitations they face are informal and regard area, strategy and investment sector. Hedge funds are usually highly specialised and as such the investor expects and requires that the fund operates in the direction (specialisation and competence) pre-selected and declared by him.
- *Remuneration of managers*. Mutual funds generally pay managers a percentage of the amount of money they manage. The manager receives an annual management fee of 1% to 2% and

Table 2.6   Main differences between hedge funds and mutual funds

Mutual Funds	Characteristics	Hedge Funds
Large	*Industry size*	Small: they represent about 4% of the total world asset under management
Long	*Average life of the product*	Short: around 7 years
According to the market in which they invest	*Classification*	According to the management style of the fund manager
Secondary	*Manager importance*	Enormous
Fixed and predefined	*Manager compensation*	Variable: it depends on the fund's performance
Large	*Number of underwriters*	Restricted and selected
No limits are imposed	*Fund size*	Limited at an average of USD 50 million, to render operation fast and flexible
Constrained by the regulatory body	*Investment possibility*	Constrained by the fund's regulations
Complete	*Management information*	At the manager's discretion. Not periodical

a bonus only partly linked to the results achieved. In contrast, hedge funds remunerate managers mainly on the basis of the returns they achieve for the fund. Indeed, money managers receive a "performance fee" of around 20% of profits achieved in a given period which nevertheless takes into account losses registered in previous years.

- *Correlation with the markets.* Mutual funds cannot protect portfolios from falls in the markets unless they sell and reduce their exposure. Hedge funds on the other hand have little correlation with market direction and, depending on the strategy adopted, can both cover themselves against market contractions and register profits during periods of falling markets. Where the markets experience negative trends, a mutual fund can at the most reduce its percentage of long positions. However, the fund will nevertheless be exposed to the risk of further reductions in the value of the remaining long positions in the portfolio. A hedge fund on the other hand could rebalance its portfolio, by increasing the weighting of the short positions and therefore take advantage of such market conditions.

Table 2.6 shows the principal characteristics of the two financial instruments, highlighting the similarities and major differences.

The structural differences between hedge funds and mutual funds as described are sufficient to explain the current trend of substituting a percentage of mutual fund investment within portfolios with investment in speculative funds. A better understanding of the competitive advantages that hedge funds are gradually developing over traditional investment funds is achieved through the objective analysis of the increasingly evident defects of the asset management sector.

The boom of mutual funds and their rapid growth in terms of assets under management and numbers of new products coming to market was a direct consequence of falling interest rates that forced banks to revise their strategies and search for financial products capable of delivering more attractive returns.

Asset management and particularly investment funds were identified as offering the opportunity to generate significant commissions of every type (e.g. subscription fees, management fees, redemption fees, etc.).

However, the spread of traditional funds (which could only hold long positions in equities and bonds) has had negative implications on the market because of the enormity of certain

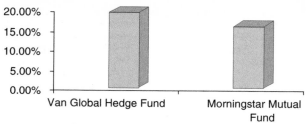

Source: Bluehedge News, reproduced with permission.

Figure 2.6   Hedge funds vs. mutual funds, performance

mutual funds, capable of creating huge market distortions as they review their asset allocation. Moreover, many mutual funds are managed by the same managers. Certain managers not only manage the funds of their own company but also the SICAV and multi-manager funds of smaller institutions. They therefore have great influence over investment decisions.

In this context, the transfer of capital elsewhere cannot but help to stabilise and limit distortions and information inefficiencies that too often facilitate arbitrages on financial markets. In market conditions such as those seen today, specialised hedge funds and uncorrelated funds of hedge funds distinguish themselves by their performance. Economic recessions and unexpected crises linked to unforeseen events such as the terrorist attack on the World Trade Centre have shown how hedge funds can outclass traditional funds.

An analysis conducted by UBS Warburg over a period of 12 years (1988–2000) produced extremely interesting results. The study consisted of adding, when the S&P 500 fell, on the one hand the performance of the Van Global Hedge Fund Index and on the other hand the performance of the Morningstar Mutual Fund Index.

Figure 2.6 shows how in the period under consideration, the Van Global index of hedge funds beat the Morningstar index of mutual funds. The results are all the more evident since the comparison is made between the two investment types during negative market conditions.

Hedge greatly outperformed American mutual funds when the S&P 500 registered quarterly losses. This data reflects the ability of hedge fund managers to preserve capital when the major equity markets experience negative trends. A successive analysis takes into consideration the S&P 500 over an 11-year time span, 1990 to the second quarter of 2001, for the quarters in which the index registered negative performance. The accumulated losses achieved by the index amounted to 67.72% over 12 negative quarters. In the same period, the returns achieved by the hedge fund industry (using the Van US Hedge Fund Index produced by Van Hedge Fund Advisors) were compared to those achieved by American mutual funds. As a reference index for mutual funds, the Morningstar Average Equity Mutual Funds Index provided by Morningstar Inc. of Chicago was used.

The mutual fund index, during the 12 quarters in which the S&P 500 registered losses had 10 quarters of losses and only in two quarters did the index register positive returns. Total losses for the 12 quarters were 67.20%. In half the cases, the Morningstar Average Equity Mutual Fund Index obtained lower returns than those achieved by the S&P 500 index. The Van US Hedge Fund Index registered losses in five quarters, of which only one quarter's results were worse than those registered by the S&P 500. In the remaining seven quarters hedge funds

Table 2.7 Hedge funds vs. mutual funds during market contractions

Quarters with Negative Performance	S&P 500 (%)	Van US Fund (%)	Morningstar Equity Mutual (%)
1T90	−3.00	2.20	−2.80
3T90	−13.70	−3.70	−15.40
2T91	−0.20	2.30	−0.90
1T92	−2.50	5.00	−0.70
1T94	−3.80	−0.80	−3.20
4T94	−0.02	−1.20	−2.60
3T98	−9.90	−6.10	−15.00
3T99	−6.20	2.10	−3.20
2T00	−2.70	0.30	−3.60
3T00	−1.00	3.00	0.60
4T00	−7.80	2.40	7.80
1T01	−11.90	−1.10	−12.60
	−62.72	**−0.40**	**−67.20**

Source: Van Hedge data, elaborated by Bluehedge.com, 2001, reproduced with permission.

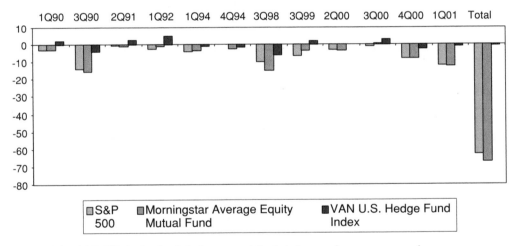

Figure 2.7   S&P 500, hedge funds index, mutual funds index: performance comparison

achieved positive returns. Indeed, in three quarters, the difference between that obtained by the S&P 500 and that reported by the Van US Hedge Fund Index was more than 10% (3T90 4T00 and 1T01). Hedge funds over the 12 quarters registered a total loss of 0.40%. See Table 2.7 and Figure 2.7.

This analysis clearly shows how the ability of the hedge fund managers succeeds in preserving invested capital during times of contracting markets. Hedge funds are extremely flexible instruments when compared to mutual fund investments in that, within the world of hedge funds, the managers may pursue different strategies which cannot be implemented by managers of mutual funds.

Table 2.8   Hedge funds vs. mutual funds: performance comparison

Performance	Hedge Funds (%)	Mutual Funds (%)
Best 10 funds	62.2	51.5
Best 10%	46.3	27.2
Best 25%	36.3	20.3
Worst 25%	6.4	5.6
Worst 10%	0.7	4.0
Worst 10 funds	−4.4	−16.1

These strategies and financial instruments, which are in many cases used with the view of protecting the fund from possible falls in equity prices, generally enable hedge funds to obtain superior performance to traditional investment classes. Indeed, Table 2.8 shows a comparison between hedge fund and mutual fund returns and for this table, we have considered the best and worst performers for the period 1995–1999. As you can see, hedge funds offer better prospects in terms of returns.

2.5   MARKET POTENTIAL

In recent years, we have seen demand for hedge funds increase from both private and institutional clients. The increase in interest in this investment class began in the United States and is rapidly spreading across Europe. The US market for hedge funds is currently larger than that of Europe: US institutional and private clients have invested for some time in the hedge fund market attracted above all by the positive opportunities offered in terms of asset allocation, absolute returns and very low levels of volatility.

In Europe, the hedge fund market is growing rapidly. Analysis from March 2001 reveals that the number of European institutional investors that have invested in hedge funds has almost doubled. According to the survey, almost a third of institutions interviewed invested in hedge funds against 17% in the previous year.

The countries where hedge funds enjoy the greatest success are Switzerland and France, (Figure 2.8) whilst in Italy, the number of managers who invest in these products is still very low. The United Kingdom is also starting to embrace alternative investments.

If the numbers of institutional investors who use these instruments in order to balance their portfolios are growing, the percentage of total assets under management invested in alternative investments is still very low. In Europe, the amount invested in hedge funds is between 0.2% and 0.3% of the entire portfolio. This figure is much higher for American institutions which, depending on the portfolio, invest 5–10% of total assets in hedge funds.

It is quite probable that institutional clients are still in the early stages of taking on such products. Even if hedge funds have for a long time been vaunted by the more important financial reviews, the institutional manager would appear to still be somewhat uncertain. The institutions that seem most interested in these products would appear to view them from the perspective of hedge funds not as an investment instrument but as a vehicle to attract client money. The number of banks and asset management companies that are launching hedge funds or funds of hedge funds to complete the range of products they can offer to their private clients is constantly increasing.

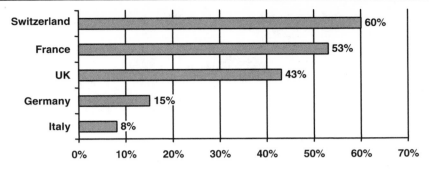

Figure 2.8   Percentage of European institutions with investments in hedge funds

The main sources of resistance can be summarised as follows:

- The perception of the volatility of hedge funds;
- A lack of experience on the part of the same institutions;
- A lack of transparency and regulation.

Notwithstanding the fact that the hedge fund market has yet to take off, the prospects for growth in Europe are extremely interesting. In Italy, for instance, where the size of the market is still negligible, the prospects are very encouraging. By beginning with an analysis of the US market, we can make two hypotheses on the evolution of this market. If, in the United States, the hedge fund market represents around 5% of the market, in Italy, annual growth of around 80% would see the amount of assets invested in hedge funds reach 1.05% by 2005.

Table 2.9 shows the current market situation and growth prospects for the next four years. Currently, the hedge fund industry accounts for 0.1% of total assets managed by Italian intermediaries, equating to €500 million.

It is interesting to evaluate how these growth forecasts will affect institutional portfolios. The intention of our analysis (Figure 2.9) is to estimate the current and future distribution of hedge funds within institutional portfolios. In 2001, the managers that make the greatest use of alternative investment instruments are banks, whilst hedge funds rarely appear in the portfolios of insurance companies, pension funds and private clients.

Laws designed to protect the small investor (considered as belonging to the "private client" category) apply above all to high net worth individuals, i.e. people with extensive financial resources, a propensity for risk and who have their own private banker who manages their capital. The number of such investors is quite small and tends to rise somewhat slowly.

Table 2.9   Marketing projections for the hedge fund market in Italy

	Annual Growth	2001	2002	2003	2004	2005
Mutual funds	10%	535,000	588,500	647,350	712,085	783,294
% Hedge funds of the total	80%	0.10%	0.18%	0.32%	0.58%	1.05%
Hedge funds in million of €		535	1.059	2.097	4.153	8.223

Source: IntesaBci, 2001, reproduced with permission.

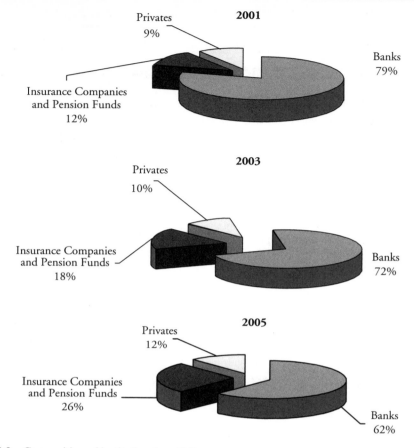

Figure 2.9   Composition of institutional portfolios

The hypothesis of evolution in the distribution of hedge fund investments shows a continuous rise in the use of these instruments both by insurance companies and pension funds. The interest on the part of insurance companies is the main driver behind the growth in innovative insurance policies and the continuous search for new structured instruments to satisfy their ever more demanding clients. In the next few years, we foresee significant development in insurance policies linked to stakes in hedge funds or funds of hedge funds. In this way, insurance companies on the one hand diversify their offering and on the other hand can propose new and innovative products.

However, the pension fund market is certainly more likely to play a larger part in the uptake of hedge funds. Notwithstanding the law which came into effect around eight years ago, open ended pension funds are still a young product (in reality, they are around two years old), with exceptional growth prospects. Two factors may radically alter this scenario:

- The desired equal treatment of open pension funds and tradable pension funds.
- The liberalisation of severance pay, which would offer all parties full autonomy in managing their assets.

The characteristics of hedge funds may be particularly attractive for pension funds. An investment of around 15% in hedge funds, diversified between the different strategies is capable of optimising the risk/return profile. Moreover, their characteristics of low correlation with traditional investments facilitate stable returns and a reduction in volatility. Considering that pension funds have a long time horizon for their investments, this opportunity will be crucial if they want to ensure consistent returns for their clients, even in times of crisis.

We can conclude that the European hedge fund market is still in its embryonic phase but has extremely interesting growth prospects. The players who will benefit most in the immediate future will be mainly the managers of institutional funds such as banks and insurance companies. After the initial period, which will see increased understanding and accurate evaluation of the potential of the product, it is estimated that 10% of institutional portfolios will be destined for alternative investments.

3

The European Market

The development of hedge funds in Europe is a natural step for the investment management sector. After the fantastic returns for 1999 and the beginning of 2000, managers are actively seeking investment instruments capable of providing superior returns while offering a higher degree of protection. Seen before as highly risky investment instruments, hedge funds are now viewed as the only opportunity to achieve the returns we have become used to during the bull market. Many mutual fund managers are leaving the established asset management companies to create their own speculative funds, further reinforcing this rapidly expanding phenomenon.

The growth of the alternative investment sector has come about in the main because of the events that have characterised the investment climate in Europe. Of these, the drastic fall in global equity markets caused mainly by the globalisation of the technology and telecommunications sectors comes first. The introduction of the single currency is another factor, eliminating the benefits of cross-border investment in Euro zone bonds.

The growing demand for alternative investments could lead to a situation of over-capacity for providers that would doubtless result in the expansion of this area. This is mainly due to the fact that hedge fund investors include not only high net worth individuals but also institutional investors and pension funds.

The fascination of hedge funds also derives from the fact that commissions are far higher when compared to the fees of other types of investment funds. This helps to counterbalance the strict regulations affecting many retail mutual investment funds and will lead to increased capital flows from mutual fund managers and large banks to alternative investments. Indeed, many managers see hedge funds as an excellent opportunity to expand their horizons.

In many countries, laws exist preventing direct marketing of hedge funds. Distribution is usually achieved using private placements. There now exist openings in certain markets and many countries are producing legislation on alternative investments. In particular, the institutional market would appear to view these products with ever keener eyes.

3.1 MARKETING OPPORTUNITIES – THE REASONS FOR THE BOOM

As far as alternative investments are concerned, Europe is the prime target for distributors. Interest on the part of high net worth individuals and institutional investors stems from the same reasoning: the fall in equity markets and the high volatility levels reached by traditional markets have triggered unprecedented demand for these products.

With the view of identifying certain trends, we shall first discuss three specific aspects:

1. Interest for alternative products in so much as they are not correlated to traditional investments.

2. A big push from the major players in asset management, stemming from reduced margins on traditional products and investor indifference to these products.
3. The gradual relaxation of regulation by the relevant European authorities for alternative investment instruments.

We shall firstly justify the strong interest in hedge funds from professional managers and private banking clients. The implosion of the Internet bubble brought severe falls in the markets. Within this overwhelmingly negative climate, only alternative investments have proven themselves to be safe havens for our capital. The major intermediaries as well as sophisticated investors have approached the world of hedge funds, desiring a better understanding of these products. They accept that high risk is not implicit in many of these products, but that hedge funds represent a diverse amalgamation within which it is as likely to identify low-risk products as products with high levels of volatility. To provide the reader with a way to gauge this, we need only refer to the world of traditional funds. Within the world of asset management, we can find low-risk funds such as currency funds but also bond funds and funds with higher volatility such as equity funds. However, it would be a mistake to associate all equity funds with the same level of risk. A global equity fund that invests in large cap companies offers lower risk than an emerging markets or technology fund. The same applies for the world of hedge funds where certain products offer completely different risk/return profiles.

The second growth factor is shown by the increasing interest on the part of mutual fund managers to offer clients alternative products. This trend is very evident in Italy, where from 2001 we saw intermediaries racing to create speculative SGRs. In Europe, all the major players in asset management have developed alternative investment management units following the launch of new hedge products.

Schroders, Gartmore, Deutsche Bank, UBS Warburg, Zurich, Scudder, Julius Bär to name but a few have all created new divisions to manage hedge funds and have started to offer these products to their private and institutional clients. There are three reasons for this rush on alternative products:

- The inherent quality of these products.
- The necessity of offering clients saleable products against the backdrop of falling equity markets and low demand for traditional solutions.
- The necessity and desire to find products that provide managers with higher margins. Indeed, hedge funds are far more profitable than traditional funds.

The third factor behind the growth in this industry is attributable to the increased understanding of these instruments on the part of the supervisory authorities in the various countries (FSA, Consob, CNVB, etc.) that are united in their desire to bring these products under their control. Otherwise, these funds are destined to embrace the favourable conditions and opportunities offered by offshore centres.

In this way, the various legislators are offering greater protection of private investors, who must otherwise rely on themselves. The progress thus far achieved has been significant but nevertheless insufficient for us to begin talking of obstacle-free investment in hedge funds for private clients.

However, the right route is being taken and the first products will come to market aimed at affluent investors and not only reserved for an elect few and institutional investors.

3.2   MARKET OPPORTUNITIES, LAWS AND FISCAL CONSIDERATIONS IN THE MAJOR EUROPEAN COUNTRIES

3.2.1   The Market and its Opportunities

To analyse the opportunities and hunger for alternative products in different European countries in detail, we must begin with the assertion that as yet, asset managers are unable to offer these instruments in total freedom to individual savers as well as to institutions. However, the existence of hedge fund conferences and the growing demand on the part of institutional investors will ultimately result in the disappearance of these barriers, with demand and supply finally meeting unrestricted.

In general, soliciting investment in alternative investment products that are not regulated by domestic supervisory authorities is forbidden. It is not however forbidden for investors to request information on these products and make investment decisions in total freedom. Indeed portfolio constraints are different from country to country, depending on which category the investor belongs to.

Before proceeding to a detailed analysis of the opportunities and obstacles that exist in each country, it would be opportune to define the main investor categories in order of size:

- High net worth individuals, i.e. the wealthiest private investors, comprising the most active investor class in these products. Traditionally, they were comprised of do-it-yourself investors of sound knowledge and competence. Today, we are witnessing the increasing institutionalisation of this category through family offices or banks and private banking departments.
- Pension funds, which have always been focused on achieving returns over the long term and on diversifying their investments.
- Traditional portfolio managers keen to insert this class of activity into their portfolios, to improve performance and lower volatility.

A recent survey conducted by Ludgate Communications on 100 institutional investors provides interesting data on the attitudes of the main players towards hedge funds. In particular, the countries with the highest concentration of hedge fund investments are France (33% of institutions), Switzerland (30%) and Holland (20%), closely followed by the UK, Scandinavia and Germany. With an eye towards investment in the near future, Scandinavia (67%) and Holland (60%) are followed by Italy with 60% of institutions interviewed expressing a desire to invest in hedge funds in the short term.

3.2.2   Legal and Fiscal Aspects

As European legislation is very complex and continually evolving, it is difficult to disentangle the various regulations. The objective of this chapter is to give a general view on how the hedge fund phenomenon has been received by the different legislators. This is in part due to the EU directive of 1985, which did not insist on regulatory uniformity within the different member countries. Instead, the directive defined a structure which member states must follow, but allowed them autonomy to regulate their national equity markets. However, this does not discourage cross-border transactions between member countries.

Certain countries do not allow hedge funds to be established and avoid this obstacle by creating "funds of funds" that function in the same way as mutual funds investing in offshore funds. In certain cases such as Italy, the reason why hedge funds have yet to take off is down to the lack of competent depository banks. As a consequence, real hedge funds are managed in places where these brokerage services are available. For example, in Germany, investment funds can use futures and options investments to hedge positions as there are fewer restrictions on their use. The fund of funds therefore does not violate this regulation.

Whilst many of these laws attempt to evade the European directive of 1985 (which defined the determination standard for the European equivalent of a registered investment company, known also as an Undertaking for Collective Investment in Transferable Securities (UCITS)), the directive makes it rather difficult for non-traditional investment strategies to be employed within the UCITS structure. If, however, a fund is authorised by the directive, it is possible to freely distribute it in all member countries. This is called a "fund with a European passport". Since not all countries conform to the European directive, there remain substantial differences between fund management methods.

Moreover, it seems that different definitions are used for alternative investments and for the investors who can buy them. Regulation of these funds seems to change constantly in order to adapt to demand. The growth in interest in these products has been seen by many countries as an opportunity and yet has encouraged more indulgent regulation of onshore funds. Many countries recognise this opportunity and do not intend to lose it to offshore tax havens. As the laws are not yet standardised, even if attempts have been made in this direction, it is still possible for Europe to become an interesting and attractive market, domicile or administrative centre.

In the following sections, the factors relevant to hedge funds within the major European markets will be presented in terms of regulation and business opportunities.

3.3   THE MAJOR EUROPEAN COUNTRIES

3.3.1   United Kingdom

The Market

The UK market has recently seen many domestic players including Schroders, Gartmore and Abbey National create alternative investment activities and offer new products to the market. Such products are typically used in the portfolios of high net worth clients, be it through SIPS (Self Investment Pension Schemes) or through managed accounts. There also exist hedge funds in which clients can invest through ISAs, a type of individual pension fund with certain fiscal advantages. Normally, hedge funds used in this way must be listed on a domestic or international stock exchange (usually in Ireland) under the form of an Investment Trust, a type of holding that invests in alternative investment funds.

Legal Aspects

The UK is one of the most accessible markets for all investment instruments. With London being the financial centre of Europe and with the Channel Islands and Ireland so close, the UK is an exceptional market in which to introduce new investment products.

Standardisation of financial market regulation was not easily achieved in Europe and particularly in the UK even if progress has been made regarding funds. Once authorised by the FSA (Financial Services Authority), funds have a sort of "passport", as stated in the European Directive of Investment Services, enabling the activity to be developed throughout the European

Union. This does not mean that the fund can be sold in Europe, and it needs to meet the marketing regulations of individual countries.

In the UK, alternative investment funds are considered "unregulated collective investment schemes" and include UCITS, unit trusts authorised in the UK and open ended investment companies. Only those companies that have been approved by the FSA to distribute these types of funds may do so.

In any case, in the UK, it is not possible to set up an onshore hedge fund, whilst it is possible to sell offshore hedge funds with prior approval from the FSA.

Fiscal Considerations

When a person invests in an offshore hedge fund, they must include capital gains and every other revenue deriving from fund participation when they declare their total income. The same fiscal conditions are applied to juridical persons whose revenue (capital gains or revenue deriving from switch transactions or sales of assets) is added to company revenue. Revenues distributed to non-resident investors or deriving from the liquidation of fund holdings are not subject to any withholding taxation.

3.3.2   Channel Islands

The Market

Directly linked to the UK market, we find the offshore world of the Channel Islands where many UK expatriates or UK impatriates manage their own money, using to varying degrees offshore trusts or life policies. These products can be used in the form of capital protected bonds, which do not pay a coupon but offer a capital gain at maturity. The reasons for this preference are mostly to be found in tax law, which taxes coupons at the same rate as taxable income by the investor whilst lower taxation rates are applied on capital gains.

3.3.3   Switzerland

The Market

This is the most interesting country for hosting these types of product. Fewer restrictions have resulted in a dense concentration of high net worth client monies, portfolio managers and competing private banks. Switzerland has always been the largest European market for alternative investments, thanks primarily to the presence of offshore funds of international clients. The alternative product offering is quite liberated, most of all in terms of authorised intermediaries and the high level of culture and sophistication demonstrated by these companies. Many private banks, having used these products in client portfolios for many years, have created alternative investment management divisions for both hedge funds and funds of funds to offer them in-house as well as to external clients. Amongst the various companies to have done this are UBS, Union Bancaire Privée, Banque Syz, HSBC Republic, Zurich and Julius Bär.

Following changes in the legislation and regulation of Swiss pension funds, these companies can increase their exposure to alternative investments so long as the investment philosophy does not contravene the "Prudent Man Rule". This regulation finds its origins in US legislation and determines the rules of conduct for trusts, which must invest with prudence and impartiality to safeguard the investment but most importantly, control risk. The Swiss hedge fund market is by size the largest in Europe but offers in all probability a lower growth rate in the medium term when compared to other countries. Certainly it is the most established market and is the place where hedge fund managers can achieve the greatest success in the short term.

Legal Aspects

The Swiss market has great potential for alternative investment products in the short term. The main characteristic of this market is the fact that the "reticent" nature of hedge funds does not bother the Swiss, used to secrecy from their banking structure. Whilst not a member of the EU, Switzerland is looking to bring its banking legislation in line with UCITS in order to maintain its competitiveness.

In Switzerland, the fund sector is regulated by the Swiss federal act on investment funds, which controls every product offering or distribution activity for the sale of stakes in overseas investment funds. This law states that the Swiss Banking Commission regulates relevant companies.

The Swiss Banking Commission considers all promotional and marketing activity related to hedge funds as a distribution activity except in exceptional circumstances:

- Investors subscribe to the fund on their own initiative, which could be stimulated by a consultation with a bank or investment manager.
- The asset manager subscribes on behalf of his/her clients. The manager cannot have a distribution agreement with the fund. Neither can he be subject to restrictions regarding funds issued by the same promoter.

In Switzerland, it is generally permitted to set up and sell onshore hedge funds as well as sell offshore hedge funds. These funds may be formed in accordance with the 1995 Federal Act of Investment Funds. Onshore funds may take the judicial form of a Collective Investment Agreement.

Funds may only be open ended and they are not restricted to specific categories of investor as often happens in other countries. Relative freedom of investment is one of the fundamental advantages of Switzerland, making it one of the best countries in Europe to commercialise hedge funds.

Other relevant legal considerations impede the listing of hedge funds, impede the manager from delegating the management of operations and make a clear distinction between the capital of the fund and that of the company that manages the fund.

Fiscal Considerations

In Switzerland, revenues from hedge fund investments have no effect on direct taxation nor on the rates of alternative taxes. The fund is considered transparent to taxation and benefits from double taxation treaties (i.e. the advantage that taxes are only payable in one country). As concerns the taxation of individuals, all profits (excluding capital gains realised by the investor through the transfer or liquidation of holdings) are subject to 35% taxation if realised through fund participation so long as the fund was distributed by a domestic intermediary. These profits are included in the taxable income of the investor who will benefit from a tax credit. In the case of juridical persons, revenues (distributed by the fund or deriving from the transfer or liquidation of stakes) are included in taxable income without the application of a retainer or tax credit. Finally, in the case of non-residents investing in the fund, the revenue is subject to a 35% tax rate, which is rebated in accordance with taxation treaties. However, should more than 80% of the revenues of the entire fund be generated overseas, the foreign investor can request the non-application of the 35% Swiss retainer.

3.3.4 Luxembourg

The Market

The Luxembourg market is more interested in domiciling products than placing them. It represents without doubt a major opportunity for all those who want to create funds aimed at institutional clients throughout Europe, because of the farsightedness of the Luxembourg authorities that do not impose taxes on these types of product. The market is interesting in terms of location because of the high concentration of private banks.

Legal Aspects

It is therefore possible to constitute onshore hedge funds and sell offshore hedge funds even though there are no specific regulations dealing with these products. Hedge funds can be created under the following Luxembourg legislation:

- The law dated 30th March 1998, part 2: funds offered to the public without specific reference to investment limits as established by community directive number 85/611 (of non-harmonised funds).
- The law of July 1991: funds dedicated to institutional investors.

Onshore hedge funds can take one of the following juridical forms:

- Fonds commun de placement (FCP);
- Société d'investissement à capital variable (SICAV);
- Société d'investissement à capital fixe (SICAF).

The supervisory authority with powers to regulate and authorise onshore hedge funds is La Commission de Surveillance du Secteur Financier (CSSF). The above-mentioned funds can be open or closed ended and are not restricted to specific categories of investor. They must however have a minimum level of initial capital (1,240,000 Euro).

The regulations of the Grand Duchy place limits on managed assets, a somewhat different approach than that adopted by the rest of Europe. The fact that the capital of the fund must be segregated from that of the company that manages the fund is also relevant. Moreover, the fund manager can delegate the management of the fund (in part or entirely) to third parties. Finally, funds may be listed.

Fiscal Considerations

A hedge fund set up in Luxembourg is not affected by direct taxation but pays a taxe d'abbonement (registration tax) of 0.06% on the net capital of the fund. The fund is considered transparent to taxation only if it has been formed as an FCP, thereby benefiting from the double tax treaty. It cannot report losses and must complete a fiscal declaration so that the taxe d'abbonement can be applied.

If the investor is a physical person, all revenue distributed by the fund and capital gains realised through the transfer or sale of the stake in the fund are included in taxable income without the benefit of tax credits. In the same way, revenue distributed to a juridical person and capital gains realised through the transfer or sale of the stake in the fund are included in total revenue without the possibility of tax credits. Regarding revenues for non-resident investors or deriving from the sale of stakes in funds, taxes are not applied.

3.3.5   Ireland

Given its offshore status, Ireland became the home of the first hedge funds set up in Europe. Ireland hosts the majority of life assurance companies linked to British assurance groups. Life and unit-linked policies are more attractive if investments are made in alternative products such as hedge funds. Obviously, the fiscal advantages and the possibility of switching from one investment to another without incurring transaction costs remain the same. Further, we have capital protected investments, which provide a taste of alternative investments with the security of capital protection.

Finally, the Irish market offers excellent opportunities in terms of listing products on the Irish Stock Exchange in Dublin, a factor which often opens the door to investments originating from other countries whose regulations demand that funds be listed in order to accept capital inflows (e.g. Spain and the UK).

Legal Aspects

In Ireland, it is possible to set up and sell onshore hedge funds as well as sell offshore hedge funds. There are no special regulations for this type of fund, therefore general laws apply. Onshore funds can take two juridical forms:

- Company
- Trust

In Ireland, the Central Bank of Ireland authorises the sale of these funds. Legislation permits both open and closed ended funds and makes a distinction between the capital of the fund and that of the company that manages the fund. As with certain other countries, Irish law allows the manager to delegate fully or in part the management of the fund to third parties and, as already stated, funds can be listed.

Fiscal Regulations

Taxes cannot be applied to the revenues of hedge funds set up in Ireland. However, in taxation terms, the fund is not considered transparent in so much as a 20% tax rate is applied to dividends and 23% to other profits.

The fund may enjoy the benefits of the double tax treaty and must complete a tax return so the above-mentioned taxes can be applied. Indeed, no other taxes are payable by the investor other than those mentioned. If these taxes are not applied, the investor must declare profits in a tax return. In the case of juridical persons, the returns achieved by the fund must be stated in a tax return and a tax credit is applied if taxes are deducted by the fund. In the case of investments by non-residents, no taxes are applied.

3.3.6 France

The Market

The French market has always represented an attractive market for hedge funds thanks to the propensity of banks to arbitrage interest rates, currencies and commodities. Both institutional investors and large corporations have always sought to invest their capital. Recently, the market opened to private investors (mainly clients of private banking operations). Currently, the most interesting products are offered to institutional clients in the form of capital protected bonds, the returns of which are linked to a range of hedge funds. The main players in this market are the large French investment banks such as Société Générale and BNP Paribas, who have always been active in creating bond structures linked to series of funds, be they traditional or as currently fashionable, of the hedge fund kind.

Legal Aspects

France represents the largest investment fund market in Europe, but also the most difficult to penetrate for non-francophones. The market is somewhat complex and governed by legislation that covers different types of funds. Certain funds necessitate registration with the Commission des Operations de Bourse, whilst for others, the submission of the prospectus to this commission immediately following the launch of the fund is sufficient. The marketing of hedge funds requires, in the majority of cases, authorisation from the Commission des Operations de Bourse.

French banks prefer to develop products in-house and this is one of the reasons why this market is extremely difficult for foreign companies to penetrate and is still somewhat slow (the French banking sector has always imposed barriers to entry on foreign operators).

The French desire to develop financial products has led them to produce various financial instruments that fall outside the EU directive of 1985. As with many other countries, France continues to seek to create instruments and laws that evade the directive. As for example with the launch of funds, listed below, which are subject to their own rules and regulations and not to the EU directive. In as much as the directive was aimed at regulating investments, instruments such as hedge funds are not included, since they do not fall under the UCITS definition.

- FCPR (fonds commun de placements à risques) are private equity funds which can invest in non-listed securities with different rules dependent on whether the funds are targeted at the general public or expert investors. As well as these funds, there are private equity funds which are not subject to restrictions as they are structured according to the American model and are limited companies.
- FCIMT (fonds commun d'intervention sur les marches à terme) are open ended funds that invest in commodity futures and financial instruments. Use of financial leverage is not limited, but 50% of the fund's assets must be invested in frozen liquid assets to meet margin requirements. Whilst there are no minimum specified investments, marketing of this fund to private clients is restricted. Indeed, it can only be sold through private placements in France.
- Funds of funds are authorised to invest in other investment schemes although this is restricted to 35% of capital in each scheme. These can be UCITS or non-UCITS funds. There is also a feeder fund which can invest 100% of assets in French or European funds.

- OPCVM (organismes de placement collectif en valeurs mobilières) are funds with "simplified procedures". These funds are only available to expert investors, do not require prohibitive governmental authorisation and are subject to more flexible limits than UCITS funds. These funds can be set up in a few days simply because they do not need to be authorised by the government, a depository bank or asset management company. The only condition is that a copy of the prospectus must be sent to the COB once the fund has been launched.

3.3.7   Germany

The Market

The German market is potentially one of the most interesting markets for hedge funds in Europe. The extent of traditional mutual fund investments bears witness to the potential of these products which as yet cannot be sold directly to retail investors. The major players are nevertheless preparing themselves to manage these products in-house, directly and through funds of funds, and will soon begin to offer products constructed specifically for smaller investors. Thus far, the greatest interest has come from private banks and insurance companies. However, certain products aimed at retail investors are about to be launched. For example, we have the Zertifikat, a sort of packaged security whose performance is linked to the rise or fall in an underlying basket of funds of funds. These products are currently at the research stage in various investment houses, particularly those active in warrants.

Deutsche Bank recently launched Xavex and Barclays offered a Zertifikat whose performance was linked to an index of hedge funds especially created and managed by BCI for the occasion.

The portfolios of insurance companies and pension funds also represent another potentially enormous market. Typically traditional and conservative, these companies are increasingly open to these products. Currently, the proportion of alternative investments making up these portfolios is in the order of a few percentage points and offers, unlike more developed markets, huge growth potential.

Legal Aspects

In Germany, it is not possible to set up onshore hedge funds whilst offshore hedge funds can be sold in accordance with legislation relevant to overseas investments (Auslandinvestment-Gesetz). The authority that supervises and authorises the sale of offshore hedge funds is the Bundesaufsichtsamt fur das Kreditwesen. Such funds are not restricted to specific categories of investor. The laws that regulate overseas investment funds in Germany are the Distribution of Stakes in Overseas Investments Act and Taxation on returns. Whilst the law differentiates between public offerings and private placements in the way in which they are regulated, it does not provide a clear and complete definition.

The German Federal Supervisory Office for Securities Trading has however provided guidelines to facilitate the differentiation between public offerings and private placements. In an official declaration, a public offering is defined as the sale to an indefinite number of people, e.g. through advertisements, circulars, etc., who *a priori* are unknown to the seller. Private placements are defined as offers made to a limited number of expert private clients and/or institutional investors who waive their rights to protection. An offer can be aimed at a limited number of investors only if the seller has existing personal relationships with them, and they are not selected on the basis of individual criteria.

It would seem advantageous to make the fund appear as a private placement, above all because this does not require extensive marketing activities. In Germany, private placements can be conducted without the obligation of notifying the German authorities (BAK). Therefore, a UCITS fund is presented to institutional investors through a public offering, even if through a limited offering; notification is unnecessary and if the fund is not registered, it is unnecessary to nominate a German paying agent.

To avoid the obligation to register the fund, it is necessary that certain criteria be satisfied. First of all, the potential investor must be informed that the fund has been offered to a limited number of investors and that therefore, stakes in the fund may not be offered to the public. Further, the company cannot conduct any marketing activity to attract public interest. If the company has an existing relationship with a local bank, this would facilitate access to the wider public whilst still appearing as a private placement.

Fiscal Considerations

In fiscal terms, overseas funds are classified as "medium level" or "grey", "low level" or "black" funds. The first of these are not registered in Germany and cannot be marketed to the general public. In each case, these funds have a tax representative in Germany and periodically publish taxable revenues, which must be referred to the competent authorities. Those comprising the second category not only are not registered in Germany, but also do not have a tax representative and do not periodically publish their taxable revenues.

If a hedge fund is classified as a "grey fund", the investor is fully responsible for taxes deriving from profits on revenues, interest, etc. He is moreover responsible for taxation related to capital gains made by the fund on the sale of securities. These proceeds are called "deemed distribution".

Relative taxation is effected by percentage points, with the progressive application of marginal rates. If revenues are received through a bank, a retainer of 30% is applied at the source. The deemed distributions that were not distributed but rather accrued by the same fund are taxable for the investor at the end of each period, at a rate based on the marginal rate paid by the investor. Moreover, the capital gains realised by the redemption or transfer of fund holdings by the investor are exempt (so long as the investor has held the stake for at least one year). This exemption does not however include the sum deriving from interim profits (i.e. matured interest but as yet not drawn by the fund) and from deemed distribution (regarding the untaxed part) which is instead included in the total declared income of the investor.

Where hedge funds are classified as "black funds", they will be subject to taxation, deemed distribution as well as 90% of the increased value of any stake held by the investor (calculated as the difference in value at the beginning and end of the year). In any case, the minimum taxable revenue cannot be less than 10% of the latest market value of the stake. In this case, therefore, taxes are applied to fictitious revenue and as such penalise the investor.

Where the stake is transferred or cashed in, 20% of this value is included in the total taxable income of the investor. This revenue is always subject to a 30% retainer, if paid through a bank. In Germany, hedge funds can be subjected to capital gains tax or to the marginal rate of income tax (up to 53%). For non-residents, no taxes are applied to revenues.

3.3.8 Austria

The Market

This is a restricted but very interesting market in which to set up banks and insurance companies, which have a traditional propensity for investing in alternative funds. The first domestic capital protected life policies linked to hedge funds were launched in the fall of 2001. The market is less regulated than in other European Union countries but there are nonetheless restrictions on offering hedge fund products to private clients. The presence of offshore clients from neighbouring countries and in particular from Eastern Europe nevertheless feeds this activity of managing portfolios within which these products are often used.

3.3.9 Spain

The Market

The Spanish market also offers quite a high level of interest in hedge products. Restrictions on the promotion of these products are very strict. The most innovative players have however begun to invest a part of their client portfolios in funds domiciled in Luxembourg or Ireland. Alternatively, they can use funds listed on the Irish Stock Exchange (less than 5%).

Legal Considerations

It is not possible to set up hedge funds in Spain. It is also difficult for offshore hedge funds to obtain the necessary authorisations from the Commission Naçional del Mercado de Valores in order to distribute in Spain.

To gain authorisation to sell their offerings, non-harmonised overseas funds must fall into one of the categories recognised by the Spanish legislator and which protect the investor in the same way as funds registered in Spain. Moreover, a certification issued by the authorities must be obtained from the country in which the fund is based.

As a consequence, notwithstanding the fact that the sale of offshore funds is technically possible, it remains very difficult to implement.

Fiscal Considerations

As hedge funds are not regulated in Spain, the legislator has not dealt with the problem of taxation of profits on hedge funds yet.

3.3.10 Portugal

Portugal has gone far in developing this market. It is not possible to set up onshore hedge funds and only funds of funds authorised in other countries are available on the market. The market leader is ESAF – Espirito Santo Activos Financieros, the management arm of Banco Esprito Santo, one of the largest Portuguese banks. They offer funds of hedge funds domiciled in Ireland through their Irish operation. These are called Caravela and are differentiated by their risk profile.

3.3.11   Sweden

The Swedish market is the most attractive from a regulatory perspective. In Sweden, offshore hedge funds can be publicised even if it is required that the fund be run directly by the issuer or otherwise overseas without the involvement of a local operator. Funds can therefore be offered to private clients. Swedish and Norwegian institutional investors are especially open to these types of investment and they are currently beginning to allocate a part of their portfolios to alternative instruments.

Legal Considerations

In Sweden, onshore hedge funds can be set up and sold even though there are no specific regulations related to such funds. Instead, they can be set up in accordance with the general rules as set out in Swedish law (Mutual Fund Act, 1990). The legal structure used to create onshore hedge funds is that related to contracts. The authority that regulates and guarantees such products is the Finansinpektionen. Unlike in other countries, authorisation to sell hedge funds is not required.

Another important factor for the European market is the possibility to promote these offshore hedge funds to the general public. It is not however permitted to sell these products to intermediaries based in Sweden. Therefore, a Swedish investor wishing to acquire a stake in an offshore hedge fund must contact the foreign issuer directly. These funds may only be open ended and not restricted to specific categories of investor. Moreover, there are no limits relative to the investment of the funds' assets. As in other countries, the funds' assets must be separated from those of the company managing the fund. The fund manager may delegate partial or full control of the management of the fund. However, funds may not be listed in Sweden.

Fiscal Regulations

Hedge funds set up in Sweden are subject to taxation. In particular, revenues derived from the fund (except for capital gains) are subject to a 30% corporate tax rate. In fiscal terms, hedge funds are not considered transparent and can benefit from the double tax treaty. Moreover, the fund must complete a tax return in order that corporation tax be applied. It is not permitted for the fund to register losses.

All profits achieved by a physical person (including capital gains) in the investment are distributed by the fund after a 30% tax rate has been applied. These revenues are included in the taxable income of the person and tax credits are applicable.

For juridical persons, all revenues deriving from the investment are included in company revenue without taxes being applied in advance, and therefore without the need for tax credits.

For non-residents investing in hedge funds domiciled in Sweden (be they individuals or entities), the same fiscal regime is applied.

3.3.12   Italy

The Italian market for alternative investments was officially born in the second half of 1999 following the *Decreto del Ministro del Tesoro, del Bilancio e della Programmazione Economica No. 228 del 24 maggio 1999* and the *Provvedimento della Banca Centrale Italiana del 20 settembre 1999*. With this decree and Italian Central Bank regulation that followed, new investment types were introduced to the market: speculative funds and restricted funds. These two investment vehicles were also permitted to function outside the limits imposed by the Italian legislature on the asset management sector to protect the investing public.

Through this new law, the Italian market for hedge funds was officially opened. Until that date, whoever wished to invest in hedge funds had to look offshore, i.e. to funds domiciled in countries other than Italy.

The efforts made in this field by the Italian authorities are significant in that they represent the first time in Europe that legislature has stated its intent to assume responsibility for and intervene to regulate these types of funds. Thanks to this law, Italy is seeking to recover the gap that has developed with the international financial community in recent years regarding the use of these alternative investment products in asset management.

The merit of this law is that it has awakened the Italian financial community to this investment vehicle that has both positive aspects as well as defects, but which clearly has unique characteristics. It was a little understood investment instrument even to those working in the financial industry. In the United States, the home of hedge funds, as well as in the rest of the world, hedge funds have operated for many years, hidden from the wider investing public. Until a few years ago even in the United States, hedge funds were a phenomenon directed mainly at high net worth individuals.

In defining this law, the Italian legislature took inspiration from the US hedge fund market, from which it has adopted numerous aspects. An important innovation introduced by the Italian legislature was the definition of hedge funds. These have been termed "speculative funds". This term is not used to signify hedge funds in the American financial community nor in any literature. Moreover, in Italian the term "speculative" has exclusively negative connotations whilst in English, this is not the case. This definition was probably chosen to have an effect on potential investors in order that they distinguish between traditional and speculative funds. Apart from a certain perplexity as to the name on the part of market professionals, the general feeling about this choice is decidedly positive.

Italian market professionals have admired the authorities' efforts to formulate the first law in Europe on hedge funds as it has enabled domestic operators both to align themselves with the European financial community and participate effectively in the European hedge fund market.

In 1999, this law generated great interest from many operators who thereupon began to consider launching speculative funds. The peculiarity of the Italian market resides in the fact that as soon as it became possible to launch hedge funds, many players became interested in these financial instruments. Amongst these are small private operators as well as the large banking groups. The large banking groups that have been accused of not keeping up with their European competitors have in this case been motioning for some time and have taken advantage of the launch of this legislation to close the gap on American institutions and set up divisions dealing with hedge funds.

The Italian market in terms of hedge fund offerings consists of medium/small operators such as Kairos, Ersel, Invesclub exemplifying the hedge fund spirit, large banking groups such as Unicredito, IntesaBci and SanPaolo Imi and major traditional asset managers, all setting up significant operations in order to launch hedge funds.

Notwithstanding the fact that the law became effective in the second half of 1998, the Italian market had to wait almost a year and a half before the first hedge fund or speculative fund was registered. The problem was essentially that the Bank of Italy wanted to jump headlong into the process of authorisation whilst it was aware that once authorised, these funds would be free to operate outside the limits imposed on mutual investment funds. The Bank of Italy did not want foreign operators entering the market simply to take advantage of its favourable laws, but rather to facilitate the setting up in Italy of "home-grown" funds. The Bank of Italy moreover wanted to be certain of the preparation and competence of those operators that obtain authorisation so that it didn't find itself with novices driving Ferraris. Last but not least, the Bank of Italy has proceeded slowly because it wants to avoid having to intervene to "save" certain imprudent funds because the possibility of funds collapsing and going into liquidation could cause serious problems in the credit system. In short, the Bank of Italy has no intention of repeating the dramatic experience of the Federal Reserve in the case of the LTCM collapse.

In the six months since the first speculative management company was launched, the number of operators on the market has risen to four offering a total of 12 funds of hedge funds. Kairos Alternative Investments SGR, run by Paolo Basilico, has beaten the competition on time to market. In April 2001, he launched three funds of funds to which he added a fourth in May. By the summer, Kairos was followed by Ersel Hedge SGR, a company of the Ersel Group that also opted to launch three funds of funds. The same number of funds was also put in place by Akros Alternative Investments, the speculative SGR of Banca Akros, which is linked to the Banca Popolare di Milano Group. The fourth company to launch was Investar run by Paolo Catafalmo with his speculative SGR Invesclub. As for the other funds, Catafalmo decided to name his funds of hedge funds after signs of the zodiac.

All four operators have launched funds of funds, seeking to achieve different risk/return profiles. Indeed, the cross-section is made up of more conservative funds, which seek to achieve good performance whilst maintaining low volatility to more aggressive funds, which seek to achieve more substantial returns. However, each of the speculative SGRs seeks low correlation with traditional investments in order that they be easily inserted into global portfolios.

The Problem of Prime Brokers in Italy

Many foreign observers have wondered why the first funds launched on the market were funds of hedge funds as opposed to pure or single manager hedge funds. The reasons for this peculiarity stem from the problem of prime brokers. In the United States but also in many other financial centres, brokerage houses have for many years provided stock lending facilities. As discussed in the first chapter, short selling is fundamental for managers using these types of strategy in that it enables them to construct short portfolios in order to reduce or neutralise market risk, whilst providing the possibility of generating returns from short selling securities.

A second problem regards the law as applied in Italy on the restrictions imposed on hedge funds registered in Italy:

• The minimum investment threshold that the legislator has set at €1 million;
• The limit of 100 investors.

The combination of these two restrictions has created certain problems for operators in so much as these products are also interesting to private clients, HNWI and institutional operators.

Experienced private investors have not encountered major problems in that for them, investing one million Euro does not appear to be a difficult threshold to meet.

Institutional investors, convinced of the advantages in terms of asset allocation that hedge funds can provide (in terms of reducing risk, low correlation and increasing the returns of a traditional portfolio) have attempted to inset these funds in the managed assets of their clients. In this way, they are contravening the Bank of Italy's interpretation of the law. This is because if a money manager chooses to insert a speculative fund into his portfolio for clients, or directly into the different portfolios of his clients, when the number of investors is calculated, the money manager will not be counted. Instead, each investor represented by the manager will be counted.

This, in the judgement of the professionals is limiting the development of the hedge fund market. A little before the summer of 2001, two different routes were taken:

- The issue of a structured product linked to hedge funds with capital protection;
- The use of hedge funds within insurance policies.

Assogestioni asked the Bank of Italy if it were possible to create a capital protected bond note, the returns of which would be entirely linked to a basket of funds or to a fund of funds registered in Italy. The Italian Central Bank answered that it was not currently possible to authorise this type of activity.

A second attempt was made consisting of inserting funds of hedge funds into an insurance policy in the form of unit and index-linked insurance policies but the response of the Italian authorities was the same.

Future Developments in Italy

In the last few months, we have witnessed the arrival on the Italian market of the large banking groups that have already obtained authorisation for speculative SGRs. These include Unicredito, SanPaolo Imi, IntesaBci and Monte dei Paschi. In addition to these institutions, there are also small management companies, bringing the number of Italian participants to around 15.

In the next few months, when a larger number of operators will be active in the market, the Italian authorities may take into consideration the calls for changes in current regulations or soften the current restrictions, thereby providing the Italian hedge fund market with greater impetus. The future appears extremely positive in that the operators are satisfied in the reaction from private clients, other hedge fund companies and from the distribution they have already achieved.

Legal Aspects

The regulations that govern collective investments can be found in Article 36 and the Legislative Decree No. 58, 24th February 1998. This decree assigned responsibility for establishing general rules and criteria that must be observed by collective investment schemes. These regulations regard:

- The object of the investment;
- The categories of investor eligible to be offered fund stakes;
- Subscription methods for open and closed ended funds;
- If applicable, the minimum and maximum maturity of the investment.

Simultaneously, the Treasury established its regulations with Decree 288, 24th May 1999. This decree represents a cornerstone for collective investments in that the following two fund classifications were established:

- Reserved funds
- Speculative funds (Art. 16)

As regards hedge funds, the Treasury states that:

- The "Società di Gestione del Risparmio" (SGR) that launches hedge funds may only be active in the formation and management of such funds. In this case, limits are imposed on invested capital.
- Fund prospectuses must mention the risk factor and that the fund neither falls under the categories prohibited by the Bank of Italy nor is subject to the rules regarding non-prudent investments.
- Fund prospectuses must indicate the asset classes in which the fund will invest and the subscription and liquidation procedures.

All of the above-mentioned regulations were created mainly to safeguard investors who should nevertheless have adequate experience in this area in that the minimum hedge fund investment as fixed by the decree is €1,000,000.

Finally, the decree declares that a fund may not have more than 100 investors and that subscriptions to the fund may not be offered to the general public. As a consequence, no offerings, invites or publicity drives may be undertaken.

Fiscal Regulations

The first aspect to consider regards the possibility of extending (under Italian law) the tax regulations for non-speculative collective investment schemes to hedge funds. Many legislative decrees have been introduced on taxation: 461/97, 259/99 and 221/2000. Moreover, the 342/2000 and 388/2000 laws were also passed. The regulations that follow refer specifically to open ended funds, closed ended funds, reserved funds and also to hedge funds because, as will be explained in the following paragraphs, under tax law, Italian hedge funds receive the same treatment as traditional mutual funds.

The Italian legislature began with the fact that every investment fund or each constituent part of any fund forms an autonomous asset group, totally separated from the capital of the asset management company, from investors' capital and from any shareholdings owned by the same company. It is for this reason that funds are not subject to income tax. Indeed, taxation of funds comes in the form of the asset management company applying a 12.5% retainer to the annual profits of the fund. Moreover, the fund must also pay tax on bank interest so long as the total deposited annually is not more than 5% of the average of assets under management.

A special regime was introduced for funds with under 100 subscribers, so long as the investors are classified as follows:

- Corporate
- Banks, brokers
- SGR
- SICAV
- Pension funds
- Insurance companies
- Other banking institutions

None of these may exceed 50% of the funds' capital.

Regarding hedge funds domiciled overseas, the tax rate applied will be different from and will not take into account whether the fund is European or extra-European. In any case, the offshore hedge fund, classified as a non-harmonised fund, will follow the following scheme:

- Physical persons: returns must be included in general income and are taxable at marginal tax rates.
- Juridical persons: returns must be added to company income without the application of a tax credit.

3.4   OFFSHORE DOMICILES FOR HEDGE FUNDS

When setting up hedge funds in Europe, one must consider many factors. Firstly, the fund must be set up and commercialised in a country with flexible registration regulations. Funds are generally not set up in a given country in order to be distributed to that country's investors. The majority of funds are set up in the European countries that offer the greatest degree of freedom regarding the trading of the instruments considered appropriate for the implementation of a given strategy. Many fund companies choose to set up funds in countries with more flexible regulations.

There are only a few countries in Europe that are truly specialised in alternative investment funds: Ireland, Luxembourg and the Channel Islands. Another factor that could favour the selection of Europe over the Caribbean (British Virgin Islands, Cayman Islands) or Bermuda as the domicile of a fund is the time zone (only one or two hours away from that of Finland or Portugal).

Ireland, the Cannel Islands and Luxembourg have maximised the combination of location and regulation, making their territories amongst the most attractive in which to domicile a hedge fund. The decision to domicile an offshore or onshore hedge fund is however dependent on many factors. Essentially, the choice is mainly based on fiscal considerations.

Table 3.1 gives an idea of the key factors when choosing to set up a hedge fund in one's home country or offshore (i.e. in Ireland, Luxembourg, the Channel Islands, BVI, Cayman, Bermuda, etc.).

Therefore, the distinguishing factor is the lack of fiscal advantages within onshore structures, which in itself provides enough incentive to locate the management of the company abroad.

Table 3.1   Key factors in choosing hedge fund locations

Offshore Advantages	Onshore Advantages
• Fiscal benefits that depend on the various legislation authorities	• The management company can operate also as an advisory company • Lower costs of management of the structure
Disadvantages	Disadvantages
• Higher costs of maintenance of the structure created to operate offshore • The efficiency deriving from savings on taxation depends on the regulations of the country of origin which require that management and control of these activities are actually done outside the country • Often there is the need to create many companies dedicated to offshore activities	• Lack of fiscal advantages

Source: Bluehedge News, reproduced with permission.

The other major choice to be made is whether to domicile a fund in a country under European jurisdiction, such as in Dublin or Luxembourg, or in a less-regulated domicile, such as the British Virgin Islands, Bermuda or the Cayman Islands. The manager can also opt for an intermediary legislation, i.e. that of the Channel Islands or the Isle of Man. If the managers expect the fund only to be sold to sophisticated investors (institutions, high net worth individuals), then the regulatory framework will not be the most important factor to evaluate and the likeliest choice will be to base the company in a less-regulated environment. Nevertheless, increasing importance is now attributed to the domicile/regulatory framework by clients.

The following sections highlight the most important aspects and the main prerequisites for basing funds in each of the above-mentioned jurisdictions.

3.4.1   Cayman Islands

The fund must fall under the definition of a "mutual fund" as stated in the Cayman Islands' "Mutual Fund Law" (revised in 1996). However, the fund is not obliged to request a licence and the registration process is far simpler if the minimum subscription level for fund participation is at least $50,000. The principal obligations of the fund are:

- Register the fund with the monetary authority of the Cayman Islands;
- Register with the same authority details of prospectuses, public offerings as well as any relevant changes;
- Register annual accounts with the authority;
- Pay the registration tax ($875).

There is no requirement to create a management company nor actually carry out any of the activities linked to the fund in the Cayman Islands.

3.4.2   British Virgin Islands

The law that regulates all fund activities is the Mutual Funds Act, 1997. The two relevant categories for alternative investments are:

- Private funds
- Professional funds

The regulatory act states that both fund types be recognised in the Registrar of Mutual Funds. Recognition is provided when the Incorporation Certificate, Articles and Memorandum are submitted. A private fund may have up to 50 investors whilst a professional fund is only targeted at professional investors holding stakes worth at least $100,000. Professional investors are classified as those investors with at least $1,000,000 in assets.

There are no specific requirements to found a management company in the BVI or to run activities linked with the fund business. However, a fund registered in the BVI must nominate a representative based full time in the BVI. The annual registration fee is $350.

3.4.3   Bermuda

In Bermuda, the category with fewest restrictions and regulations is called the "Institutional Scheme". This investment category is subject to $100,000 minimum investment. Moreover, the minimum fund size must be at least $50,000,000. Where the fund fails to meet these requirements, it is classed as a "Standard Scheme" and is subject to the normal regulations of the Bermuda Monetary Authority (BMA). These include the obligation (with some exceptions) to nominate a Bermudan company to handle the custody operations.

A fund based in Bermuda need not be managed from Bermuda but must run certain administrative activities in Bermuda. The other requirements of the BMA are related to the publication of compulsory information, which must be inserted in the prospectus.

3.4.4   Ireland

The Irish Stock Exchange has a history over centuries but became autonomous only in 1995. Before 1995, it was simply a subsidiary of London's International Stock Exchange. The Irish Bourse is not only the most popular place to list hedge funds, but also one of the preferred places to set up hedge funds.

The popularity of Ireland is in part due to the programme approved by the European Union to create the International Centre for Financial Services in Dublin. The choice of the centre's headquarters was initially made to create jobs in Ireland and prevent the drain of professional financiers to other countries. Because of this desperate need to create jobs, regulations are less rigid and we must remember that financial service companies pay only a 10% tax rate.

To be listed on the Irish Stock Exchange and sold to individuals, a fund must be domiciled or authorised in one of the following countries: EU member countries, the Channel Islands, Isle of Man, Bermuda or Hong Kong SAR. If the fund is not authorised in one of these countries, it can only be offered to sophisticated investors and not to the wider public.

Another factor to consider is the ease with which funds can be registered in Ireland. Moreover, listing a fund on the Irish Stock Exchange is a sort of publicity and enables the fund to address many of the needs of institutional investors as well as providing the fund with the sort of exposure that otherwise it would not have.

3.4.5   Luxembourg

Luxembourg has the double advantage of being part of the EU and housing a huge number of private banks. Though Luxembourg lacked the support and structures provided to Ireland by the EU, it imposed itself on the world of hedge funds by taking advantage of the success enjoyed by the mutual investment fund sector. The mutual fund background, the reputation of Luxembourg's private banking sector as well as its membership of the EU have ensured that Luxembourg is one of the best places to domicile hedge funds.

As well as offering these advantages, Luxembourg was the first country to adhere to the European directive. This would seem to lead to Luxembourg's pre-eminent position in the investment sector in that it is amongst the leaders in the electronic international distribution of funds.

The laws that govern the investment funds in Luxembourg reflect the 1985 European Directive. Therefore, by registering funds in Luxembourg, they become authorised in all other European member states. The March 1998 law reflects the regulations of the directive, with specific reference to UCITS. These laws and regulations fall under the jurisdiction of La Commission de Surveillance du Secteur Financier (CSSF, which is the legislative organ in Luxembourg).

A vast range of funds can be set up in Luxembourg (Table 3.2). The main difference in the legal structure that regulates them is whether they fall into the UCITS or non-UCITS category.

Table 3.2   Investment funds in Luxembourg classified by strategy

Investment Strategy	Net Assets in USD m	Market Share
Fixed income	7320	33.76%
Equity	9217	42.51%
Mixed (equity and bonds)	1867	8.61%
Venture capital	10	0.05%
Unlisted companies	69	0.32%
Funds using leverage	79	0.36%
Funds of funds	1239	5.71%
Money market	1542	7.11%
Liquidity	216	1.00%
Real estate	87	0.40%
Futures and options	35	0.17%
Total	**21,681**	**100.00%**

Source: Bluehedge News, reproduced with permission.

The first is subject to part I of the law while the second is subject to part II. Hedge funds and funds of funds both belong to the second category (non-UCITS funds) and for this reason are subject to greater restrictions than other fund types.

Investment funds that intend to sell stakes to Luxembourg's public can only do so after completing a prohibitive authorisation process with the CSSF. Once the fund has received official approval, it will be registered in the list of authorised investment schemes. The list of funds and successive amendments are published in the official Luxembourg gazette, *The Memorial*. In order to obtain approval, requests must be made to the CSSF.

Obtaining approval for funds set up in accordance with foreign laws must be done through the relevant authorities in the funds' country of origin. When developing investment activities in Luxembourg, it is necessary to obtain authorisation from the local supervisory authorities.

3.4.6   Channel Islands

The Channel Islands have always had a reputation as a tax haven for financial products and although generally classified together, the laws of each of the islands are different. Jersey and Guernsey seem to be the right place for investment funds in general and particularly for hedge funds and products that fall outside the UCITS definition. Almost all the laws permit distribution in the UK and now also in the rest of Europe.

As for all investment products, the more competent the target investor, the more flexible the regulations regarding the commercialisation of the product. The riskier the investment, the likelier that the laws will limit the offer only to professional investors.

Hedge funds are considered risky for the majority of investors so in this area are defined as non-classified funds. It must however be noted that funds of funds belong to the recognised fund category and can therefore be sold directly to the public.

Investment funds in Jersey are governed by two different laws, depending on which category they fall into. Whilst not part of the EU, the regulatory standards and the supervision of investment funds have been recognised by numerous overseas authorities. Agreements have been made with various jurisdictions to facilitate the authorisation of funds based in Jersey within these countries. This is done on a case by case basis.

3.4.7 Isle of Man

The Isle of Man's Financial Supervision Commission is responsible for the authorisation and supervision of investment funds. There are different levels of regulation that depend on the category and structure of the fund. For example, the "Exempt Fund" and "Professional Investor Fund" are not subject to approval by the authority and both represent the main categories of alternative investments. The professional investor funds are set up specifically for institutions and for other professional investors. They are not subject to any restrictions regarding the number of investors, although these funds have a minimum investment equivalent to $100,000. They can only be sold to professional investors (HNWI and market professionals). The exempt funds are private funds restricted to a maximum of 50 investors. The Isle of Man is the only tax haven that forms part of the European VAT system. Inclusion in this system makes conducting business with Europe much easier. Whilst not belonging to the EU, the Isle of Man has a special agreement that enables other countries to develop financial activities and take advantage of special fiscal treatment. In all cases, the fund must be administered in the Isle of Man.

3.5 FUTURE PROSPECTS

The creation of laws by the EU for the investment sector indicates that hedge funds and other investment funds will soon take off. There has been a desire to create a single European financial market by 2005. If this happens, the European Union will have to take many factors into consideration, such as levels of transparency, regulation and risk management.

Another aspect to consider is the influence of the Internet. In the investment sector, we are referring to the remote marketing of financial services. In the meantime, the EU is working on its latest modifications of the last directives on the subject from 1997 and 1998. The most difficult aspect of this regulation is the fact that it must take into account the laws of the different countries. Until we witness the standardisation of this directive, it will continue to be modified.

The European Union has a long way to go. As regards the financial services sector, the objective is to remove barriers inhibiting the cross-border marketing of collective investment units and offer a greater range of products.

In the next chapter, we will explore the information possibilities and marketplaces deriving from the mother of all the networks.

4

Information in the World of Hedge Funds

Within the world of hedge funds and alternative investments, we are seeing the emergence of a series of associations, web sites, organisations and specialised organisations whose objective is to provide information, research, reports, databases and organise conferences and events. This small world has often been compared to the specialist field which grew up around "online finance". There are of course substantial differences in the target audience of these providers. Indeed, in the hedge fund sector, information, analysis and research services are in many cases subscription only whilst their peers in online finance saw rapid growth because their services were free. It is important to note that for specialised hedge fund web sites, it is impossible to draw advertising revenues from the major players in the market as almost all relevant laws prohibit companies from communicating with and soliciting business from the wider public.

4.1 ASSOCIATIONS AND ORGANISATIONS

The major associations and organisations focused on hedge funds are based in the United States and the UK. Members of these associations include fund managers, investors and individuals in back office and processing activities for hedge funds.

4.1.1 Hedge Fund Associations

One of the principal American associations is the Hedge Fund Association (http://ww.thehfa.com/) which describes itself as an "international non-profit association of hedge fund managers, service providers and investors". The objective of the organisation is to unite the hedge fund industry to increase the potential for hedge fund investment. Hedge funds are still viewed with suspicion by certain investors, convinced of the high volatility of these products (a feeling fuelled by the media which concentrates attention on the swift and risky attacks by macro funds). The association's objective is to educate savers and legislators throughout the world on the real benefits and potential risks associated with investments in the various hedge fund strategies. Membership costs $500–1000, providing benefits deriving from the association's influence within the hedge fund industry, full access to the association's official web site as well as a newsletter reserved for subscribers.

The web site (Figure 4.1) enables subscribers to express opinions in a forum and to access information (including contact info) on all upcoming events. There are in fact many conferences organised throughout the world with the view of explaining the structure of these products, procedures, regulation and the investment criteria that form the basis of the choices made by managers. It is therefore quite important to stay up-to-date with events in so much as they can provide important insights into new tendencies and developments within the alternative investment industry. Moreover, members of the association receive discounts for such events as well as specialised sector reviews.

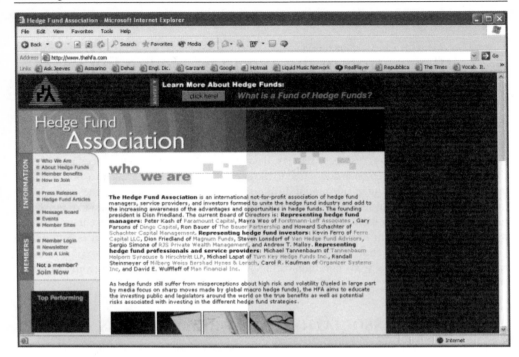

Figure 4.1   The web site for the Hedge Fund Association, reproduced by permission of the Hedge Fund Association Ltd

4.1.2   AIMA

The Alternative Investment Management Association (AIMA) is the global, not-for-profit trade association dedicated to the hedge fund community. Established in 1990, the objectives of AIMA are to increase investor education, transparency and promote due diligence and related best practices, and to work closely with regulators and interested parties to better promote and control the use of alternative investments. All activities are non-commercial and include: the commission and distribution of research, the *AIMA Journal*, generic due diligence questionnaires, industry discussion forums, invitation-only, educational events for the investor community and communication with regulatory bodies on proposed developments. AIMA also negotiates discounts to commercial conferences and publications for its membership as well as endorsing select items which it believes to be of a high standard.

AIMA's corporate members are spread throughout Europe, North America, Asia, Australia and the Middle East, and comprise fund managers, brokers, lawyers, administrators, institutional investors and other service providers. Members meet nationally/regionally throughout the year and, through their elected council members, are able to directly influence the activities and direction of AIMA. Through this democratic process and the invaluable input of members throughout the years, AIMA has become the industry's global, professional body.

AIMA has an extensive website (www.aima.org) which contains a wealth of additional information including articles, research, a library and bibliography.

4.2   PUBLICATIONS

Regarding publications relevant to this sector, the experience has been somewhat different than that seen by the associations. Development in this area has come through economic reviews on the asset management sector. In the following pages, we will detail the most important sources of information specialised in alternative investments.

4.2.1   Hedge Fund Alert

This is a weekly newsletter focused on the hedge fund industry. It is edited in New Jersey and is considered one of the main information sources for the American market. It provides a complete view on the launch of new funds, expectations, market monitors and an in-depth study of hot topics in the hedge fund sector.

4.2.2   Bluehedge News

This European newsletter, published weekly, has 30,000 subscribers and is similar to *Hedge Fund Alert*. See www.bluehedge.com for details (Figure 4.2). The newsletter provides exclusive interviews with protagonists from the world of alternative investments and hedge fund performance figures for the previous month. *Bluehedge News* offers news and research on the Italian and European markets and is suitable for both experienced and inexperienced investors.

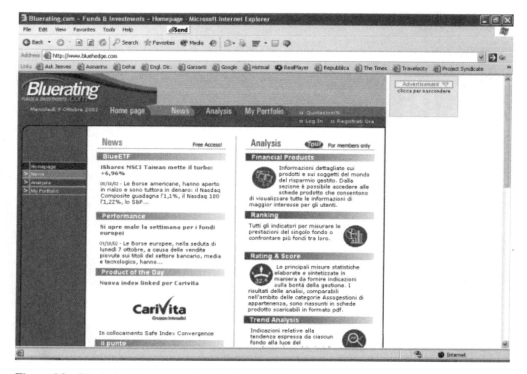

Figure 4.2   Bluehedge News, reproduced with permission

4.2.3   Portfolio International and Hedge Funds International

Founded in 1986, *Portfolio International* is an authoritative guide for market professionals and international distributors of investment products, providing commentary, analysis and qualified opinion on the political and regulatory developments influencing the financial product industry. Thanks to strong relationships with fund companies in Luxembourg and Ireland, it is well positioned to be the primary source of information on the pan-European investment fund market.

Portfolio International was launched as a monthly magazine specialised in the banking and offshore sectors. With the advent of alternative investment products in the UK, it began to dedicate a section of the monthly magazine to hedge funds – *Hedge Funds International*. Both the magazine and its various supplements provide news, analysis and interviews on various products as well as information and news on hedge fund managers which in this sector, often means the difference between success and failure.

In September 2001, *Portfolio International* also launched the web site www.portfolio-international.com (Figure 4.3). The web site covers daily news and analysis and serves as a first point of contact for readers. The web site also allows users to consult a comprehensive database on offshore funds as well as useful contacts for companies with offshore offices.

Portfolio International is therefore a reference for both the British and European markets. Subscribers include many professionals based in Italy, Germany, France, Switzerland and Luxembourg.

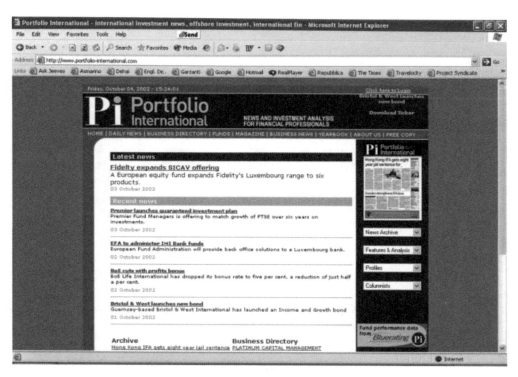

Figure 4.3   *Portfolio International*'s web site, reproduced by permission of Portfolio International

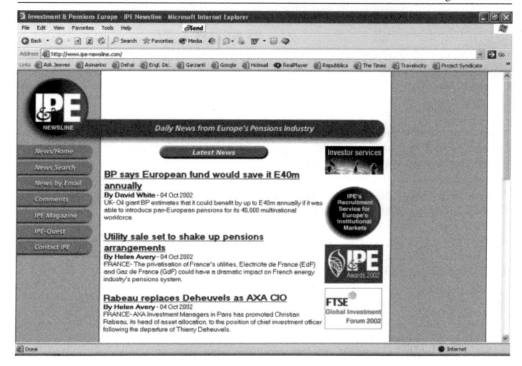

Figure 4.4   IPE Newsline web site, reproduced by permission of IPE International Publishers

4.2.4   Investment & Pensions Europe

Investment & Pensions Europe (IPE) is one of the most authoritative monthlies for pension funds and asset management. IPE also focuses on alternative investments and often publishes articles and supplements on hedge funds and their use within pension funds. Moreover, IPE organises many conferences and seminars including events on hedge funds. IPE runs two web sites. Firstly, there is www.ipeonline.com, effectively the electronic archive for the magazine, also providing information on conferences and seminars organised by IPE and other companies. As it provides information on the major events in the calendar, it is considered an important source of information for the business community in London. The second web site, www. ipe-newsline.com (Figure 4.4) is entirely dedicated to news, providing news flashes on the latest developments in the financial sector.

4.2.5   Hedge Funds Review

This British monthly newsletter is essentially divided into four sections:

- The first gives an overview of company activity and management during the previous month with news and trends for the hedge funds sector.
- The second analyses the cover story and explores current themes, be they on legal matters or on specific products.
- The third is dedicated to statistics, breaking down by strategy the best performing funds and providing commentary on the reasons for their performance.

- The final part is dedicated to the hedge fund directory, providing contact information for prime brokers, alternative service providers and hedge funds.

Overall, this publication differs from the others for its analytical approach, particularly regarding statistics.

4.2.6   Financial News

The weekly publication *Financial News* is the leader in the UK for information on funds and investment banking. It recently decided to devote a section to hedge funds in each edition, with the view of providing a more complete view of innovations in structured products and funds of hedge funds. *Financial News* also offers an electronic edition (www.efinancialnews.com). That many UK-based journals have expanded their activities shows how seriously the European financial industry is taking the advent of hedge funds.

4.3   RESEARCH WEB SITES

4.3.1   Tremont-TASS

The colossus Tremont-TASS provides analysis, information and research through three web sites. The two sites of Tremont (www.tremont.com) and TASS (www.tassresearch.com) provide detailed information on the hedge fund market, including reports and in-depth research. Moreover, the sites allow you to subscribe to the database, providing in-depth information on more than 2500 hedge funds. This database is recognised as the most comprehensive and accurate source of information available today and is continually updated by a team of 15 people.

   The third site, www.hedgeindex.com (Figure 4.5), is more interactive and provides free access to information on the CSFB/Tremont index of hedge funds, on all the subindexes relating to the various strategies as previously discussed. The site enables users to download certain Excel files on the historical performance of the main as well as subindexes. All data is updated monthly and sent via e-mail to all registered users. The site's interactive graphs allow users to compare all data on the CSFB/Tremont index with that of the subindexes and the principal world indicators such as the MSCI World, S&P 500, Dow Jones, NASDAQ and Russel 2000. Commentary from Tremont Advisors is offered on all hedge indices, highlighting the relationship between volatility and performance.

4.3.2   MAR

MAR was founded in 1979. Its newsletter provides qualitative and quantitative information on the performance of futures, trading advisors and funds.

   In January 1994, *MAR Hedge* was launched and was the pioneer in tracking alternative investments. The newsletter contains news, profiles of managers, alternative investment fund rankings and analysis. *MAR Hedge* publishes a twice-yearly directory on the performance and valuations of hedge funds in conjunction with *La Porte Asset Allocation*. It covers more than 1500 hedge funds and funds of hedge funds. MAR also offers *Hedge Fast*, a thrice-monthly faxed update providing news on the world of hedge funds. This also provides data on the monthly performance of hedge funds within two days of the end of the month.

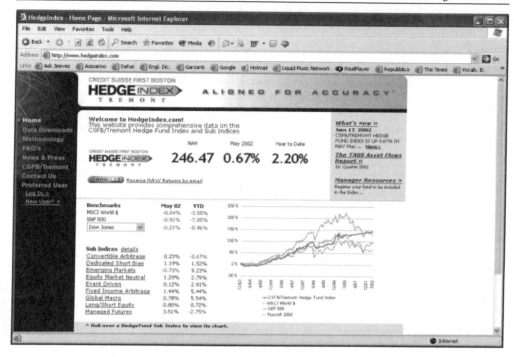

Figure 4.5   The Hedge Index web site, www.hedgeindex.com. Reproduced by permission of CSFB

In July 1998, MAR launched its third publication, *MAR Sophisticated Investor Strategies*. This is a newsletter dedicated specifically to family offices and high net worth individuals. In 2001, MAR was acquired by the Zurich group.

4.3.3   Van Hedge Fund Advisors International

Van Hedge is a company based in Nashville, TN, specialised in research and analysis on hedge funds. Van Hedge also publishes hedge fund indexes and uses data on more than 4000 hedge fund products. On the web site www.vanhedge.com (Figure 4.6), you can find a great deal of information on the company and its services, which can be divided into four sections:

- Research
- Analysis
- Information
- Consultancy

Detailed reports on the markets and hedge funds, tables with analysis, interesting articles from the press, educational material and everything that may be useful to increase understanding and keep you updated on the subject are all provided. Moreover, Van in its capacity as a consultancy offers investors the possibility of constructing customised and "benchmarked" portfolios.

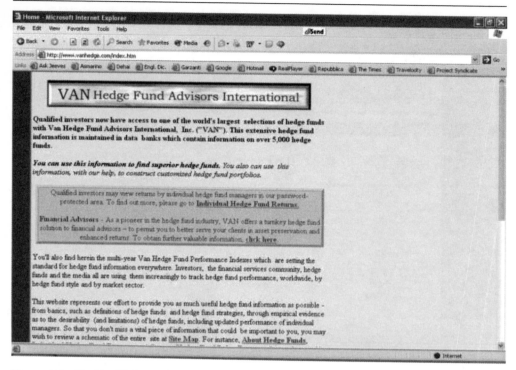

Figure 4.6 The Van Hedge web site. Van Hedge Fund Advisors International, Inc. and/or its licensors, Nashville, TN, USA, reproduced with permission

4.3.4   Hennessee Group

Hennessee is a famous American company specialised in advising on alternative investment products. The company, founded in 1987, is amongst the most expert in the field of consulting and has launched Hennessee Hedge Fund Indices, often used by hedge fund managers to make comparisons, analyses and decisions on portfolio selection.

Hennessee publishes monthly and annual research on hedge funds. The most important of these are:

- *Monthly Hennessee Hedge Funds Review*
- *Timely Manager Due Diligence Report*
- *Annual Hennessee Hedge Fund Manager Survey*
- *Annual Hennessee Hedge Fund Investor Survey*

In particular, the *Hennessee Hedge Funds Review* which is published monthly is dedicated to investors, family offices, foundations, pension funds and other institutions. It provides hundreds of interviews with managers, drilling down to specifics and explaining how managers succeed in registering gains. It provides technical and fundamental analysis of the investment styles of hedge funds, all 22 Hennessee hedge fund indices (split by investment style) as well as information on new opportunities arising in business linked to the world of alternative investments.

The official site (www.hennesseegroup.com) provides a presentation of the company as well as an interesting section on discussion forums regarding the regulation of hedge funds

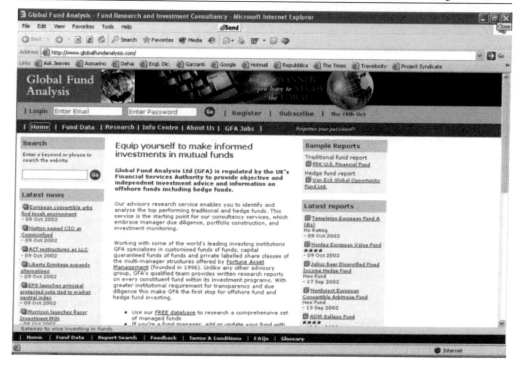

Figure 4.7   Global Fund Analysis web site, reproduced by permission of Global Fund Analysis

and the development of this market. All of the indexes can be downloaded with monthly data retrievable from 1993 onwards and yearly data prior to 1993.

4.3.5   Global Fund Analysis

Launched in 1996, Global Fund Analysis is a company dedicated to the research and analysis of hedge funds and traditional funds. In particular, it is possible to purchase and consult extremely detailed qualitative reports on many funds through the web site www.globalfundanalysis.com (Figure 4.7). A free database is available with a search engine enabling users to view and select funds by flexible criteria. Users may choose between traditional funds and hedge funds. Moreover, there is a free news section providing a great deal of accurate information. It differs from other fee-based web sites in that it allows you to purchase individual reports.

4.4   INFORMATION SITES

Interest in hedge funds in Europe has brought new business in connection with the Internet. It was only a few years ago that the advent of online finance for European investors resulted in the development of large numbers of web sites dedicated to traders of varied experience and providing all manner of financial information from technical to fundamental analysis, portfolio optimisers to real time pricing, breaking news to efficient portfolio management. In short, there arose a range of services that increasingly used the web to reach investors and thanks to the cost savings facilitated by the web, resulted in lower commission structures across the board. These business models were more or less based on advertisement revenues in that they have always offered their services free of charge. Recent market contractions and economic restrictions have stopped the development of these sites, with many closing or utterly changing their business models, transforming them from free portals into real information and service supermarkets.

The logic of the web as applied to hedge funds is quite different and more in line with the target audience. This is in part due to the experience gained by the more traditional financial web sites and in part because of the types of individuals interested in these services. Investors in alternative instruments are quite prepared to buy information and analysis services in that with such investments, high returns can be achieved so long as care is taken in their selection. The added value of sites dedicated to hedge funds is therefore to provide help and information in choosing these products, which is otherwise unavailable in this sector.

The first stage in analysing hedge fund sites should be to understand the development of the most important American sites and then to look at their European equivalent.

4.4.1   Hedge World

This is perhaps the top web site on hedge funds in that it has succeeded in identifying the needs of investors, fund managers, service providers and intermediaries, creating for each of these categories a dedicated site (Figure 4.8). Many of the services offered are fee-based and prices vary depending on the category.

In general, the information offered is very selective and composed of:

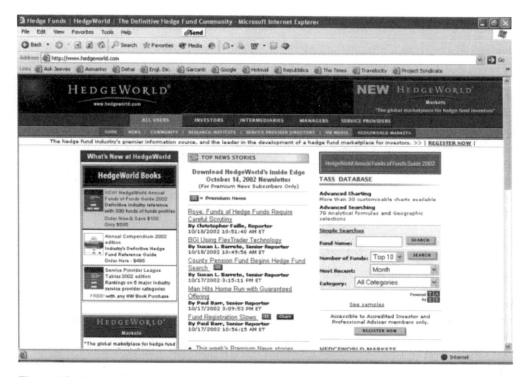

Figure 4.8   Hedge World web site, reproduced by permission of Hedge World

- News: accessible to all users, offering an extensive overview of the latest innovations in terms of products and companies. The section is divided into daily news, international news, accounting news and legal news.
- Community: there is a section dedicated to the Hedge World community offering the possibility to interact in a forum and pose questions to the experts.
- *Alternative Edge* Newsletter: this is the weekly contact between Hedge World and its registered users. A newsletter in pdf format provides information on all the relevant events of the week.
- Bookstore, Education and Research: this section is free and provides important sources of material on alternative investments. Here we find many reports from major brokerages as well as a list of books published on the world of finance and a complete glossary on hedge funds.
- TASS Database: one of the functionalities restricted to investors/fund managers. It allows users to obtain all information publicly released by the companies in question as well as a series of exclusive analyses.
- Events: this is a continually updated section dedicated to upcoming events. As the site is recognised internationally, details of all conferences throughout the world are available.

4.4.2   Bluehedge.com

The site www.bluehedge.com (Figure 4.9) was launched in 2001 as a section of Bluerating.com, the leading Italian web site for information and analysis on asset management. Initially, the

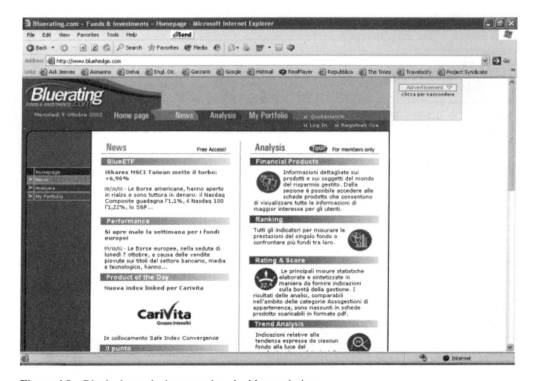

Figure 4.9   Bluehedge web site, reproduced with permission

section provided news and interviews with experts from the field who had explored the hedge fund phenomenon in Italy. The objective of the site is to lead to a better understanding of the field for a wider public. Bluehedge.com resides in the pages of Bluerating.com, which in turn provides qualitative and quantitative analysis as well as style analysis on investment funds. With the growth of the European hedge fund market, Bluehedge was created to complete the offering of information, analysis and data on the site.

4.4.3   Mondo Hedge

This is one of the Italian sites specialised in hedge funds and is dedicated entirely to these products (Figure 4.10). Access is almost totally reserved for subscribers. The content is comprised of:

- Editorials;
- News from *MAR Hedge* translated into Italian;
- An extensive database on hedge funds and speculative funds;
- Education and legislation;
- Community: newsletter, links, detailed information, events, library.

It is interesting to note that this site is the first in Italy dedicated to alternative investments. It has followed the same model as the original American sites in that it seeks to be the most comprehensive information source.

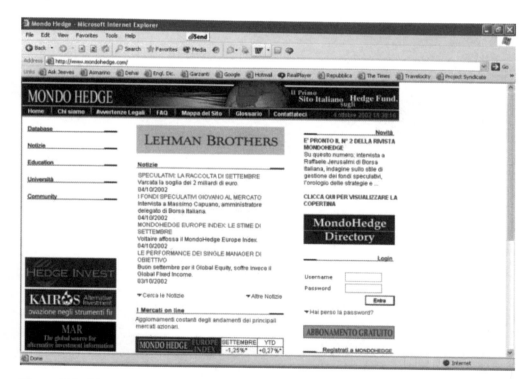

Figure 4.10   Mondo Hedge web site, reproduced by permission of MondoHedge SpA

4.4.4   eHedge

eHedge is an independent company based in Frankfurt, offering hedge fund investment solutions to institutional clients. www.ehedge.de was the first site in Germany to be entirely dedicated to the alternative investment market. The ambition is to be the main European marketplace for the sector over the next few years. eHedge enables investors to contact hedge fund managers and conduct business independently and securely. eHedge is not part of the dot. com phenomenon but a pure financial service, strongly supported by its online functionality. The peculiarity of the site is to condense an entire trading desk onto one address. It is divided into four sections:

- News and in-depth research;
- A complete hedge fund database;
- The possibility to request a price, view the offerings and assign mandates;
- The possibility to monitor your portfolio and access reports on your positions.

It is therefore a real alternative investment supermarket, quite unique in both Europe and America.

4.4.5   Hedge Fund Intelligence

This is a British site providing information on alternative investment products. Hedge Fund Intelligence offers (for a fee) in-depth reports and analysis on European hedge funds as well as providing a monthly newsletter which updates fund managers, investors and service providers on:

- News;
- Profiles of new funds;
- People;
- Industry analysis;
- Performance profiles (analysis of investment strategies and results);
- Research;
- Trends in and evolution of the market.

4.5   HEDGE FUND INDICES

As has already happened for mutual funds, in recent years, indices can represent benchmark performances for these funds. Indices have in general two functions. The first is to quantify the returns of a given class of activity. In this case, an index can be of use when deciding where to allocate financial resources. The second is to evaluate the abilities of the manager in relation to performance. An index constructed with this objective tends to focus on a particular strategy or investment style. This section is dedicated to the analysis of certain indices.

4.5.1   CSFB/Tremont Hedge Fund Index

The information and materials presented herein have not been reviewed by CREDIT SUISSE FIRST BOSTON TREMONT INDEX L.L.C. (the "Index") or its affiliates, subsidiaries, members or parents ("affiliates") and is not sponsored, endorsed or approved by the Index or its affiliates. This was the result of the combined efforts of Credit Suisse First Boston and Tremont Advisors. Published in August 1999, data has been analysed back to 1994. It is currently

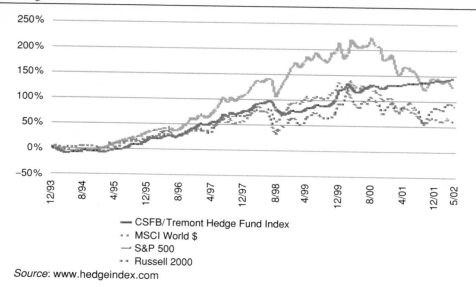

published monthly. The CSFB/Tremont index is the only index weighted in terms of assets under management. This methodology consists of assigning to each fund a weighting that is relative to the total assets managed by that fund. It is a criterion that enables us to have a more accurate framework compared to equal weighted indices.

The universe of hedge funds to be quantified was taken from the TASS database that values approximately 2600 funds and including only those funds with more than $10 million under management and updated figures. The funds are divided into subcategories corresponding to different investment styles. The index is re-balanced monthly and the funds are re-selected quarterly. Funds based in all countries are considered, be they open or closed ended and performance is calculated net of commissions. When a new fund is inserted, this does not result in the recalculation of the index's past performance but only contributes to the index from the moment it is added.

The principal characteristics of the CSFB/Tremont index are:

- The index is asset weighted;
- Constituent funds must have at least $10 million under Management;
- The fund balances must be reviewed;
- Funds are re-selected quarterly;
- Funds are not removed from the index unless they are liquidated or no longer satisfy the conditions set out by CSFB/Tremont. To minimise the problem of survivorship bias, a fund can only be removed if:
- The fund does not provide monthly performance figures or state the investment classes used;
- The fund violates the rules regarding the provision of financial Information;
- The fund ceases its activity.

As stated, the index has been calculated from 1994 (Figure 4.12) and as of 31st May 2002, it was made up of 385 hedge funds, subdivided according to investment style:

- Convertible Arbitrage: funds that seek to obtain profits from positions in convertible bonds and in the underlying companies.
- Dedicated Short Bias: funds that short sell equities and derivative instruments.
- Equity Market Neutral: funds that aim to obtain neutral returns relative to the beta, taking advantage of the correlation between long and short positions.
- Event Driven: funds that aim to take advantage of events affecting companies such as mergers & acquisitions, financial crises, etc.
- Fixed Income Arbitrage: funds that aim to generate profits by taking advantage of pricing anomalies between correlated fixed income securities.
- Global Macro: funds that invest in multiple securities and other Instruments.
- Long/Short Equity: funds that invest in both long and short positions and focus on specific sectors, regions or markets.
- Managed Futures: known as CGTAs (Commodity Trading Advisors), these funds invest in futures contracts on stipulated financial instruments and commodities.

The CSFB/Tremont index is located on the Internet at www.hedgeindex.com.

4.5.2   MSCI-FRM Index

At the end of January 2001, the MSCI-FRM indices on hedge funds were announced. These indices were the result of a joint venture between Morgan Stanley Capital International and Financial Risk Management (a consultancy based in London). The approach used to construct these indices was based on a triple classification:

- Process used to generate profits;
- Class of activity;
- Geographic area.

The first classification concerns the management style: hedge funds are assigned in relation to portfolio strategies (Table 4.1).

Table 4.1   First classification

Investment Styles	Description
Stock selection	Long bias
	No bias
	Short bias
	Variable bias
Specialist credit	Distressed debt
	Positive carry
	Private placements
Relative value	Convergence arbitrage
	Merger arbitrage
	Statistical arbitrage
Directional trading	Discretionary
	Macro
	Systematic
	Fundamental
	Systematic technical

Table 4.2   Second classification

Investment Category	Subcategories
Equity	Equity (includes warrants and other derivatives)
	Convertibles (warrants, etc.)
Fixed income	Credit insensitive
	Credit sensitive
	Mortgage-backed securities
Commodities	Agricultural
	Energy
	Metals
Currencies	Developed markets
	Emerging markets

The second classification regards the type of investment pre-selected by different strategies depending on whether they are equities, bonds, currencies or commodities (Table 4.2).

The third subdivision regards the geographic area. More specifically, this concerns the geographic area where the hedge fund expects to invest and generate profits and not where the manager or instruments used are based. For example, if a French company quoted on the New York Stock Exchange is held by an American manager, it is considered a European investment. The categories are derived directly from the MSCI World index:

- Europe
- North America
- Japan
- Asia Pacific ex Japan
- Emerging Markets
- Global Developed
- Global

4.5.3   Zurich Hedge Fund Index

This index is different from the others in that it focuses on those managers more likely to be considered by institutional and qualified investors. Further, this index selects those funds that employ negligible levels of financial leverage and rarely use derivative instruments. This index covers five hedge fund strategies and is currently made up of 60 funds selected from the thousands in existence. It was launched in 2001, data has been backdated to 1998 and the index was constructed according to the following principles:

- Not ambiguous: the hedge funds included in the index and the weighting assigned to them are public information. Changes in the composition of the index are made in advance.
- Attractive to investment: it is expected that the investor can obtain positive returns by investing in any of the constituent funds, with low tracking errors and relatively low costs.
- Measurability: investors have free access to prices and returns used to calculate the index so that the return of a single index can be verified.
- Suitability: the indices only include those funds that can be held by institutional investors.
- Verifiability: changes in the components of the index are made in accordance with previously stated procedures and proposed by a committee whose members are selected from the public.

To construct the index, a group of managers was identified, capable of satisfying the criteria established by the Zurich Hedge Fund Index. Then, management styles were identified (the classification of styles is that set out by Zurich and not as described by the managers). Clearly, these descriptions frequently overlap. The categories are as follows:

- Convertible Arbitrage
- Merger Arbitrage
- Distressed Securities
- Event Driven Multi-Strategy
- Hedged Equity

The criteria which funds must satisfy in order to be included in the index are somewhat restrictive. They generally refer to the funds' soundness and stipulate that the manager must possess infrastructure of proven quality and have a track record of attracting capital from qualified investors:

- Minimum two-year track record. A manager with less than two years' experience cannot be tested and available statistics are insubstantial.
- Assets under management. For each strategy, a minimum fund capital threshold is stipulated. Funds that fail to meet this threshold are excluded from the index.

4.5.4   Hedge Fund Research Index

Created in 1994, this is an index subdivided into 32 categories and subcategories for which data has been gathered dating back to 1990. It includes around 1100 funds selected from a database of around 1700. The methodology used seeks to offer a valid reference tool and representative benchmark of a large hedge fund universe subdivided by management style. The investment styles of individual funds are also subdivided according to both geographic criteria as well as in terms of the instruments used within the various strategies. The index also contains a separate subcategory dedicated to funds of hedge funds.

4.5.5   Van Hedge Fund Index

This is an index based on the performance of over 750 different US and offshore funds. It is subdivided into 14 strategies that are also combined to provide a general index. The admission criteria for the index consist of a memorandum presented by the fund and a series of interviews with the fund manager.

4.5.6   Standard & Poor's

In June 2002 Standard & Poor's announced plans to create the S&P Hedge Fund Index aimed at providing a transparent performance benchmark for hedge funds. The index is expected to be launched in the third quarter:

- The index will track 40 funds and will be divided into three subindices (arbitrage, event driven and tactical) representing nine strategies (macro, long/short, equity managed futures, special situations, merger arbitrage, distressed, fixed income arbitrage, convertible arbitrage and equity market neutral).
- To avoid over-representation of one individual strategy within the index all the strategies will be equally weighted.

- The constituents of the fund index will go through a quantitative screening to ensure they conform to the return and risk characteristics of each strategy. For funds to be included, fund managers will be required to offer daily investment transparency and daily valuations.

The index committee of Standard & Poor's will review the constituents on a regular basis to ensure the criteria of the index are being met and to implement any necessary rebalancing. S&P will announce the fund constituents and methodology in the third quarter.

4.5.7 Final Considerations on Indices

As you will have noted, many challenges emerge when attempting to construct an index. Each of the companies has found different though valid solutions. We can summarise the main differences as follows:

- Selection criteria: the choice of selection criteria upon which to base the index represents the first obstacle. Track records, assets under management and restrictions in terms of the publication of data are some of the criteria used to define the hedge fund universe.
- Classification: strategy definition is one of the main problems faced in the construction of an index. Each of the indexes analysed uses a particular classification.
- Weightings: what is the weighting of each fund within an index. Different weightings inevitably result in different valuations.
- Rebalancing: how to decide when to reallocate the activities of a fund. Certain indexes rebalance monthly whilst others do so quarterly or yearly.

Table 4.3 shows several differences and similarities between the indices analysed.

The first interesting piece of data deals with the classification of hedge funds. All of the indexes use different ways to subdivide funds by management style. In reality, defining the hedge fund universe poses many difficulties. There is little uniformity in the attitudes of

Table 4.3 Indices compared

	Zurich Hedge Fund Indices	HFR Hedge Fund Indices	CSFB/Tremont Hedge Fund Indices	Van Hedge Fund Indices	MSCI-FRM
Launch date	2001	1994	1999	–	2000
Data publicity	No	Yes	Yes	No	No
Classification	5	17 categories 14 subcategories	9	14	Multidimensional
Presence of the "Hedge Fund Composite"	No	Yes	Yes	Yes	Yes
Required minimum size	Variable (between $25m and $75m)	None	USD 10 m	None	None
Criteria of performance evaluation	Average	Average	Weighed average as a function of assets	Average	Average
Rebalancing	Quarterly	Monthly	Quarterly	Monthly	–
Number of funds	60	1100	372	750	–

institutional investors on which strategies can be defined as hedge fund strategies and on the classification of those funds that are considered as such. With these considerations in mind, it is possible to understand why Zurich is the only company to not construct a composite index. The other extremely important factor concerns the methods used to measure performance. The only index to weight funds according to assets under management is the CSFB/Tremont index.

In general we can confirm that the Zurich index is substantially different from the others, highlighting that previously the selection criteria were somewhat restrictive. In terms of classification, the HFR and MSCI-FRM indexes are certainly more detailed.

From this brief analysis, you will have noted that one of the main problems faced when constructing an index is the definition of the different investment strategies. This is important in that incorrect strategy definition leads to a poor representation of the market.

These indexes are the first stage in creating innovative investment products. In particular, investment in an index is a convenient and efficient way to eliminate systematic risk, which in this case is the risk of selecting the wrong fund.

Glossary

Alpha A numerical value indicating a manager's risk-adjusted excess rate of return relative to a benchmark. Measures a manager's "value-added" in selecting individual securities, independent of the effect of overall market movements. In the Jensen version (Jensen alpha), it is a measure of the manager's ability to beat the relevant benchmark.

Alternative investment Investment in asset classes other than equities, bonds or other securities. For example, art, wine and antiques.

APT (Arbitrage Pricing Theory) A model for pricing equities developed by Stephen Ross. It is based on the idea that the returns of a specific stock are determined by the stock's exposure to a series of systematic risk factors common to the whole market. The returns for the stock are therefore the sum of the premiums deriving from exposure to each of these risks.

Arbitrage An investment technique used to profit from seemingly insignificant differences between stock indexes and futures contracts on those indexes. For example, the movement of indexes, and futures contracts on those indexes, is not always synchronised. In such cases, a nimble arbitrageur can make a lot of money by buying the less expensive one and selling the more expensive.

Asset allocation An investment strategy that defines the percentages of the investment portfolio that should be allocated to stocks, bonds or other asset classes. It represents the first phase in the investment process. Strategic – defines the allocation for macro-classes of financial instruments with a medium to long time horizon (3–5 years) and establishes a benchmark with which to compare performance. Tactical – a short-term expression of the strategic approach (1 month–1 year) that focuses on specific investment opportunities.

Asset class A type of security or market sector in which investments can be made. Examples of asset classes are equities, bonds, cash or real estate.

Back-end load Some mutual funds impose a load, or sales charge, when you sell shares in the fund. That is called a back-end load, or a contingent deferred sales load. Typically, the charge, which is a percentage of the value of the assets you have in the fund, applies only during the first few years you own your shares. In most cases, too, the percentage you pay declines each year during that period and then is dropped. Shares in back-end load funds are sometimes described as Class B shares to distinguish them from front-end load funds, which are known as Class A shares, and level-load funds, called Class C shares.

Back office   The administrative activities of brokerage houses. This includes confirming all executed trades, updating positions and developing administrative activities.

Bank of Italy   The central bank of Italy. It was formed as a private company limited by shares in 1893. Since 1936 it has been a public law institution. In its century-long life it has progressively acquired functions and responsibilities, transforming it from its original status as a currency issuing institution into a modern central bank. Today its functions are: currency issue; banking and financial supervision; market oversight; safeguarding competition in the credit market; economic and institution analysis, research and study; and, jointly with the European Central Bank, oversight over payment systems. In the sphere of economic policy, the bank performs high-level consultation for the legislative and executive branches. It also provides the treasury service for the central government. Together with the other national central banks of the EU member countries and the European Central Bank, the Bank of Italy forms part of the European System of Central Banks, where it helps to determine monetary policy stance and decisions for the entire Euro area; and in accordance with the principle of subsidiarity, it implements that policy in Italian money and financial markets.

Basis point   Yields on bonds notes and other fixed income investments fluctuate regularly, typically changing only within hundredths of a percentage point. These small variations are measured in basis points, or gradations of 0.01%, or one-hundredth of a percent, with 100 basis points equalling 1%. For example, when the yield on a bond changes from 12.72% to 12.65%, it has dropped seven basis points. The term is also used to describe small changes in the interest rates charged for mortgages or other loans, and to indicate your percentage of ownership in certain kinds of investments, where each basis point equals 0.01% of the whole investment.

Beta   Beta is a measure of an investment's relative volatility. The higher the beta, the more sharply the value of the investment can be expected to fluctuate in relation to a market index. For example, Standard & Poor's 500 Stock Index (S&P 500) has a beta coefficient (or base) of 1. That means if the S&P 500 moves 2% in either direction, a stock with a beta of 1 would also move 2%. Under the same market conditions, however, a stock with a beta of 1.5 would move 3% (2% increase × 1.5 beta = 0.03, or 3%). But a stock with a beta lower than 1 would be expected to be more stable in price and move less. Betas as low as 0.5 and as high as 4 are fairly common, depending on the sector and size of the company. However, in recent years, a number of experts have disputed the validity of assigning and using a beta value as an accurate predictor of stock performance.

Bond   Bonds are debt securities issued by corporations and governments. Bonds are, in fact, loans that you and other investors make to the issuers in return for the promise of being paid interest, usually but not always at a fixed rate. The issuer also promises to repay the debt on time and in full. Because bonds pay interest on a regular basis, they are also described as fixed income investments.

Borrowing capacity   The amount of money that a hedge fund can borrow from a broker, dealer or other moneylender. For example, according to the Federal Reserve Board's T regulation, a maximum of 50% of the value of the security may be borrowed (depending on the security).

Capital   The total assets of a hedge fund net of losses but including fees owed to the hedge fund manager.

Capital gain   When you sell an asset at a higher price than you paid for it, the difference is your capital gain. For example, if you buy 100 shares of stock for $20 a share and sell them for $30 a share, you realise a capital gain of $10 a share, or $1000 in total. If you sell an asset at a lower price than you paid for it, we refer to this as a "capital loss".

Capitalisation   As regards an individual stock, it equals the number of shares listed on an exchange multiplied by the share price. As regards the capitalisation of a market or index, this equals the sum of the values of the constituents of that index.

Capital protected or guaranteed fund   This is a particular type of fund that guarantees a minimum return to the subscriber. This minimum return, generally in line with interest rates, is achieved by the management company by buying put options on the benchmark of the same fund and investing part of the capital in government debt or similar instruments.

Capital structure arbitrage   An investment strategy that seeks to take advantage of inefficiencies in the capital structure of a company. The strategy therefore comprises the acquisition of undervalued stocks and the sale of overvalued stocks with the expectation that the price difference between the two will converge.

CAPM (Capital Asset Pricing Model)   A theoretical model for pricing equities, according to which the expected return from a security is the same as the returns deriving from a risk-free investment, plus a premium relating to the security's exposure to systematic risk. The systematic risk exposure coefficient is called the beta and is calculated for each security. Its value can theoretically be from zero to infinity, even if the value is most frequently around 1. A security with a zero beta is a risk-free asset (generally found in 3-month bonds issued by debtors with the highest credit ratings. The greater the exposure to systematic risk, the higher the beta, the greater the expected returns of the security. The strong hypotheses behind this model are the homogenous outlook of investors and their aversion to risk. However, one of the starting points is that the only type of risk to which the market assigns a premium is systematic risk, because this specific component can be eliminated through diversification.

Commission   The fees paid by the client to the intermediary when buying or selling financial products. This generally takes the form of a percentage of the total value bought or sold. In asset management, there are various specific types of commission:

- *Subscription fee*, paid when the client subscribes to a stake in a fund.
- *Management fee*, paid periodically to the asset management company. Represents the compensation for the "active management" of the fund's capital.
- *Performance or incentive fee*, paid to the asset management company if within a certain period, returns exceed the benchmark.
- *Redemption fee,* paid by the client when he sells his stake in a fund.

Concentration   This happens when a significant percentage of the portfolio is exposed to the same or similar market or other risk factors, raising the likelihood of the fund registering losses because of economic events or adverse markets influencing these risks.

CONSOB (Commissione Nazionale per le Società e la Borsa)   The public authority responsible for regulating the Italian securities market. Its activity is aimed at the protection of the investing public and in this respect CONSOB ensures the transparency and correct behaviour by securities market participants, disclosure of complete and accurate information to the investing public by listed companies, accuracy of the facts represented in the prospectuses related to offerings of transferable securities to the investing public, and compliance with regulations by auditors entered in the Special Register. It conducts investigations with respect to potential infringements of insider dealing and market manipulation law.

Convertible arbitrage   Investment strategy that seeks to exploit pricing inefficiencies between a convertible bond and the underlying stock. The manager will typically long the convertible bond and short the underlying stock.

Convertible bonds   Convertible bonds are corporate bonds that you can convert into common stock of the company that issues them rather than redeeming them for cash when they mature. These bonds have a double appeal for investors concerned about volatility and high stock prices: their prices go up if stock prices go up but usually drop less than the underlying stock price if that price should fall. And while convertible bonds typically provide lower yields than regular bonds, they provide higher yields than the underlying stock. You can buy convertibles through a broker or choose a mutual fund that invests in them.

Counterparty   A third party that trades with a hedge fund.

Credit provider   Usually a bank or financial institution that provides credit to a hedge fund or in connection with the financing of an acquisition of shares or other instruments by the hedge fund. A counterparty can be seen as a credit provider when it facilitates an OTC derivatives trade with a hedge fund.

Custodial arrangement   Agreement between a hedge fund and a depository bank that defines the relationship between the two parties.

Custodian   A bank or other financial institution responsible for the custody of hedge fund capital. A custodian provides multiple services from cash management, dividend payments, carrying out payments on behalf of the hedge fund, safekeeping of share certificates and investment transfers, exercising rights and options. In reality, the hedge fund's capital is often held by various brokers acting as subcustodians.

Dealer   A trader that trades for his own account. With regard to brokers, dealers take positions in the hope of selling them at a higher price. This activity is high risk, and dealers are subject to certain supervisory obligations.

Depository bank   With respect to discretionary portfolio management, the depository bank is a credit institution charged with effecting checks and guarantees. In particular, it must safekeep securities and liquid assets, regulate trading activities and check that all trades conform to fund legislation and other laws.

Derivative   Derivatives are hybrid investments, such as futures contracts, options and mortgage-backed securities, whose value is based on the value of an underlying investment. For example, the changing value of a crude oil futures contract depends on the upward or downward movement of oil prices. Certain investors, called hedgers, are interested in the underlying investment. For example, a baking company might buy wheat futures to help estimate the cost of producing its bread in the months to come. Other investors, called speculators, are concerned with the profit to be made by buying and selling the contract at the most opportune time. Derivatives are traded on exchanges, over the counter (OTC) and in private transactions. The most common derivative products are futures, options, swaps and warrants.

Disclosure   The submission of all relevant information regarding a company in accordance with the regulations established by a country's supervisory authorities (SEC, FSA, CONSOB) or with respect to a contract.

Distressed securities investing   Investment strategy focusing on troubled or restructuring companies at deep discounts through stocks, fixed income, bank debt or trade claims. Seeks to exploit possible pricing inefficiencies caused by the lack of large institutional investor participation.

Efficient frontier   This is the graphic representation of efficient portfolios. The axes represent risk and returns. The area below the efficient frontier represents inefficient portfolios.

Emerging markets   Countries in the process of building market-based economies are broadly referred to as emerging markets, though there are major differences among the countries usually included in this category. Some emerging market countries, including Russia, have only recently relaxed restrictions on a free-market economy. Others, including Indonesia, have opened their markets more widely to overseas investors, and still others, including Mexico, are expanding industrial production. Combined, they have stock market capitalisation of less than 3% of the world's total.

Emerging markets investing   A generally long-only investment strategy which entails investing in geographic regions that have undeveloped capital markets and exhibit high grow rates and high rates of inflation. Investing in emerging markets can be very volatile, and may also involve currency risk, political risk and liquidity risk.

Endowment   A fund organised by an institution (usually a university) to finance study programmes or doctorates.

Equity market neutral investing   Equity investing on both the long and short side, with equal dollar amounts. Will attempt to neutralise market risk, and isolate a manager's alpha, to achieve absolute returns.

Ethical fund   These are socially responsible funds in that they invest in financial instruments issued by companies that observe certain principles. These principles include their environmental or social approach and the treatment of specific categories of worker.

European equity investing   A hedge on European shares using long and short investments. Seeks to hedge certain market risks and obtain absolute returns.

EVCA   Acronym for the European Private Equity and Venture Capital Association. Its role is to promote private equity and venture capital activities through its research, publications and lobbying activities.

Event driven investing   Investment strategy seeking to identify and exploit pricing inefficiencies that have been caused by some sort of corporate event, such as a merger, spin-off, distressed situation or re-capitalisation.

Exchange traded fund   Exchange traded or closed end funds behave like mutual funds in some ways and like stocks in others. Like other mutual funds, exchange traded funds buy and sell individual investments in keeping with their investment objectives. But the funds resemble stocks in the way they are traded, since they raise money by selling a fixed number of shares when the fund is first issued. Then the shares trade in the secondary market, either on a stock exchange or in an electronic market. The market price of shares of a closed end fund fluctuates not only according to the value of its underlying investments but also in response to investor demand.

Fixed income arbitrage   An investment strategy that seeks to take advantage of inefficiencies in the price of fixed income securities and related derivative instruments. Typically, the manager longs the fixed income securities or similar instruments that he feels are undervalued and shorts a security or instrument that is similar to a fixed income security.

Fund of funds   A fund that invests in other investment funds.

Futures   A futures contract obligates you to buy or sell a specified quantity of the underlying investment, which can be a commodity, a stock or bond index, or a currency, for a specific price at a specific date in the future. But you can usually sell the contract to another trader or offset your contract with an opposing contract before the settlement date. Futures contracts provide some investors, called hedgers, with a measure of protection from the volatility of prices on the open market. For example, wine manufacturers are protected when a bad crop pushes grape prices up on the spot market, provided they have a futures contract to buy the grapes at a set price. Similarly, grape growers are protected if prices drop dramatically – if, for example, there's a surplus caused by a bumper crop – provided they have a contract that sets the price at a higher level. Unlike hedgers, speculators use futures contracts to seek profit on price changes. For example, speculators can make (or lose) money, no matter what happens to the grapes, depending on what they paid for the futures contract and what they can sell it for.

General partner   Managing partner of a limited partnership, responsible for the operation of the limited partnership. The general partner's liability is unlimited.

Global macro investing   Investment strategy that seeks to profit by making leveraged bets on anticipated price movements of global stock markets, interest rates, foreign exchange rates and physical commodities.

Harmonised   Those funds that observe the community directive on OICR. These funds can be domiciled in any EU country.

Hedge/hedging   A method (often sophisticated) employed to minimise investment risk. Holders of a given stock might reduce risk on a relatively basic level, for instance, by buying a put option or selling a call option on that same stock; if the stock goes down, the option will rise in value, providing a "hedge" against losses.

Hedge fund   This name derives from the first funds of their kind, which emerged in the forties and fifties. These funds were particular in that they protected themselves from possible falls in the market. They were normal equity funds other than for the fact that they sold short and used financial leverage. With financial leverage, the manager could invest more capital in securities that he viewed as promising, short selling securities that were likely to fall in price. The ultimate objective was to protect the fund from possible market falls. Hedge funds are private investment partnerships open to institutions and wealthy individual investors. These funds pursue returns through a number of alternative investment strategies, including hedging against market downturns by holding both long and short positions, investing in derivatives, using arbitrage, and speculating on mergers and acquisitions. Some hedge funds use leverage, which means investing borrowed money, to boost returns. Because of the substantial risks associated with hedge funds, securities laws limit participation to individuals with incomes of at least $200,000 a year ($300,000 for couples) or those who have a net worth of at least $1 million.

Hedge fund manager   Acts as investment advisor for a hedge fund to manage the funds investments and assets. Offshore hedge funds usually operate with a legally separated hedge fund manager whilst many American hedge fund managers form an integral part of the structure of the hedge fund (i.e. general partner of a limited partnership or director of a limited company).

Hurdle rate   The minimum investment return a fund must exceed before a performance allocation/incentive fee can be taken. For example, if a fund has a hurdle rate of 5% and annual performance of 15%, incentive fees will only be applied to the 10% performance achieved above the hurdle rate.

Incentive fee   This is the fee calculated on the profits achieved by the fund during the period under consideration. For example, if the initial investment was 1,000,000 dollars, the fund achieved 25% during that period (creating 250,000 dollars of profits) and the incentive fee is 20%, then the fund receives 20% of the 250,000 dollars, therefore equalling USD 50,000.

Information ratio   One of the most important ratios to show the efficiency of a portfolio as compared to the benchmark. The differential between the returns of the managed portfolio and the benchmark is known as the tracking error volatility.

Junk bonds   Junk bonds carry a higher-than-average risk of default, which means that the bond issuer may not be able to meet interest payments or repay the loan when it matures. Except for bonds that are already in default, junk bonds have the lowest ratings, usually Caa or CCC, assigned by rating services such as Moody's Investors Service and Standard & Poor's (S&P). Issuers offset the higher risk of default on junk bonds by offering substantially higher interest rates than are being paid on investment-grade bonds. That is why junk bonds are also known, more positively, as high-yield bonds. Michael Milken made his fortune on the back of these bonds before they became the centre of scandals and legal actions. There are nevertheless overseas mutual funds that still invest exclusively in this bond category.

Leverage   Using leverage is an investment technique in which you borrow money to increase the size of your investment. The expectation is that you will realise a much greater return than you could by investing your own money alone. In addition, using leverage lets you wield greater financial power without putting your own money at stake.

Liquidity   This is the characteristic of a financial instrument that enables it to be quickly converted into cash.

Lock-up   This is the period in which the investor may not sell or cash in his investment.

Long biased manager   Investment managers with a long directional market philosophy. Short selling and hedging are not the main components of their investment portfolio.

Long/short   An investment strategy that controls exposure to a particular asset class, taking both long and short positions. These positions can be equal and opposite, in which case, the exposure to the asset class would be equivalent to zero. Alternatively, the combined position can be leveraged or futures contracts can be used. The manager should be able to construct a negative (short) position when he identifies an overvalued stock and a positive position when he identifies an undervalued stock. This flexibility to take advantage of stock price movements, be they positive or negative, should maximise the opportunities for the manager to generate returns and add value.

Managed futures funds   Futures investments managed in accordance with a predetermined plan.

Management fee   This is the fee received by the manager on the investment's entire capital value. For example, if at the end of the investing period the investment is valued at 1 million dollars and the management fee is 1%, the fee will therefore be 10,000 dollars.

Market neutral investing   Investing in financial markets through a strategy that will result in an investment portfolio not correlated to overall market movements and insulated from systematic market risk.

MSCI   Morgan Stanley's Capital International group (MSCI) provides benchmarks to track stocks traded in 45 international stock markets. They are considered the benchmarks for international stock investments and mutual fund portfolios. The strong performance of the Europe and Australasia Far East Equity Index (EAFE) between 1982 and 1996 in relation to Standard & Poor's 500 Stock Index (S&P 500) is often credited with generating increased US interest in investing in overseas markets.

NAV   The value of one share of a mutual fund. It is calculated by totalling the value of all the fund's holdings and dividing by the number of outstanding shares. That means the NAV changes regularly, though day-to-day changes are usually small. With no-load funds, the NAV and the offering price, or what you pay to buy a share, are the same. With front-load funds, the offering price is the sum of the NAV and the sales charge per share. The NAV is also the price per share the fund pays when you sell back, or redeem, your shares.

Offshore   With this term, we can identify an investment company or financial intermediary registered in a country characterised by a lack of legislation, controls and low tax regimes. Typical offshore centres are the Cayman Islands, British Virgin Islands, the Bahamas, Bermuda and Bahrain.

Open ended and closed pension funds   Open ended pension funds are run by companies authorised to manage assets. Unlike closed pension funds, they are not accessible only by a specific category of worker but rather are open to all investors.

Option   Buying an option gives you the right to buy or sell a specific investment at a specific price, called the strike price, during a preset period of time. If you buy an option to buy, which is known as a call, you pay a one-time premium that is a fraction of the cost of the actual transaction. For example, you might buy a call option giving you the right to buy 100 shares of a particular stock at a strike price of $80 a share when that stock is trading at $75 a share. If the price goes higher than the strike price, you can exercise the option and buy the stock, or trade the option to someone else at a profit. If the stock price doesn't go higher than the strike price, you don't exercise the option, and it expires. Your only cost is the money that you paid for the premium. Similarly, you buy a put option, which gives you the right to sell the underlying investment to the person who sold the option. In this case, you exercise the option if the market price drops below the strike price. In contrast, if you sell a put or call option, you collect a premium and must be prepared to buy or sell the underlying investment if the investor who bought the option decides to exercise it. You can buy or sell individual stock options, stock index options, and options on futures contracts, currency and Treasury securities interest rates.

Over the counter (OTC)   A transaction between two parties executed off-exchange. Such transactions are negotiated in private in accordance with a two-way agreement signed by both parties. For example, the shares of small companies, forward contracts and other derivatives are often traded OTC.

Performance trigger   A contractual clause that specifies the consequences of hedge fund performance should the value of that fund fall below an established level.

Portfolio manager   The person who invests and manages an amount of capital raised by the hedge fund manager. The portfolio manager can be employed by the hedge fund or by external asset managers actively controlled by the hedge fund manager or with whom he places a passive investment.

Prime broker   A brokerage company that provides multiple services for hedge funds, exceeding the custody, clearing, settlement and research services of traditional brokers.

R squared   Numerical value indicating correlation to a benchmark index. Statistically defined as deviations from the mean of a dependent variable that can be explained by deviation from the mean in an independent variable. Computed via ordinary least squared regression analysis.

Security market line   The graphic representation of the relationship between the expected returns of a given security and the underlying market, using the beta of the specific security within the CAPM pricing model.

Sharpe ratio   One way to compare the relationship of risk and reward in following different investment strategies, such as emphasising growth or value investments, is to use the Sharpe ratio. To figure the ratio, you subtract the risk-free return from the average return of an investment portfolio made up of these investments over a period of time, and then divide the result by the standard deviation of the return. A strategy with a higher ratio is less risky than one with a lower ratio. This approach is named for William P. Sharpe, who won the Nobel Prize in Economics in 1990.

Short selling   To sell a security without owning it, with an obligation to buy the security at a later time, and repay the security creditor who had lent it for sale. Profits will result if the investor is able to buy it back later at a lower price.

Sortino ratio   The Sortino ratio is similar to the Sharpe ratio except that it uses as its denominator only the downside volatility and not the upside volatility. It is considered a refinement on the Sharpe ratio and is calculated as the difference between the returns of the fund, those deriving from a risk-free activity and downside risk, which in its turn is calculated as the average downside movement of fund returns. It indicates the ability of the manager to provide the investor with superior returns (in line with additional risk) to those deriving from risk-free activities.

Structured financial product   This is a financial instrument obtained by combining two or more financial instruments in a way that unifies the advantages of each in a single investment. A typical example comes in the form of equity-linked bonds, created by putting together regular bonds and call options. In general, these types of investments are difficult to value because of their composite nature.

Trust   Person or entity that holds assets on behalf of others. It can have the legal authority to take financial decisions on behalf of others.

Umbrella funds   In this kind of structure each compartment, or subfund, forms part of one sole legal entity and yet can operate in accordance with a distinct investment policy. Umbrella funds offer a straightforward method of asset allocation and allow many operational cost savings together with a good product management. In addition, this type of fund offers a particular attraction for fund promoters since it can cater for a range of different investment strategies within the umbrella of the same product. The investor can exchange units in one compartment for units in another. For little or no charge, he can thus switch investments according to market opportunities.

Volatility   Volatility indicates how much and how quickly the value of an investment, market or market sector changes. For example, stocks of small, newer companies are usually more volatile than those of established, blue chip companies because their values tend to rise and fall very sharply over short periods of time. The volatility of a stock relative to the overall market is known as its beta, and the volatility triggered by internal factors, regardless of the market, is known as a stock's alpha.

Warrant   For a small fee, you can purchase a warrant that allows you to buy a company's stock at a fixed price. The warrant is valid for a specific period of time, often for several years. Sometimes there is no expiration date. For example, a warrant priced at $1 per share might guarantee you the right to buy a certain stock at $10 within the next 10 years. If the price goes up to $15, you can exercise, or use, your warrant, save $4 per share, and resell the security at a profit. If the price of the stock falls over the life of the warrant, however, the warrant becomes worthless.

Yield   Yield is the rate of return on an investment, paid in dividends or interest and expressed as a percentage. In the case of stocks, the yield on your investment is the dividend you receive per share divided by the stock's price per share. With bonds, it is the interest divided by the price. In the case of bonds, the yield on your investment and the interest rate your investment pays are sometimes – but by no means always – the same. If the price of a bond moves higher or lower than par, the yield will be different from the interest rate. For example, if you pay $950 for a bond with a par value of $1000 that pays 6% interest, your yield is 6.3%. But if you paid $1100 for the same bond, your yield would be only 5.5%. Yield can usually be calculated by dividing the amount you receive annually in dividends or interest by the amount you spent to buy the investment.

Index

Compiled by Annette Musker

THE BLUE BOOK
YOUR ANSWER TO PARKING PROBLEMS

The City of Westminster

The Royal Borough of Kensington & Chelsea

The London Borough of Camden

The London Borough of Islington

The City of London

Southwark

The London Borough of Lambeth

Wandsworth

The London Borough of Hammersmith & Fulham

YOUR GUIDE THROUGH THE CONFUSION OF PARKING IN LONDON

The Blue Book has been compiled by conducting extensive field surveys and with the generous & uncomplaining help of the following people and administrative bodies

The Parking Committee for London
The Traffic Director for London
Jag Patel and Westminster City Council
John Stewart and the Royal Borough of Kensington and Chelsea
Gary Griffiths and Mr.Ralli and the London Borough of Camden
Chris Harry and the London Borough of Islington
Ken Jones and the Corporation of London
Terry Dale and Southwark Council
Brian Hildrew at Wapping
Bill Hunt at Spitalfields
Graham Burrel at Bethnal Green
Peter Friend and Mr. Bhamber at Hammersmith and Fulham
Johnny Asada at Hackney

We would also like to thank the following for their infinite patience and tireless support towards Pathmedia Communications Ltd in producing this atlas
Alessandra Galtrucco
Steve Nickson
Yasmin Tuazon
Andrew Rogoff
..and thanks to the Parking Committee for London for the idea of the Glossary of Signs
1st edition November 1993
© Pathmedia Communications Limited 1993

Published by Pathmedia Communications Limited of Unit 12, Chelsea Wharf, 15 Lots Road, London SW10 0QJ
ISBN 0 9522309 0 9

Cartography supplied by Dorling Kindersley Limited, London

Every effort has been made to ensure that the information contained in this book is as up to date as possible at the time of going to press. However, information such as tariffs, controlled hours, opening hours, prices etc. are liable to change. The publishers cannot accept responsibility for any expense or loss arising from the use of this book.

The Blue Book has been designed to clear up any confusion in the mind of the London driver over parking and his rights. Our goal is to help make the clamping companies a little less profitable and the motorist a little more confident. Inside you will find a full explanation of the current parking rules, the new rules that are being introduced, your rights with respect to clamping or towing away, and a full Central London street atlas showing one way streets, parking meters, petrol stations and car parks.

THE BLUE BOOK CONTENTS

How to use the Blue Book

To make the Blue Book as easy to use as possible we have used symbols in the margin so you can quickly and easily find the information you need to know.

 Where ?   Clamping situations   £ Cost

(?) When ?   🚚 Towing away situations   Attention !

How long ?   🅸 Advice & parking tips   Meter penalties

Believe it or not, parking policy in London is co-ordinated and organised by government. The bad news is that it is done by each borough, so what should be a smooth system, is a patchwork of regulations and tariffs. We will show you the regulations as they exist in Westminster, Kensington & Chelsea, Camden, Islington, Southwark, Lambeth, Hammersmith & Fulham, Wandsworth and the City of London.

When and where you can park

 When & where you can park is determined by the term, "Controlled Hours", listed under a 🚫 symbol on roadside signs (see Glossary for examples)

 "Controlled hours" means the times during which you cannot park on any yellow lines and in order to park safely, you must use a meter or, if you have the right permit, a resident's bay.

As soon as Controlled Hours end you can park on nearly all single yellow lines, and all meters and residents bays free of charge. Parking restrictions for double yellow lines extend beyond Controlled Hours and are listed on roadside plaques.

Controlled Hours vary across London. Moreover, Controlled Hours in Bayswater and Soho have been extended to 10pm and 8.30pm respectively Monday to Saturday for residents' bays only; preventing non-permit holders from parking there well after the 6:30pm watershed.

 Controlled hours across the city are shown on our London atlas by coloured areas and a plaque underneath "CH".

METER PARKING

In addition to variable times of restriction in the capital there are a variety of different prices for parking time at meters.

 You can save a lot of money by consulting the Blue Book map for the cheapest meter rates near your destination.

 Most meters and Pay & Display machines in London allow a maximum stay of two hours. However there are 4 hour meters scattered around the city as well as 4 hour pay and display machines. Consult the atlas to see if there is one near your destination. Also check on our car park index to see if it is cheaper to go to a nearby car park if you are staying longer than 2 hours.

 • Before leaving for your destination consult our street index for meter spaces and coins accepted.
• Wrong change when you get to a meter? Look on our map for Pay & Display machines - they accept most coins.
Don't forget to check if hourly meter prices or car parks are cheaper nearby.

LONDON IN A STATE OF CHANGE

 The current rules for meters, excess periods, tickets and clamping are in the process of fundamental change. Unfortunately for the motorist each Borough is introducing the new rules at a different time.

THE CURRENT RULES
These operate in Westminster, Kensington & Chelsea, Islington, the City of London until July 1994. They also operate in Camden, but only until the 6th of December, and in Southwark until February 1994.

THE NEW RULES
These are already in operation in Hammersmith & Fulham and Wandsworth.
Camden will introduce the new rules on the 6th December.
However by law, Camden has 6 months in which to change all its signs and meter displays. So be very careful when visiting the theatre or Bloomsbury.

 Our **London Parking Map** shows which boroughs operate which rules.

THE CURRENT METER AND PAY & DISPLAY RULES

These rules are in operation in Westminster, Kensington & Chelsea, Islington, Lambeth & the City of London until July 1994.

These rules are also in use in Camden until the 6th of December 1993.
Southwark also operates these rules, but plans to change in February 1994.

• After your time has run out at the meter you go into the Excess Period and may get an Excess Charge Notice (ECN). The Excess Period is either shown by a yellow flag on mechanical meters or a digital "EXCESS" display.

• ECNs are written by Traffic Wardens or council employed contractors.

Excess Charge Notices cost about £30 (£25 Kensington & Chelsea)

In Westminster ECN fines vary according to meter tariffs.
Where meter prices are £2 per hour the fine is £30
Where the price is £1.50/£1 per hour the fine is £20
In 60p per hour areas the fine is £10

• During the Excess Period you cannot be clamped or towed away. The Excess Period lasts 30 minutes (1 hour Kensington & Chelsea and Southwark).

After the Excess Period is over you enter the Penalty Period. You may now also get a Fixed Penalty Notice (FPN).

Fixed Penalty Notices at meters are £30

Only Traffic Wardens currently write FPNs for meters. You have 28 days to pay the FPN before it increases by half.

You may now be towed away (frequently done at Christmas and in busy shopping areas to keep meters free).

2 hours after you enter the Excess Period the police may legally clamp you.

Check on your ticket to see that the clamping time limit has been observed. Complain if it has not and you may get a refund.

THE NEW METER AND PAY & DISPLAY RULES

The following rules are now in operation in Hammersmith & Fulham and Wandsworth and will apply all over London from July 1994.

Camden is introducing these rules from the 6th of December & Southwark from February 1994. However, councils have six months in which to change signs and displays on their meters. So, you might park at a meter for the theatre or in Bloomsbury and the meter might show an Excess Period but you would in fact be in the new Penalty Period.

All other central London boroughs will operate this system after July 1994.

Under these new rules the Excess period is abolished.

Once paid-for-time is over, you enter the Penalty Period. You may now get a Penalty Charge Notice (PCN). The PCN is the new parking ticket.

Penalty Charge Notices cost
£20 Wandsworth, Hammersmith & Fulham

If you do not pay the PCN within 14 days the price doubles.

15 minutes after you enter the new penalty period:

You may be clamped or

You may be towed away

All enforcement of meter regulations and all clamping and towing away will pass to local councils. Expect ticketing and clamping to increase.

WHAT TO DO AT OUT OF ORDER OR FULL METERS

These give 2 hours free parking only if they are the mechanical variety and they do not have an "Out of Order" bag over them You can also park for free at meters without a "meter-head". So, the rule is:

At mechanical but At digital

RESIDENTS' BAYS

Outside Controlled Hours anyone can park at residents' bays.

Controlled Hours for residents' bays are the same as for meters and single yellow lines, except in Bayswater and Soho where restrictions last until 10pm and 8.30pm respectively. Check signs near residents' bays for times.

THE CURRENT RULES

If you park at a resident's bay without the right permit you will either get a Fixed Penalty Notice of £30

or

Notice of Intended Prosecution (NIP) around £30

NIPs are given out in boroughs that use private contractors to patrol meters and residents' bays. NIPs have no fixed fine. The amount must be settled in court.

If you are in the clamping zone (see Clamping Rules) you can be clamped if you park in a resident's bay without the right permit.

You can also be towed away.

THE NEW RULES

If you park at a resident's bay without the right permit you will get a

Penalty Charge Notice   £20 Hammersmith & Fulham and Wandsworth

                                £30 provisionally set for Camden from 6/12/93

You may be clamped or towed away

YELLOW LINES

The simple rule is that parking is forbidden at

- • Broken lines for some of the Controlled Hours (usually peak times)
- • Single yellow lines for all of the Controlled Hours
- • Double Yellow lines for all of the Controlled Hours & extra times -not necessarily 24 hours/day (Times listed on roadside plaques).

Always look for a yellow plaque on a pole by the yellow line or lines. This will tell you the times when parking is forbidden. **If there is no plaque then it is forbidden for the duration of Controlled Hours for that area.**

DROPPING OFF OR PICKING UP? (KERB STRIPES)

If you want to pause not park, then you can stop for up to 20 minutes at any meter, resident's bay or yellow line - provided you take note of the yellow stripes on the kerb - and provided you are loading "bulky items".

 "Bulky items" is loosely defined as objects you would **need** a car to transport, it does not mean getting cash or parcels. **Traffic Wardens should watch the car for 5 minutes before writing a ticket.** Stick a note in the car window that you are loading.

 Always check yellow stripes on the kerb. They prohibit loading. Check times on roadside plaques.Any loading is prohibited where there is:

 • One stripe for some of the Controlled Hours (usually peak times).
 • Two stripes for all of the Controlled Hours.
 • Three stripes for all of the Controlled Hours and extra times
(Always check times on nearby roadside plaques).

 Cost of yellow line parking: £30 Fixed Penalty Notice or Penalty Charge Notice - if the borough operates the new parking rules.

You can then be clamped or you can be towed away

RED ROUTES

 Some roads now have red lines. There is **no stopping** on a red route except in specially drawn roadside boxes. Restricted parking hours on red routes are unique to each road and do not correspond to the Controlled Hours zone they fall into. Roughly, there is no stopping:

 • on a single red line 7am to 7pm. Outside these hours you can park
 • on a double red line 24 hours a day.

 If you stop on a red route you may get a £40 Fixed Penalty Notice.

 If the car is left unattended the police will tow you away.

 Signs showing restricted parking hours on red routes are typically small and legible only when you stop so check your journey on our London Parking Map.

CLAMPING RULES

You may be clamped if you park during Controlled Hours at:

- A meter and you do not pay (except when loading).

"I was just going for change" will not help you.

- An out of order digital meter or a meter with an Out of Order bag over it.
- A meter and pay, but your car is not fully within the designated space.
- The same parking place within one hour of leaving it.

A "parking place" refers to a rank of spaces enclosed by double white lines at either end. Do not just move your car one meter down after your time is over, you may still be clamped.

- A meter and go back to buy extra time (meter feeding).
- A resident's bay without the right permit.
- Single or Double Yellow lines.

> **Cost: £38 + Fixed Penalty Notice or Penalty Charge Notice = £68**

THE CURRENT RULES

The following clamping rules apply to all central London boroughs (with the exceptions of Hammersmith & Fulham and Wandsworth).

The Clamping Zone: clamping is only allowed in Westminster, Kensington & Chelsea, Camden south of the Euston Road and the City of London.

The Police cannot clamp you for 2 hours after your meter time has run out.

THE NEW RULES

The new rules are now in operation in Hammersmith & Fulham and Wandsworth. Camden will be introducing these rules on the 6th of December 1993 and Southwark plan to introduce them in February 1994. All other central London boroughs will operate this rules after July 1994. **All boroughs operating these rules have the right to clamp.**

The Excess Period is abolished and you may now be clamped 15 minutes after you have entered the Penalty Period.

TOWING AWAY

During Controlled Hours you can be towed away in the same places you can be clamped i.e. residents' bays and yellow lines. You can also be towed away as soon as you enter the penalty period on a meter.

Outside Controlled Hours you can also be towed away for

- Obstructing the road
- Parking on pavements, watch out around Soho
- Parking at a diplomatic bay (24 hours a day)
- Parking at disabled or doctors bays

Cost: £105 + Fixed Penalty Notice or Penalty Charge Notice = £135 + £12 per day storage.

Towing away is more unusual from a meter, due to removal costs. The probability of being towed away rises if you park in a resident's bay without a valid permit and almost becomes a certainty if you park illegally on yellow lines.

Breaking down: Call the police or tell a Traffic Warden. Put a note on your car while you go and look for one. The police will then move your car for free and call a breakdown service. If you don't tell the police you will be towed away and charged the full removal fee.

THE CURRENT RULES

You can be towed away in any borough that operates the current rules. Some boroughs who are not allowed to clamp under the present rules, will tow away illegally parked cars instead.

Towing away is supervised by the police.

THE NEW RULES

Under the new rules any borough can apply for, and be granted, the right to tow away.

There is no Police involvement in towing away under the new rules. All vehicle removals will be undertaken by council employed contractors.

YOUR RIGHTS

TICKETS

Details of complaint procedures are listed on tickets.

CLAMPING

In boroughs that operate the current rules - see London Parking Map - and provided you initially paid for meter time then you cannot be clamped until 2 hours after the end of your meter time.

In boroughs that operate the new system then the time limit is reduced to 15 minutes.

Whichever system a borough uses, if you return to your car and the clampers are fixing the clamp to your car, but the padlock has not been closed, then you can compel them to remove the clamp.

TOWING AWAY

If you return to your car to find the tow truck poised beside it, ready to start towing away, but all the wheels of your car are still on the ground then you can legally prevent them from towing away the car.

SPECIAL CASES - CLAMPING ON PRIVATE LAND

The rules laid out in this book do not apply to clamping on private land, for instance at supermarket or railway station car parks.

If whoever owns the land intends to clamp trespassing cars then there must be signs to that effect somewhere in the car park. These signs, however, can be very small, so make a thorough search before parking.

Clamping on private land is becoming more and more common, There are however little or no legal safeguards for the unwitting driver, in particular the lack of any apparent ceiling on the amount a landlord can charge for de-clamping.

PARKING TIPS

MUSEUMS

Councils have helpfully placed large concentrations of four hour parking meters close to exhibition centres and museums.

Look on our atlas for streets shaded to show four hour meter concentrations.

WEEKEND PARKING

Always check on our atlas for the Controlled Hours plaque and the zone as defined by the shaded background area. If your destination is near a less restrictive zone then look for parking there.

For example if you are going to Sloane Square then the Controlled Hours for this area are 8:30am to 6:30pm on Saturdays. However by consulting the blue book atlas you can find free parking nearby after 1:30pm on Saturdays.

If you were coming for the day then you could find a four meter on the Blue Book map, park at 9:30am and confidently leave the car for the whole day!

BRINGING DOWN THE COST OF PARKING

If you are parking close to a boundary between one borough which clamps and another which doesn't, for instance at Tower Bridge, then look on the Blue Book for the border between the two - shown by different Controlled Hours zones - and then you can park as close to your destination as possible without running the risk of getting clamped.

Check the meter tariff areas on the atlas for the nearest cheap meters to your destination so you can better plan your journey. Pay and Display machines, as they take most coins, offer greater flexibility for your money than a meter that accepts only £1 coins.

You can also lessen the chances of a clamp by parking in boroughs with longer Excess Charge Periods. The best example of this is the difference between Kensington and Chelsea and Westminster. If you are visiting the South Kensington museums, for instance, then it might be better to park on the Kensington side of the Exhibition Road where the Excess Period is 1 hour as opposed to 30 minutes on the Westminster side, the Excess Charge is £25 as opposed to £30.

THE PARKS

All the parks in central London are administered by a separate parks authority. As a consequence they have different and often less restrictive Controlled Hours to the surrounding boroughs - a good place to park for shopping in Knightsbridge during the day.

PARKING QUIRKS AND TROUBLE SPOTS

Parking enforcement and regulations differ enormously between boroughs. To complete our parking guide we therefore provide a brief outline of the main problems you might find that are peculiar to each borough.

To recognise which borough you are in you can either look at the street name plates at junctions or on a parking meter "head".

WESTMINSTER

Westminster has the most variety of Controlled Hours and tariff zones of any of the central London boroughs. Things to watch for:

Westminster meters accept £1 coins only in £2 per hour areas or £1 & 20p coins in all other areas.

The Excess Period in Westminster is 30 minutes. The Excess Charge varies according to which meter-tariff zone you are in (these are shown on the Blue Book Atlas)

£2/hour	£30 Excess Charge Notice
£1.00-£1.50/hour	£20 Excess Charge Notice
60p/hour	£10 Excess Charge Notice

Westminster is part of the current clamping zone (see Clamping Rules).

Residents' bays in Bayswater and Soho have special times of restriction.

Map pages 8/9	Bayswater	8:30am-10pm	Monday-Saturday
Map pages 10/11	Soho	8:30am-8:30pm	Monday-Saturday

For nearly all single yellow lines and meters parking is free and unrestricted after 6:30pm on weekdays and 1:30pm on Saturdays.

Map pages 11/12   **White meters** are only to be found on the Embankment around Temple Bar. They allow meter parking at off-peak times. During the "rush hour" in the early morning and late afternoon they should be treated as single yellow lines. The precise times of restrictions will be listed on the meter "head".

Enforcement of Excess Charges and residents' bays is handled by the council. Regulations are enforced with gusto.

KENSINGTON & CHELSEA (K&C)

 K & C meters accept either £1 & 20p coins or 20p coins only.

 The Excess period in K & C lasts for 1 hour as opposed to 30 minutes in most other boroughs. So if you do overstay and are ticketed you have twice as long before you receive a fixed penalty notice. The Excess Charge in K & C is £25.

 K & C is part of the current clamping zone (see Clamping Rules).

 Around the Portobello Road there are Pay & Display machines that have special restrictions on the weekends for antique dealers, so, when parking in this area, read the signs carefully.

Enforcement of regulations in K& C is handled by government employed Traffic Wardens.

CAMDEN

 Camden meters accept £1 & 20p coins.

 Camden introduces the new parking rules on 6th December so be very careful when visiting the theatre or Covent Garden, as clamping can then take place 15 minutes after your meter time is up. Camden has provisionally set the price of its Penalty Charge Notice after the 6th of December at £30.

 Camden south of the Euston Road is part of the current clamping zone until 6th December. After the 6th of December clamping will be extended to the whole of the borough.

Map pages 3/11   Camden has the only London parking zone where Controlled Hours extend beyond 6:30pm on weekdays and Saturdays.

 If you find a double yellow line in this area and there is no plaque then this means that they are restricted until 8:30pm.

 Camden has some off-peak Pay & Display machines on the Grays Inn Road. Be sure to read the times on these very carefully before parking as at peak times they should be treated like single yellow lines.

Residents' bays and parking meters are enforced by council employed private contractors.

ISLINGTON

Islington meters accept £1 & 20p pieces.

The Excess Period in Islington is 30 minutes and the Excess Charge is £30.

There is a Red Route in Islington on Upper Street, which starts just north of Angel tube station. At the time of going to print it is very heavily policed, so if you do have to stop for any reason then use the specially designated roadside boxes.

Enforcement of all parking regulations in Islington is handled by government employed Traffic Wardens.

SOUTHWARK

Southwark meters accept £1, 50p & 20p pieces in digital meters and 20p pieces only in mechanical meters. Certain parts have a voucher system in operation.

The Excess Period in Southwark is 1 hour and the Excess Charge is £32.

Southwark has introduced a **voucher parking scheme**, for parts of the borough. Meters in these areas have been removed and in order to park you must buy a voucher to display in your windscreen.The same rules apply to vouchers as for meters e.g. voucher "feeding" is also a ticketable offence.

Enforcement of all parking regulations in Southwark is handled by government employed Traffic Wardens.

LAMBETH

Lambeth meters in the area shown on our map accept 20p pieces.

The Excess Period in Lambeth is 1 hour for 2 hour meters and 2 hours for 4 hour meters. The Excess Charge is £24.

Enforcement of all parking regulations in Lambeth is handled by government employed Traffic Wardens.

HAMMERSMITH AND FULHAM (H&F)

 Most of H & F now has Pay & Display machines which accept £1, 50p, 20p, 10p & 5p.

H & F now operate the new meter and clamping and towing away rules.

 H & F have the right to clamp.

 H & F also have the right to tow away.

Enforcement of all parking regulations in H & F is handled by council employed private contractors.

WANDSWORTH

 Wandsworth meters in the Putney area accept £1, 50p & 20p coins.

Wandsworth now operate the new meter and clamping and towing away rules.

 Wandsworth have the right to clamp.

 Wandsworth also have the right to tow away.

Enforcement of all parking regulations in Wandsworth is handled by council employed private contractors.

CITY OF LONDON

 City of London meters accept £1 & 20p pieces.

 The Excess Period in the City is 30 minutes and the Excess Charge is £30.

 The City is part of the current clamping zone.

 Smithfield has very peculiar Controlled Hours due to the late hours that traders work.

 The new City Police checkpoints are all shown on our atlas, see the key on atlas-pages for details.

Enforcement of all parking regulations in the City is handled by government employed Traffic Wardens.

Red Routes are to be introduced over the next two years. The roadside signs list the prohibitions on the red route. They should also list times when loading or stopping is allowed in the red-roadside boxes.

You may also see this sign, or a variation of it at bus stops with double yellow lines or with the phrase "Urban Clearway" above it. Stopping is prohibited where you see this sign.

Roadside plaques list the times that you may park. If a yellow line does not have a plaque then the hours correspond to those of the Controlled Hours for the whole area.

Controlled Zone signs are placed at the borders between areas with different Controlled Hours. The sign lists the Controlled Hours for all the single yellow lines, meters and resident's bays in one area.

Residents' bays have the same Controlled Hours as meters unless otherwise stated on the plaque. Be very careful when parking in Bayswater and Soho.

Plaques by the yellow kerb stripes list the hours during which you can't park in order to load or unload - see Dropping off or Picking up. **Roughly** the rules are:

> **No loading**
> **Mon - Fri**
> **8:30am - 10:30am**

Single kerb stripes limit loading for some of the Controlled Hours - usually during the peak morning and afternoon periods.(Officially, it is limited for "Part of the working day")

> **No loading**
> **Mon - Fri**
> **8:30am - 6:30pm**

Double kerb stripes limit loading for all of the Controlled Hours.(Officially, "All of the working day").

> **No loading**
> **At any time**

Three kerb stripes limit loading for all of the Controlled Hours and extra times.(Officially, "More than the working day")

CENTRAL LONDON CAR PARKS

Map ref	Car park	Hours	Weekend	Min time	£ /2hr	£ /6hr	Evening
age Ref							
A2	Acacia Garage Sterling	24 hrs		2hrs	£ 1.60	£ 4.60	£2 from 6pm
A5	Bell St Sterling	24 hrs		2hrs	£ 1.70	£ 4.90	£2 from 6pm
A5	Church St Sterling	7.30am-7.30pm	Closed Sun	2hrs	£ 2.00	£ 7.40	£2 overnight
C5	Crawford St NCP	8am-8pm	Closed Sat & Sun	2hrs	£ 3.20	£ 9.60	
C5	Marylebone Rd NCP	24 hrs		2hrs	£ 4.00	£ 12.50	
B5	Old Marylebone Rd Britannia	7am-7pm	Closed Sat & Sun	2hrs	£ 2.00	£ 6.00	
B4	Park Rd NCP	24 hrs		2hrs	£ 2.30	£ 6.80	
A5	Securipark (nr Metropole hotel)	24 hrs		12 hrs	£8/12hrs		
age Ref							
E5	Devonshire Row Mews	7am-9pm	Sat 9am-3pm, Closed Sun	1hr	£ 4.00	£ 9.00	£3, 9pm-7am
D5	Chiltern St NCP	24 hrs		2hrs	£ 3.30	£ 10.00	
F5	Cleveland St NCP	8am-7.45pm	Closed Sat & Sun	2hrs	£ 4.30	£ 12.50	
F5	Clipstone Mews ML Car Parks	24 hrs		1hr	£ 3.50	£ 9.80	£2 from 6pm
D5	Cramer St NCP	8am-6.30pm	Sat to 6pm, Closed Sun	2hrs	£ 3.70	£14.80 day	
E5	Portland Pl NCP	7am-7pm	Closed Sat & Sun	day	£14.70 flat		
F5	Regent Forte Crest Hotel NCP	24 hrs		2hrs	£ 3.80	£ 11.50	£5.50 6pm-9am
F4	Stanhope St	7am-9pm		day	£8.00 flat		
age Ref							
C5	Bloomsbury Sq	24 hrs		2hrs	£ 3.50	£ 10.00	£5 from 6.30pm
C4	Brunswick Sq NCP	24 hrs		2hrs	£ 2.30	£ 6.90	£3, 6pm-9am
A3	Cardington St Sterling	24 hrs		3hrs	£4.00 / 3hrs	£20 / 3hrs+	
A3	Euston Station Sterling	24 hrs		3hrs	£4.00 / 3hrs	£20 / 3hrs+	
C5	Imperial Hotel CCP	24 hrs		2hrs	£ 2.80	£ 8.50	
C3	Judd St NCP	7am - 6.30pm	Closed Sat & Sun	2hrs	£ 2.00	£ 6.00	
B2	Kings Cross BR	6am-10pm		day	£8 flat		
B4	Marchmont St	24 hrs		2hrs	£ 2.30	£ 6.90	
A5	Ridgemount Pl NCP	8am - 6.30pm	Sat 8am-1pm, Closed Sun	2hrs	£ 4.20	£ 9.50	
B4	Royal National Hotel CCP	24 hrs		2hrs	£ 2.40	£ 7.00	
B4	Russell Ct NCP	24 hrs		2hrs	£ 2.40	£ 7.30	
age Ref							
E4	Bowling Gn Ln NCP	24hrs		1hr	£ 3.00	£ 9.00	£2, 6pm-9am
F5	Britton St NCP	7.30am-6.30pm	Closed Sat & Sun	half day	£5 half day	£9 day	
F5	Caxton House NCP	7.30am-6.30pm	Closed Sat & Sun	2hrs	£ 2.80	£ 8.60	
F5	Charterhouse Sq NCP	6am-6pm	Closed Sat & Sun	day	£7.80 flat		
F2	Elia Mews	7am-6pm	Closed Sat & Sun	1hr	£ 1.20	£ 3.60	
F4	Great Sutton St NCP	8am-6.30pm	Closed Sat & Sun	half day	£4.70 half day	£8.40 day	
F4	Hat & Feathers NCP	7.30am - 7.00pm	Closed Sat & Sun	half day	£4.60 half day	£8.30 day	
E1	Layton Rd (Parkfield St) NCP	8am-8pm	Sun 7.30am-3pm	2hrs	£ 1.60	£ 4.80	
F3	Owen St (Goswell Rd) NCP	7am - 7pm	Closed Sat & Sun	2hrs	£ 1.60	£ 5.30	
E5	Saffron Hill NCP	7am-11pm	Sat 7am-1pm, Closed Sun	2hrs	£ 2.80	£ 8.60	£1, 5pm-11pm
E4	Skinner St NCP	7am-6pm	Closed Sat & Sun	half day	£3.65 half day	£6.30 day	
F5	Smithfield St NCP	5am - 5pm	Sat 7am-1pm, Closed Sun	day	£8.40 flat		
F4	St Johns St NCP	7am-7pm	Closed Sat & Sun	2hrs	£2.30	£7.00	
E2	Tolpuddle St	24hrs		1hr	£1 per hr flat		

CENTRAL LONDON CAR PARKS

Map ref	Car park	Hours	Weekend	Min time	£ /2hr	£ /6hr	Evenir
Page Ref							
A5	Aldersgate NCP	24 hrs	all day £2.30	1	£ 3.20	£ 9.60	£2.30 5pm-9a
A5/B5	Barbican NCP	8am-12am	Sat 8am (Sun10am) -12am	1	£ 2.50	£ 9.00	
B3	Britannia Walk NCP	7.30am-6.30pm closed Sat & Sun		half day	£ 2.80 half day		
B3	Brunswick Pl	24 hrs		2	£ 2.30	n/a	
C4	Clere St NCP	7.30am-6.30pm closed Sat & Sun		day	£ 7.50 flat		
B5	Finsbury Sq NCP	24hrs		2	£ 4.00	£ 11.60	
A3	Macclesfield Rd NCP	7.30am-6.30pm closed Sat & Sun		half day	£ 2.80 half day		
C4	Paul St NCP	7am-7pm	closed Sat & Sun	2	£ 3.20	£ 5.20	
C3	Pitfield St NCP	8am-6.30pm	closed Sat & Sun	day	£ 4.40 flat		
C5	Primrose St CPS	8am-10pm	closed Sat & Sun	2	£ 4.00	£ 8.00	
C3	Tabernacle St NCP	7am-6.30pm	closed Sat & Sun	day	£ 8.50 flat		
Page Ref							
D4	Bishopsgate NCP	M-Sa 7am-7pm Sun -£1.90/2hr		half day	£ 2.80 half day £4.50 day		
D4	Holywell Ln NCP	7.30am-6.30pm closed Sat & Sun		£5.00 flat			
D4	Shoreditch High St EuroCP	24 hrs	free (owners risk)	1	£ 2 .00	£6.50 day	free from 6.15
D5	Spital Square UKCP	7am-7pm closed Sat, Sun-market rate		2	£ 3.00	£ 8.00	
D5	Whites Row CPS	24 hrs		1	£ 2.00	£ 8.00	£1.50 from 6p
Page Ref							
C5	Hornton St APCOA	24 hrs		2	£ 3.20	£ 9.60	£1.50 from 9p
Page Ref							
D1	Arthur Ct (Queensway) NCP	24 hrs		2	£ 2.30	£ 6.90	
D3	Bayswater Rd NCP	8am-10pm	8am-8pm	2	£ 2.20	£ 6.10	
E1	Colonnades NCP	8am-9pm		1	£ 2.30	£ 5.80	
E1	North Wharf Rd UKCP	7am-7pm	closed Sun	2	£ 1.70	£ 5.00	
F1	Paddington BR	24 hrs		day	£16.00 flat		
D2	Poplar Pl Cabriolet Cars	24 hrs		2	£ 2.50	£ 4.60	
D2	Queensway Sterling	24 hrs		2	£ 2.00	£ 6.20	£2.00 from 6
D5	Royal Garden Hotel NCP	24 hrs		2	£ 3.50	£ 9.50	£9.00 5pm-9a
F2	Royal Lancaster Hotel	24 hrs		2	£ 4.00	£ 8.00	
D5	Young St NCP	24 hrs		1	£ 3.20	£ 9.60	£1.40 6pm-9
Page Ref							
C1	Bilton Towers NCP	24 hrs		2	£ 4.40	£ 12.50	£5.00 6pm-9a
C2	Bryanston St NCP	24 hrs		1	£ 4.00	£ 12.50	£5.20 6pm-9a
C1	Churchill Hotel NCP	24 hrs		2	£ 2.60	£ 8.00	£6.00 6pm-9
B1	Kendal St South NCP	8am-8pm	closed	2	£ 3.10	£ 9.40	
C5	Kinnerton St ML Car Parks	24 hrs		2	£ 3.10	£ 9.40	£2.00 from 6
B5	Knightsbridge Gn NCP	8am-8 pm	closed Sun	2	£ 4.20	£12.50	
C2	North Row UKCP	24 hrs		2	£ 4.00	£ 10.00	£5.50 6pm-9
C2/C3	Park Ln NCP	24 hrs		2	£ 2.60	£ 8.40	
C5	Park Tower Hotel NCP	24 hrs		2	£ 2.60	£ 7.80	£5.20 6pm-8.30
B1	Park West NCP	24 hrs		2	£ 3.20	£ 9.50	
C5	Pavilion Rd NCP	24 hrs		2	£ 4.20	£ 12.60	£3.50 6pm-8.30
C1	Portman Sq NCP	24 hrs		2	£ 2.80	£ 8.60	
A5	Prince's Gate London & Counties	24 hrs		2	£ 4.00	£ 16.00	
B1	Seawood Garage	7am-11pm		2	£ 4.00	£ 8.00	
B1	Water Gardens NCP	24 hrs		2	£ 2.85	£ 8.90	£7.00 6pm-9

Map ref	Car park	Hours	Weekend	Min time	£ /2hr	£ /6hr	Evening
Page Ref							
F3	Arlington House NCP	24 hrs		3	£8.50/ 3hrs	£ 25.00	
D3	Audley Sq NCP	24 hrs		2	£ 4.20	£ 12.50	£6.30 6pm-9am
D5	Berkeley Hotel	6.30am-10pm	Sun 7am-12 noon	4	£8/ 4hrs	£ 12.00	
F1	Berner St NCP	7am-7pm	closed Sat & Sun	2	£ 5.50	£ 16.00	
D3	Britannia Hotel NCP	24 hrs		2	£ 4.50	£ 13.50	
F2	Broadwick St APCOA	24 hrs		2	£ 4.50	£ 12.20	
E4	Carrington St NCP	24 hrs		2	£ 4.40	£ 13.00	
E1	Cavendish Sq Sterling	6am-midnight	closed Sun	1	£ 4.40	£ 13.00	
E3	Chesterfield House NCP	8am-8pm	closed Sat & Sun	2	£ 4.40	£ 13.00	
D3	Fountain House	7am-10pm	closed Sat & Sun	2	£ 4.00	£ 16.00	
E2	Grosvenor Hill NCP	7am-8pm	Sat 8am-6pm, closed Sun	2	£ 5.20	£ 16.50	
D3	Grosvenor House Hotel	24 hrs		2	£ 5.00	£ 12.50	
E1	Harley St	24 hrs		2	£ 3.80	£ 11.00	£4.20 from 6pm
E4	Hilton Hotel NCP	24 hrs		2	£ 4.50	£ 13.00	
E4	Inn on the Park	24 hrs		1	£ 4.50	£ 9.50	
E4	Hotel Intercontinental	24 hrs		2	£ 4.50	£ 13.00	
D1	Kendall St NCP	8am-8pm	closed Sat & Sun	2	£ 3.10	£ 9.40	
D2	London Mariott NCP	7am-8pm		4	£ 8.40/ 4hrs	£ 12.50	
F3	Old Burlington St	7am-midnight	Sat -7pm, closed Sun	2	£ 4.80	£ 14.00	
E4	Old Park Ln NCP	8am-8pm	closed Sat & Sun	2	£ 4.40	£ 13.20	
F1	Sanderson House NCP	7.30am-7pm	Sat 8.30-6pm, closed Sun	2	£ 5.50	£ 16.00	
D2	Selfridges	7am-midnight	closed Sun	2	£ 4.50	£ 13.00	£3 from 6pm
E1	Welbeck St NCP	7am-8pm	Sat -7pm, closed Sun	1	£ 4.00	£ 12.00	
Page Ref							
B2	Bedfordbury NCP	7.30am-m'night	closed Sun	2	£ 4.70	£ 14.10	£7.30 6pm-9pm
A2	Brewer St NCP	24 hrs		2	£ 5.00	£ 15.80	£9.50 6pm-9am
B2	Cambridge Circus Sterling	24 hrs		2	£ 4.00	£ 11.70	£6.80 from 6pm
A2	Denman St NCP	24 hrs		2	£ 5.00	£ 15.80	£9.50 6pm-9am
C1	Drury Ln (Wintergarden) NCP	24 hrs		2	£ 3.60	£ 10.80	£6.00 6pm-9am
B1	Holborn NCP	24 hrs		2	£ 3.80	£ 11.50	£6.30 6pm-9am
A2	Poland St APCOA	24 hrs		1	£ 3.20	£ 9.60	£1.50 from 9pm
C2	Savoy Hotel	24 hrs		4	£ 8 /4hrs	£ 12.00	
A2	Swiss Center NCP	8am-2am	Sat -1pm, closed Sun	3	£ 6.30 / 3hrs	£ 12.00	
B3	Trafalgar Sq Sterling	24 hrs		2	£ 4.10	£ 12.30	£4.20 from 5pm
B2	Upper St. Martins Ln NCP	24 hrs		4	£ 8.50 /4hrs	£ 12.50	£7.80 6pm-9am
A2	Wardour St NCP	24 hrs		2	£ 4.70	£ 14.10	£7.30 6pm-9am
A3	Whitcomb St Sterling	24 hrs		2	£ 4.00	£ 12.00	£6.00 from 6pm
B1	YMCA (Adeline Pl) NCP	24 hrs		1	£ 4.00	£ 12.60	
Page Ref							
E1	Atlantic House (Shoe Ln) NCP	7.30am -7pm	closed Sat & Sun	2	£ 2.80	£ 8.50	
E3	Cornwall Rd CPS	24 hrs		2	£ 3.50	£ 8.00	£3.00 from 5pm
D3	Doon St CPS	8am-midnight	Sun £3 flat	2	£ 3.50	£ 8.50	£3.00 from 5pm
F4	Gt Suffolk St NCP	7am-7pm	closed Sat & Sun	1	£ 3.20	£7.50/day	
D3	Hayward Gallery	8am-midnight	Sun £3 flat	2	£ 3.50	£ 8.00	£3.00 from 5pm
F1	Hillgate House NCP	24 hrs		1	£ 3.50	£ 7.00	£1.30 5.30pm-7.30am

CENTRAL LONDON CAR PARKS

Map ref	Car park	Hours	Weekend	Min time	£ /2hr	£ /6hr	Evenin
Page Ref							
F2	International Press Centre NCP	8am - 8pm	closed Sat & Sun	2	£ 2.70	£ 8.00	
F5	Library St NCP	7am-6pm	closed Sat & Sun	half day	£3 half day	£5 day	
D3	National Theatre CPS	8am-2am	Sun £3 flat	2	£ 3.50	£ 8.00	£3 from 5p
F1	Paternoster Row NCP	24 hrs		1	£ 3.50	£ 10.30	
F1	Snowhill NCP	7am-8pm	closed Sat & Sun	2	£ 3.00	£ 8.90	
F5	St Georges Circus NCP	8am-7pm	closed Sat & Sun	6		£ 3.00	
Page Ref							
A1	Aldersgate St NCP	24 hrs		1	£ 3.20	£ 9.60	£2.30 5pm-9a
A2	Baynard House CPS	24 hrs		1	£ 2.00	£ 8.00	£1.50 from 6p
A2	Distaff Ln NCP	7am - 7pm	closed Sat & Sun	2	£ 3.50	£13.20 day	
B1	London Wall CPS	24 hrs		1	£ 2.00	£ 8.00	£1.50 from 6p
C4	Snowsfield NCP	24 hrs		1	£ 1.60	£ 4.50	£1.80 6pm-9a
A4	Southwark St Union Car Park	7am-8pm	closed Sat & Sun	2	£ 2.00	£ 5.00	
B3	Swan Lane CPS	24 hrs		1	£ 2.00	£ 8.00	£1.50 from 6p
B2	Vintry NCP	24 hrs	Sat & Sun £1.50 7-7	1	£ 3.20	£ 9.50	£1.50 5.45pm-9a
Page Ref							
F2	Cable St NCP	7am - 7pm	closed Sat & Sun	6		£ 3.20	
D1	Houndsditch NCP	7am-10pm	closed Sat,Sun 8am-3pm	2	£ 4.40	£13.20	
E2	Minories CPS	24 hrs		1	£ 2.00	£ 8.00	£1.50 from 6p
D1	Rodwell House NCP	24 hrs		2	£ 3.30	£ 10.00	£3.20 5.30pm-9a
E2	Royal Mint Ct	7am-7pm	N/A	day	£6 flat		
F3	Thomas More St NCP	7am - 9.30pm	closed Sat & Sun	2	£ 1.30	£5.50 day	
F3	More St	8am-11.30pm		2	£ 2.00	£ 3	
D3	Tower Hill CPS	24 hrs		1	£ 2.00	£ 8	£1.50 from 6p
E3	Tower Thistle Hotel	24 hrs		1	£ 2.50	£ 6.50	
Page Ref							
C1	Earls Court Rd	24 hrs		2	£ 1.70	£ 7.20	
C2	Fenelon Place NCP	8am-6pm	closed Sat & Sun	half day	£5.40 half day	£9.50 day	
B1	Olympia Hilton Hotel NCP	24 hrs		half day	£4.00 half day	£7 day	£3 5.30pm-9a
C4	Park Inn (Lillie Rd) LCP	24 hrs		1hr	£ 1.70	£ 5.00	
A1	Russell Rd City & Suburban	24 hrs		3hrs	£3.50/3hrs	£ 4.50	£11 up to 24 h
C4	Seagrave Rd Sterling	24 hrs		1hr	£ 3.00	£ 9.00	£5 overnig
Page Ref							
B1	Copthorne Tara Hotel	24 hrs		2	£ 3.50	£ 7.00	
E2	Forum Hotel	24 hrs		2	£ 2.50	£ 6.50	
E2	Gloucester Hotel	24 hrs		2	£ 3.50	£ 8.50	£18 overnig
F2	Harrington Rd Union CP	7am-8pm	9am-7pm	2	£ 3.00	£ 8.00	£5 overnig
E5	Lots Rd APCOA	7am-7pm	closed Sat & Sun	1	£ 1.40	£ 4.50	
D2	Swallow International Hotel	24 hrs		2	£ 2.50	£ 7.00	

CENTRAL LONDON CAR PARKS

Map ref	Car park	Hours	Weekend	Min time	£ /2hr	£ /6hr	Evening
Page Ref							
17 C1	Cadogan Place NCP	24 hrs		2	£ 4.00	£ 12.00	
C1	Hyatt Carlton Tower Hotel	24 hrs		1	£ 5.00	£ 15.00	
B2	Nell Gwyn Garage	24 hrs		5	£6/5hrs	£ 9.00	
C2	Royal Court Hotel	24 hrs		3	£5/3hrs	£ 10.00	
Page Ref							
18 E3	Abbotts M'r (Warwick Way) APCOA	24 hrs		2	£ 2.60	£ 5.60	£2 from 6pm
E2	Buckingham Palace Rd Unipark	7am-8pm	Sat 8am-6pm, closed Sun	1	£ 3.00	£ 7.00	
D2	Eaton Mews Garage	8am-10pm	Sat -6pm, Sun 9am-1pm	2	£ 7.00	£ 12.00	£21 for 24 hrs.
E2	Semley Place NCP	24 hrs		2	£ 2.50	£ 8.00	£2.40 6pm-8.30am
Page Ref							
19 B1	Abingdon St NCP	24 hrs		2	£ 2.95	£ 8.40	£3.30 6pm-9am
A3	Dolphin Sq NCP	24 hrs		1	£ 0.90	£ 4.00	
	Rochester Row APCOA	7am-midnight		2	£ 3.10	£ 9.40	£2 from 6pm
Page Ref							
20 F1	Elephant & Castle NCP	8am-7pm	Sat 8am-7pm, closed Sun	1	£ 0.60	£ 2.50	

CENTRAL LONDON SERVICE STATIONS

Map ref		Hours	Shop	Company
Page	**Ref**			
	A2	24 hrs	Yes	Mobil, Wellington Rd
	A4	24 hrs	Yes	Esso, Capital Edgware
1	A5	24 hrs	Yes	Texaco, The Vale
	B3	24 hrs	Yes	Texaco, Star Hanover Gate
	B4	24 hrs	Yes	Jet, Park Rd
	C5	24 hrs		Independent, Marylebone Rd
Page	**Ref**			
	D5	7.30am-7pm		Elf, Marylebone Garage
	E1	24 hrs	Yes	Jet, Oval Rd
2	F2	24 hrs	Yes	Esso, St Georges
	F3	24 hrs	Yes	Mobil, Euston
	F5	8am- 6pm Mon - Fri		Independent, Clipstone St
Page	**Ref**			
	B3	24 hrs	Yes	Cyma, Euston Rd
	B4	24 hrs	Yes	Elf, Woburn Pl
3	C1	24 hrs	Yes	Mobil, Goods Way
	C2	6am-10pm Mon-Fri		Gulf, York Way Motors
		6am- 9pm Sat, 10am-4pm Sun		
Page	**Ref**			
	D3	24 hrs	Yes	Shell, Mount Pleasant
4	F1	24 hrs	Yes	Jet, Essex Rd
	F2	24 hrs	Yes	Texaco, City Rd
	F4	24 hrs	Yes	Texaco, Clerkenwell Rd
Page	**Ref**			
	A4	7am-9pm	Yes	Shell, Central St.
	B4	7am-11pm Mon-Sat, 8am-10pm Sun	Yes	Shell, Old St.
5	B5	6am-9pm Mon-Fri, 7am-6pm	Yes	Q8, City Rd
		Sat, 8am-6pm Sun		
	C4	24 hrs	Yes	Texaco, East Central
Page	**Ref**			
6	D4	24 hrs	Yes	Texaco, Shoreditch
Page	**Ref**			
	A2	6am-11pm	Yes	Shell, Andrews Garage
7	B2	24 hrs	Yes	Texaco, Westbourne Grove
	C2	24 hrs	Yes	Texaco, Pembridge Villas
Page	**Ref**			
8	E3	24 hrs	Yes	Shell, Hertford
	F5	7.30am-7pm Mon-Fri, 8am-1pm Sat,	Yes	Shell, Queens Gate Mews
		8am-12 noon Sun		
Page	**Ref**			
9	B1	7am-11pm Mon-Fri, 8am-10pm Sat	Yes	Texaco, Kendal Street
		9am-9pm Sun		

HOW TO USE THE BLUE BOOK STREET INDEX

THE INDEX

The Blue Book street index tells you the page number and map reference like any other index. It also tells you the meter availability and the "chances" of finding a 4 hour parking meter at your destination.

Street Name	Map Ref	2 hrs	4 hrs	Coins
St. James's Square SW1	11 A3	Gd.		£1/P&D
Chichester Street SW1	19 A3		Gd.	£1 & 20p
Claverton Street SW1	19 A3	Gd.	Ave.	£1 & 20p

METERS

The index tells you how many meters there are in that street (all the 2 hour meters and all the 4 hour meters).

The rankings for meters are

- Gd.   10 meters and over
- Ave.   5- 9 meters
- Bd.   1-4 meters

Always make a note of the length of the street on the atlas and match that up in your mind with the number of meters in the index.

For example

- Chester Mews has a "Bd" rating. However as a mews there are likely to be less people competing for those meters and they should be easier to find.
- Shaftesbury Ave has a "Gd" rating but the street is very long and the meters are all concentrated at one end.

4 HOUR METERS

4 hour meters are difficult to find and many Londoners are unaware of their existence. This is largely because they are hardly ever grouped together, usually being sprinkled in with 2 hour meters. As a consequence they are usually occupied by drivers who only wanted a 2 hour meter.

To help you find one of these meters we have rated the ease of finding a 4 hour meter in the index.

- Gd.   Most of the meters on that street are 4 hour meters
- Ave.   You have about a 50-50 chance of getting a 4 hour meter
- Bd.   1/4, or less, of the meters on that street are 4 hour meters

A 3-course meal for 3p at Pizzaland!

We've teamed up with Pizzaland, the Italian Pizza specialists, to bring you this fabulous offer. When you buy a one, two, or three course meal at Pizzaland, the vouchers below entitle you to the same number of courses, up to the same value, for just 1p each!

If you haven't been down to Pizzaland for a while, it's time to take another look. To go with their friendly service, they've recently launched a new menu, featuring authentic Italian pizzas such as the Four Cheeses pizza and exciting new choices like Spicy Mexican Chicken. Why not start with Garlic Mushrooms Alfredo or Canneloni; and finish with Tiramisu or the new Tricolore ice cream.

It's the ideal place to relax over a leisurely meal, accompanied by a glass or two of their smooth Italian House Wine, or with a Coke for the kids. With a wide range of vegetarian options pasta dishes and a special kids menu, there's something for everyone at Pizzaland, so cut out the vouchers now and race down to your nearest restaraunt!

Pizzaland can be found all over London

STARTER FOR 1P

When you buy any starter, this voucher entitles you to another one, of the same value or less, for 1p.

Offer applies to Eat-In meals only. Voucher not redeemable conjunction with any other offer. Offer valid at all Pizzaland restaraunts, every day except Saturdays until 28th November 1993.

Pizzaland   PLU 571

PIZZA FOR 1P

When you buy any 10"Traditional or 7" Deep Pan or Gourmet Pizza, this voucher entitles you to another one, of the same value or less, for 1p.

Offer applies to Eat-In meals only. Voucher not redeemable conjunction with any other offer. Offer valid at all Pizzaland restaraunts, every day except Saturdays until 28th November 1993.

PLU 572

Pizzaland

DESSERT FOR 1P

When you buy any dessert, this voucher entitles you to another one, of the same value or less, for 1p.

Offer applies to Eat-In meals only. Voucher redeemable conjunction with any other offer. valid at all Pizzaland restaraunts, every day e Saturdays until 28th November 1993.

Pizzaland   PL

SELFRIDGES

- **Contract Parking**

- **Casual Parking**

- **Petrol Station**

- **Auto Accessories**

- **Hand Car Wash**

Selfridges Garage is located in the Heart of the West End adjacent to Selfridges Department Store.

For further details please contact George Williamson on 071 - 493 5181

SELFRIDGES GARAGE
ORCHARD STREET LONDON WIH OHB

Probably the most secure parking in the West End
Burlington Garage

3-9 Old Burlington Street, W1

The sensible solution for parking

Credit cards accepted

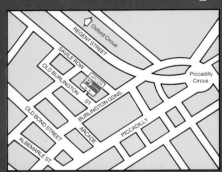

Season tickets, Contracts and storage available call 0932 789812

THE CAR CLAMP RECOVERY CLUB

The original pioneering organisation that has brought new freedom to clamped and towed away motorists.

Over 5,000 motorists make use of our services. Shouldn't you, or your company, join them?

**Join London's
Leading Recovery Club - Today**

CALL US NOW ON 071 235 990

HE LONDON PARKING MAP

The map below shows the area of London covered by the Book & Central London post code districts. The number in the corner of each box indicates the atlas page that part of London.

The map also shows which parts of the capital will be operating the new parking rules and on which dates (see "HE NEW METER RULES" & "NEW RULES" sub headings). These dates may change - so check signs on meters.

LONDON RED ROUTES

London is the first city in the UK to see the introduction of "Red Routes". Over the next 3 years a wide network of red routes will be introduced across the capital.

There is no stopping for any reason on a red route (see "Red Routes"). Look for red lines by the kerb and roadside signs telling you the hours of restriction for each red route.

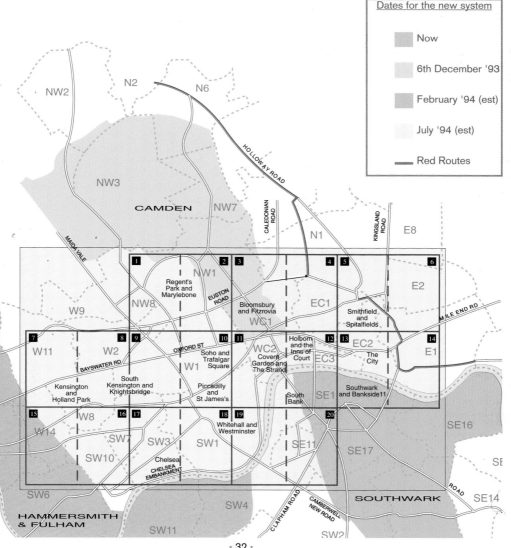

Dates for the new system

- Now
- 6th December '93
- February '94 (est)
- July '94 (est)
- Red Routes

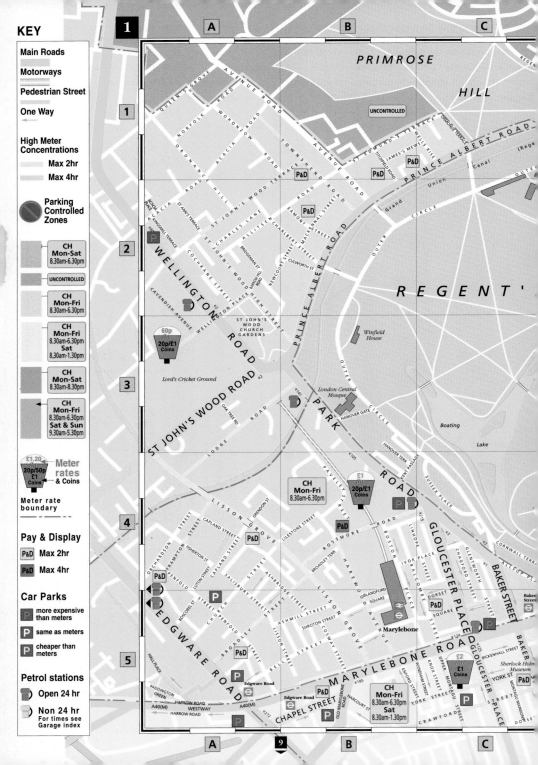

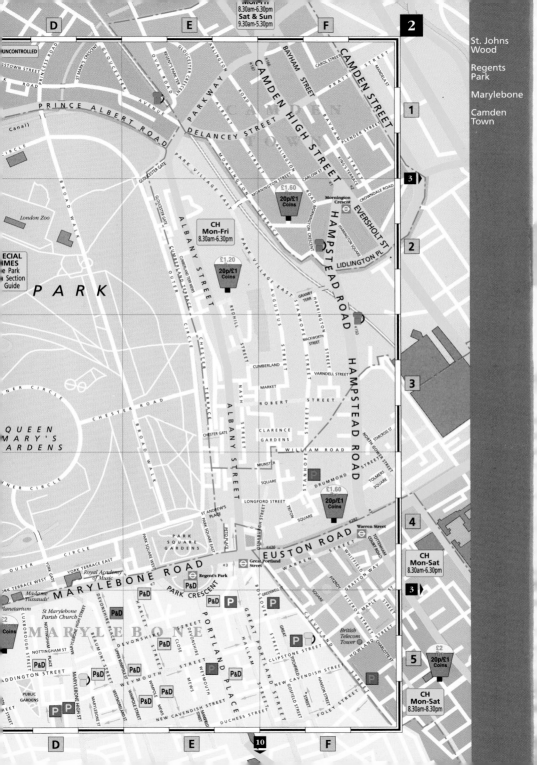

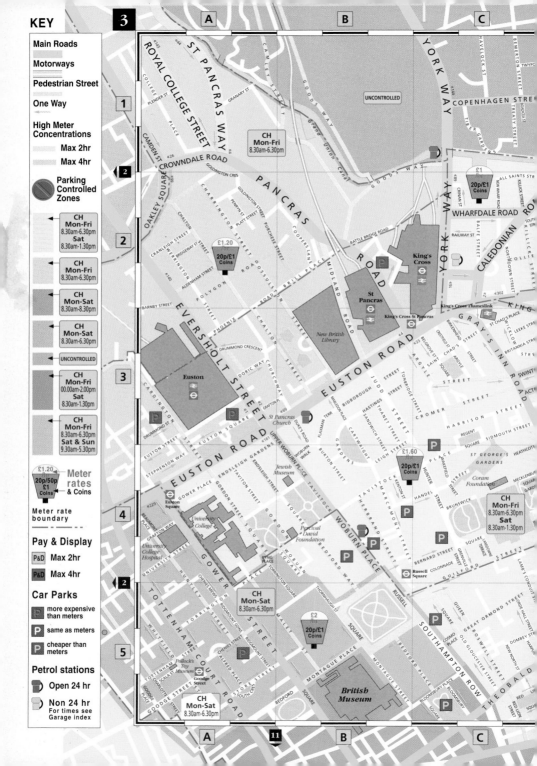

WARNING

AFTER 6 DECEMBER 1993 NEW CONTROLLED HOUR BOUNDARIES COME INTO EFFECT IN THE BOROUGH OF CAMDEN. THE PAGE OPPOSITE SHOWS THE BOUNDARIES FROM 6 DECEMBER 1993. THE MAP PAGE OVERLEAF IS ONLY VALID UNTIL 6 DECEMBER 1993.

PLEASE REMOVE THIS PAGE AFTER 6 DECEMBER 1993.

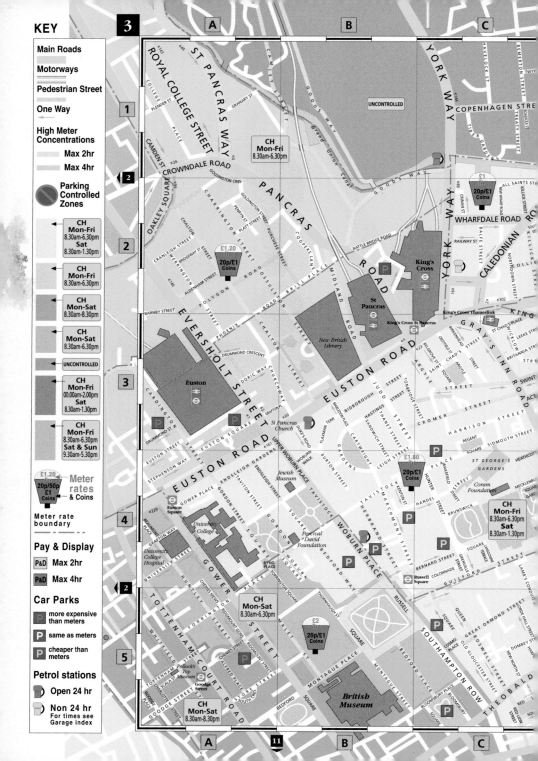

4

Euston
King's Cross
Bloomsbury
Clerkenwell
Islington
Finsbury

D   E   F

4

1

5▶

2

ISLINGTON

UNCONTROLLED

PRICE'S YARD
MATILDA STREET
HEMINGFORD ROAD
MINGFORD ROAD
ST
CALEDONIAN ROAD
2926
COPENHAGEN STREET
CLOUDESLEY ROAD
CLOUDESLEY SQUARE
STONFIELD ST
GIBSON SQUARE
ST MARY'S PATH
GASKIN STREET
PACKINGTON STREET
ESSEX ROAD
719
MURIEL STREET
CHARLOTTE TERRACE
CLOUDESLEY STREET
THEBERTON STREET
CLOUDESLEY SQUARE
LIVERPOOL ROAD
BARFORD STREET
ISLINGTON GREEN GARDENS
ST PETER'S STREET
CRUDEN STREET
RALEIGH STREET
CARNEGIE STREET
HALFMOON CRESCENT
FINSBURY
CLOUDESLEY PLACE
BATCHELOR STREET
CAMDEN WALK
GRANTBRIDGE STREET
BURGH STREET
WYNFORD ROAD
MAYGOOD ST
DEWEY ROAD
P
TOLPUDDLE STREET
ISLINGTON HIGH ST
CHARLTON PLACE
GERRARD ROAD
DANBURY STREET
P
£1
20p/£1 Coins
RODNEY STREET
CUMMING STREET
DONEGAL STREET
CYNTHIA ST
CHAPEL MARKET
GRANT GOSSON ST
RISINGHILL STREET
PENTON STREET
BARON STREET
WHITE LION STREET
419
ISLINGTON HIGH ST
849
DUNCAN STREET
COLEBROOKE TERRACE
NOEL ROAD
DUNCAN STREET
VINCENT TERRACE
GRAHAM ST
STREET
CLAREMONT SQUARE
Angel
£389
ELIA STREET
SUDELEY STREET
ELIA STREET
CITY GDN ROW
PENTONVILLE ROAD
133
PENTON RISE
CROSS STREET
VERNON RISE
PERCY STREET
GT PERCY STREET
LLOYD BAKER STREET
RIVER STREET
CLAREMONT CLOSE
MYDDELTON
ST JOHN STREET
OWEN ST
CITY ROAD
GOSWELL ROAD
NELSON PL
P
CH
Mon-Fri
8.30am-6.30pm
Sat
8.30am-1.30pm
CHADWELL STREET
P
WAKLEY STREET
£328
FRIEND STREET
PAGET ST
HEMPST STREET
HALL STREET
INGLEBERT STREET
AMWELL STREET
RIVER STREET
MYDDELTON PASSAGE
RAWSTORNE STREET
GOSWELL ROAD
MORELAND STREET
STREET
FINSBURY
LLOYD'S ROW
SPENCER STREET
ST JOHN STREET
WYNYATT STREET
WHARTON STREET
GRANVILLE SQUARE
MARGERY STREET
YARDLEY STREET
WILMINGTON SQUARE
HARDWICK STREET
GLOUCESTER WAY
MEREDITH STREET
STREET
NORTHAMPTON ASHBY ST
GOSWELL ROAD
£1.60
20p/£1 Coins
KING'S CROSS ROAD
FREDERICK STREET
CUBITT STREET
PAKENHAM STREET
ROSEBERY AVENUE
MYDDELTON STREET
SKINNER STREET
WYCLIF ST SQUARE
SEBASTIAN ST
TOMPION ST
PERCIVAL STREET
CYRUS STREET
MALT ST
AGDON ST
ATTNEVESLEY STREET
SPA FIELDS
CORPORATION ROW
WOODBRIDGE ST
SEKFORDE STREET
P
£2
20p/£1 Coins
FARRINGDON ROAD
PHOENIX PLACE
MOUNT PLEASANT
NORTHAMPTON ROAD
BOWLING GREEN LANE
SANS WALK
COMPTON STREET
DALLINGTON STREET
P
ST ANDREW'S GARDENS
WREN STREET
GOUGH STREET
BROWNLOW ST
The Dickens House Museum
COLEY ST
P&D
P&D
WARNER STREET
RAY ST
EYRE STREET HILL
CLERKENWELL CLOSE
FARRINGDON LANE
AYLESBURY STREET
CLERKENWELL GREEN
ST JOHN'S SQUARE
GREAT SUTTON STREET
BERRY ST
NORTHBURGH STREET
ST JOHN STREET
DOUGHTY MEWS
ROGER ST
ELM ST
LAYSTALL STREET
HERBAL HILL
BRITTON STREET
CLERKENWELL ROAD
P
P
JOHN'S MEWS
NORTHINGTON STREET
GRAY'S INN ROAD
RAYMOND BUILDINGS
JOCKEY'S FIELDS
GRAY'S INN GARDENS
CLERKENWELL ROAD
PORTPOOL LANE
HATTON GARDEN
HATTON PLACE
KIRBY STREET
SAFFRON HILL
TURNMILL STREET
BENJAMIN STREET
ALBION PL
EAGLE COURT
ST JOHN'S LANE
CHARTERHOUSE SQUARE
P
P&D
Farringdon
GT JAMES STREET
EMERALD STREET
BEDFORD ROW
PRINCETON STREET
BROWNLOW ST
LEATHER LANE
ST CROSS STREET
BALDWINS GARDENS
GREVILLE STREET
GRAY'S INN ROAD
GRAY'S INN
Gray's Inn
Chancery Lane
St Etheldreda's
FARRINGDON ROAD
BENJAMIN STREET
Farringdon
P
COWCROSS ST
£3
20p/£1 Coins
CHARTERHOUSE STREET
CLOTH FAIR
LONG LANE
St Bartholomew -the-Great
CH
Mon-Fri
00.00am-2.00pm
Sat
8.30am-1.30pm

D   E   **12**   F

3

4

5▶

5

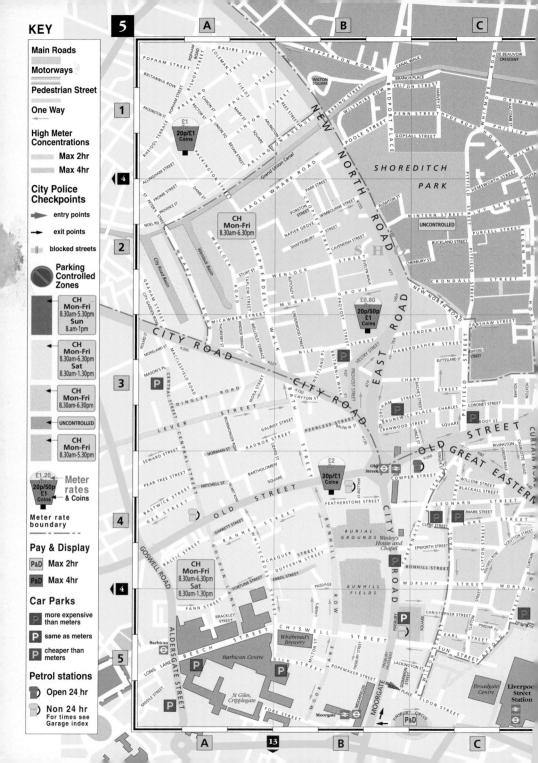

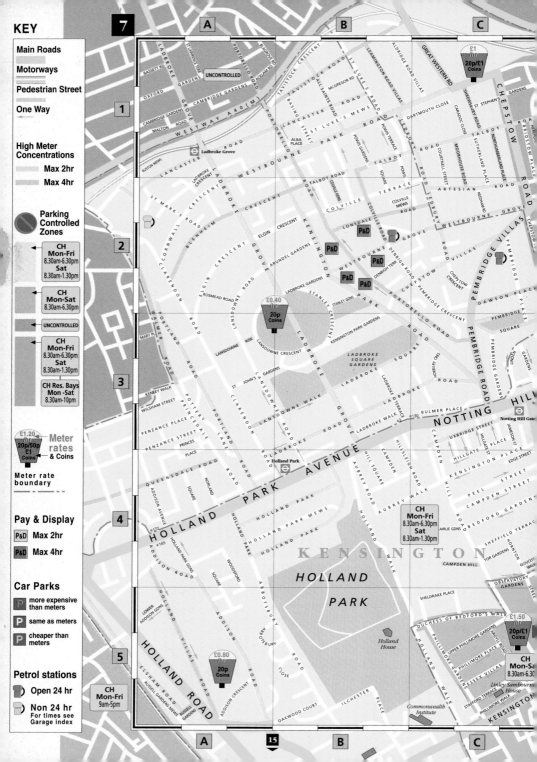

18

Chelsea

King's Road

Sloane
Square

Belgravia

Pimlico

Battersea

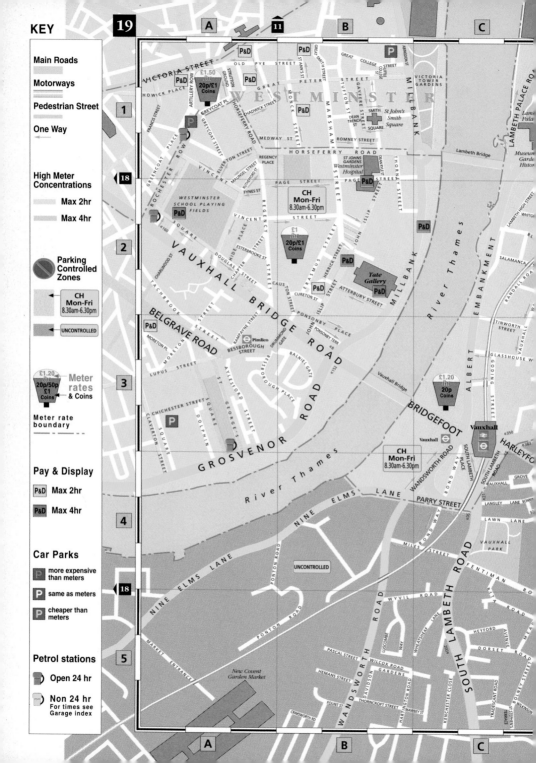

Street Name		2hrs	4hrs	Coins
Bankside Power Station SE1	12 F3 13 A3			
Banner St EC1	5 A4	Gd.	Bd.	£1 & 20p
Banqueting House SW1	11 B4			
Barbican Centre EC2	5 A5			
Barclay Rd SW6	15 C5			
Barford St N1	4 E1			
Barge House St SE1	12 E3			
Baring St N1	5 B1			
Bark Pl W2	8 D2	Ave.		£1 & 20p
Barkston Gdns SW5	16 D2	Gd.	Ave.	20p
Barnby St NW1	3 A2			
Barnet Gro E2	6 E3			
Barnham St E1	14 D4			
Barnsbury Rd N1	4 E1			
Baron St N1	4 E2	Bd.		£1 & 20p
Baroness Rd E2	6 E3			
Baron's Ct Rd W14	15 A3			
Baron's Keep W14	15 A2			
Baron's Pl SE1	12 E5			
Barrow Hill Rd NW8	1 A2	Bd.		£1 & 20p
Barter St WC1	11 C1	Ave.		£1 & 20p
Bartholomew Clo EC1	5 A5	Gd.		£1 & 20p
Bartholomew La EC2	13 B1			
Bartholomew Sq EC1	5 A4			
Barton Rd W14	15 A3			
Basil St SW3	9 C5	Gd.	Bd.	£1 & 20p
Basing St W11	7 B1	Ave.	Bd.	20p
Basinghall Ave EC2	13 B1			
Basinghall St EC2	13 B1	Gd.		£1 & 20p
Basire St N1	5 A1			
Bassett Rd W10	7 A1			
Bastwick St EC1	5 A4	Ave.		£1 & 20p
Batchelor St N1	4 E1			
Bateman's Row EC2	6 D4			
Bath St EC1	5 B3	Ave.	Bd.	£1 & 20p
Bathurst Ms W2	9 A2			
Bathurst St W2	9 A2	Bd.		£1 & 20p
Battersea Bridge SW3 SW11	17 A5			
Battersea Bridge Rd SW11	17 A5			
Battersea Park SW11	17 C5 18 D5			
Battersea Pk Rd SW8 SW11	18 F5			
Battersea Power Station SW8	18 F4			
Battle Bridge La SE1	13 C4			
Battle Bridge Rd NW1	3 B2	Ave.		£1 & 20p
Batty St E1	14 F1			
Baxendale St E2	6 E3			
Bayham St NW1	2 F1			
Baylis Rd SE1	12 E5			
Bayswater Rd W2	8 E3			
Bayswater Rd W2	9 A2			
Beak St W1	10 F2			
Bear Gdns SE1	13 A3			
Bear La SE1	12 F4	Ave.		£1, 50p & 20p / 20p
Beauchamp Pl SW3	17 B1	Gd.		£1 & 20p
Beaufort Gdns SW3	17 B1	Gd.		P & D
Beaufort St SW3	16 F3 17 A4	Bd.		20p
Beaufoy Wlk SE11	20 D2			
Beaumont Ave W14	15 B3			
Beaumont Cres W14	15 B3			
Beaumont Pl W1	3 A4			
Beaumont St W1	2 D5	Gd.		£1 / P & D
Bedale St SE1	13 B4			
Bedford Ave WC1	11 B1	Gd.		£1 & 20p
Bedford Gdns W8	7 C4	Gd.	Bd.	20p
Bedford Pl WC1	3 B5	Gd.		£1 & 20p
Bedford Row WC1	4 D5	Gd.		£1 & 20p
Bedford Sq WC1	3 B5			
Bedford St WC2	11 C3	Ave.		£1 / P & D
Bedford Way WC1	3 B4	Gd.		£1 & 20p
Bedfordbury WC2	11 B2			
Beech St EC2	5 A5			
Belgrave Ms North SW1	10 D5			
Belgrave Ms West SW1	18 D1			

Street Name		2hrs	4hrs	Coins
Belgrave Pl SW1	18 D1	Gd.	Ave.	£1 & 20p
Belgrave Rd SW1	18 F2 19 A3	Gd.	Gd.	£1 & 20p / P & D
Belgrave Sq SW1	10 D5	Gd.	Bd.	£1 & 20p / P & D
Belgrove St WC1	3 C3	Ave.		£1 & 20p
Bell La E1	14 D1			
Bell St NW1	1 A5	Gd.		£1 & 20p
Bell Wharf La EC4	13 B2			
Bell Yd WC2	12 D1			
Belvedere Rd SE1	12 D4	Ave.		20p
Bemerton St N1	3 C1			
Bentinck St W1	10 D1			
Berkeley Sq W1	10 E3	Gd.		£1 / P & D
Berkeley St W1	10 E3	Gd.		£1
Bermondesy Antiques Mkt SE1	13 C5			
Bermondsey St SE1	13 C4	Ave.		£1, 50p & 20p / 20p
Bermondsey Wall East SE16	14 F5			
Bermondsey Wall West SE16	14 E4			
Bernard St WC1	3 C4	Gd.		£1 & 20p
Berners St W1	10 F1 11 A1	Gd.		£1
Berry St EC1	4 F4	Ave.		£1 & 20p
Berwick St W1	11 A1	Ave.		£1
Bessborough Pl SW1	19 A3			
Bessborough St SW1	19 A3			
Bethnal Grn Rd E1	6 D4			
Bethnal Grn Rd E2	6 F3			
Bethwin Rd SE5	20 F5			
Bevan St N1	5 A1			
Bevenden St N1	5 C3			
Bevington St SE16	14 F5			
Bevis Marks EC3	14 D1			
Bickenhall St W1	1 C5			
Bidborough St WC1	3 B3	Gd.		£1 & 20p
Big Ben SW1	11 C5			
Billing Rd SW10	16 E5			
Billingsgate EC3	13 C3			
Bina Gdns SW5	16 E2	Ave.	Gd.	20p
Binney St W1	10 D2	Bd.		£1
Birdcage Wlk SW1	10 F5 11 A5			
Birkenhead St WC1	3 C3	Gd.		£1 & 20p
Bishop King's Rd W14	15 A2			
Bishop St N1	5 A1			
Bishop's Bridge Rd W2	8 E1			
Bishop's Rd SW11	17 B5			
Bishopsgate EC2	6 D5 13 C1			
Bishopsgate Church Yard EC2	13 C1			
Black Prince Rd SE1	19 C2			
Black Prince Rd SE11	20 D2	Gd.		20p
Blackall St EC2	5 C4			
Blackfriars Bridge EC4	12 F2			
Blackfriars La EC4	12 F2	Bd.		£1 & 20p
Blackfriars Rd SE1	12 F3			
Blackfriars Underpass EC4	12 F2			
Blagrove Rd W10	7 A1			
Blandford Sq NW1	1 B5			
Blandford St W1	10 D1	Gd.		£1
Blantyre St SW10	16 F5	Bd.		20p
Blenheim Cres W11	7 A2	Ave.	Gd.	20p
Bletchley St N1	5 B2			
Blewcoat School SW1	11 A5			
Blomfield St EC2	13 C1	Bd.		£1 & 20p
Bloomfield Terr SW1	18 D3	Gd.		£1 & 20p
Bloomsbury Pl WC1	3 C5	Ave.		£1 & 20p
Bloomsbury Sq WC1	3 C5			
Bloomsbury St WC1	11 B1			
Bloomsbury Way WC1	11 C1			
Blue Anchor Yrd E1	14 E2			
Blythe Rd W14	15 A1			
Boadicea St N1	3 C1			
Boating Lake NW1	1 C3			
Boating Lake SW11	18 D5			
Bolney St SW8	19 C5			

Each place name is followed by its postal district, its atlas reference, 2 hour meters, 4 hour meters and then by the coins accepted.

Street Name		2hrs	4hrs	Coins
Bolsover St W1	2 F5	Gd.		£ 1
Bolton Gdns SW5	16 D3	Ave.	Gd.	20p
Bolton St W1	10 E3	Bd.		£ 1
Boltons The SW10	16 E3	Gd.	Gd.	20p
Bond Way SW8	19 C4			
Bonhill St EC2	5 C4	Ave.	Gd.	£1 & 20p
Bonnington Sq SW8	19 C4			
Boot St N1	5 C3			
Borough High St SE1	13 B4			
Borough Mkt SE1	13 B4			
Borough Rd SE1	12 F5	Gd.	Bd.	£1, 50p & 20p / 20p
Borough Rd SE1	13 A5			
Boscobel St NW8	1 A5	Gd.		£1 & 20p
Boston Pl NW1	1 B4			
Boswell St WC1	3 C5	Gd.		£1 & 20p
Boundary St E2	6 D4			
Bourdon St W1	10 E2			
Bourne St SW1	18 D2			
Bouverie Pl W2	9 A1			
Bouverie St EC4	12 E2			
Bow La EC4	13 A2			
Bow St WC2	11 C2	Ave.		£ 1
Bowling Grn La EC1	4 E4	Ave.	Bd.	£1 & 20p
Bowling Grn St SE11	20 E4			
Boyfield St SE1	12 F5			
Brackley St EC1	5 A5	Ave.		£1 & 20p
Brad St SE1	12 E4			
Braganza St SE17	20 F3			
Braham St E1	14 E1			
Braidwood St SE1	13 C4			
Bramber Rd W14	15 B4			
Bramerton St SW3	17 A4	Ave.		20p
Bramham Gdns SW5	16 D2	Ave.	Gd.	20p
Branch Pl N1	5 B1			
Bray Pl SW3	17 C2	Ave.	Bd.	£1 & 20p
Bread St EC4	13 A2			
Bream's Bldgs EC4	12 E1	Ave.		£ 1
Brechin Pl SW7	16 F2	Ave.	Ave.	20p
Brecon Rd W6	15 A4			
Bremner Rd SW7	8 F5			
Brendon St W1	9 B1	Bd.		£ 1
Bressenden Pl SW1	18 F1	Gd.		£1 / P & D
Brewer St W1	11 A2			
Brick La E1 E2	6 E5			
	6 E3			
Brick St W1	10 E4			
Bridge Pl SW1	18 F2			
Bridge St SW1	11 C5			
Bridgefoot SE1	19 C3			
Bridgeman St NW8	1 A2	Ave.		£1 & 20p
Bridgeway St NW1	3 A2			
Bridport Pl N1	5 B1			
Bridstow Pl W2	7 C1			
Brill Pl NW1	3 B2			
Britannia Row N1	5 A1			
Britannia St WC1	3 C3	Ave.		£1 & 20p
Britannia Wlk N1	5 B3			
British Museum WC1	3 B5			
British Telecom Tower W1	2 F5			
Brittania Rd SW6	16 D5			
Britten St SW3	17 A3	Bd.	Gd.	£1 & 20p
Britton St EC1	4 F5	Ave.	Bd.	£1 & 20p
Brixton Rd SW9	20 E5			
Broad Sanctuary SW1	11 B5			
Broad Wlk NW1	2 D2			
Broad Wlk The W8	8 E4			
Broadcasting House W1	10 E1			
Broadgate Centre EC2	5 C5			
Broadley St NW8	1 A5	Gd.		£1 & 20p / P & D
Broadley Terr NW1	1 B4			
Broadwall SE1	12 E3			
Broadway SW1	11 A5	Bd.		£ 1
Broadway Mkt E8	6 F1			
Broadwick St W1	10 F2	Gd.		£ 1
	11 A2			
Broken Wharf EC4	13 A2			
Brompton Cemetery SW10	16 D4			
Brompton Oratory SW7	17 A1			
Brompton Pk Cres SW6	16 D4			
Brompton Pl SW3	17 B1			
Brompton Rd SW3	9 B5	Bd.		£ 1
Brompton Sq SW3	17 B1			
Bronsart Rd SW6	15 A5			
Brook Dri SE11	20 E1	Gd.	Bd.	£1, 50p & 20p / 20p
Brook Gate W1	9 C3			
Brook Ms North W2	8 F2			
Brook St W1	10 E2	Gd.		£1 / P & D
Brook St W2	9 A2			
Brooke St EC1	4 E5	Bd.		£1 & 20p
Brook's Ms W1	10 E2	Gd.		£1 / P & D
Brookville Rd SW6	15 B5			
Brougham Rd E8	6 F1			
Brown St W1	9 B1	Ave.		£ 1
Brownlow Ms WC1	4 D4	Bd.		£1 & 20p
Brownlow St WC1	4 D5			
Brunswick Ct SE1	14 D5			
Brunswick Gdns W8	8 D4	Gd.	Bd.	20p
Brunswick Pl N1	5 B3			
Brunswick Sq WC1	3 C4	Bd.		£1 & 20p
Brushfield St E1	6 D5	Bd.		£1 & 20p
Bruton La W1	10 E3			
Bruton Pl W1	10 E3			
Bruton St W1	10 E3	Gd.		£1 / P & D
Bryanston Ms E. W1	9 C1			
Bryanston Pl W1	9 B1	Gd.		£ 1
Bryanston Sq W1	9 C1	Gd.		£1 / P & D
Bryanston St W1	9 C2	Gd.		£1 / P & D
Buck Hill Wlk W2	9 A3			
Buckingham Gate SW1	10 F5	Bd.		£ 1
Buckingham Gate SW1	11 A5			
Buckingham Palace SW1	10 F5	Ave.		£1 & 20p
Buckingham Palace Gardens SW1	10 E5			
Buckingham Palace Rd SW1	18 E2			
Buckingham St WC2	11 C3	Ave.		£ 1
Buckland St N1	5 C2			
Bull Wharf La EC4	13 A2			
Bulls Gdns SW3	17 B2			
Bulmer Pl W11	7 C3			
Bunhill Fields EC1	5 B4			
Bunhill Row EC1	5 B4	Gd.	Bd.	£1 & 20p
Burdett Ms W2	8 D1			
Burgh St N1	4 F2	Ave.		£1 & 20p
Burial Grounds EC1	5 B4			
Burlington Arcade W1	10 F3			
Burlington Gdns W1	10 F3			
Burnaby St SW10	16 F5	Gd.	Bd.	20p
Burnsall St SW3	17 B3			
Burnthwaite Rd SW6	15 C5			
Burrell St SE1	12 F3	Bd.		£1, 50p & 20p / 20p
Burslem St E1	14 F2			
Burton St WC1	3 B4	Gd.		£1 & 20p
Burton's Ct SW3	17 C3			
Bury Pl WC1	11 C1	Ave.		£1 & 20p
Bury St EC3	14 D1	Ave.		£1 & 20p
Bury St SW1	10 F3	Ave.		£ 1
Bush House WC2	12 D2			
Buttesland St N1	5 C3			
Buxton St E1	6 E4			
Byward St EC3	14 D2			
Byng Pl WC1	3 A4	Gd.		£1 & 20p
C				
Cabinet War Rooms SW1	11 B4			
Cable St E1	14 F2			
Cadogan Gate SW1	17 C2	Ave.	Bd.	£1 & 20p
Cadogan Gdns SW3	17 C2	Gd.	Bd.	£1 & 20p
Cadogan La SW1	18 D1	Bd.	Gd.	£1 & 20p
Cadogan Pier SW3	17 B4			
Cadogan Pl SW1	17 C1	Gd.	Ave.	£1 & 20p
Cadogan Sq SW1	17 C1	Gd.	Bd.	£1 & 20p
Cadogan St SW3	17 C2	Gd.		£1 & 20p
Cale St SW3	17 A3	Gd.	Bd.	£1 & 20p/20p
Caledonian Rd N1	3 C2			
	4 D1			
Callender Rd SW7	8 F5			
Callow St SW3	16 F4	Ave.	Bd.	20p
Calshot St N1	4 D2			
Calthorpe St WC1	4 D4			

Street Name	2hrs	4hrs	Coins
Calvert Ave E2 6 D3			
Calvin St E1 6 D5			
Camberwell New Rd SE5 20 E5			
Cambridge Circus WC2 11 B2			
Cambridge Gdns W10 7 A1			
Cambridge Pl W8 8 E5			
Cambridge Sq W2 9 A1			
Cambridge St SW1 18 F3	Ave.		£1 & 20p
Camden High St NW1 2 F1			
Camden St NW1 2 F1	Gd.	Bd.	£1 & 20p
3 A1			
4 F1			
Camden Wlk N1 4 F1			
Camera Pl SW10 16 F4	Ave.	Gd.	20p
Camlet St E2 6 D4			
Camley St NW1 3 A1	Gd.	Ave.	£1 & 20p
Campden Gro W8 7 C4	Gd.	Ave.	£1 & 20p
Campden Hill W8 7 C4	Gd.	Gd.	20p
Campden Hill Rd W11 7 C4	Ave.		20p
Campden Hill Sq W8 7 B4	Ave.	Bd.	20p
Campden St W8 7 C4	Gd.	Bd.	20p
Canadian Embassy SW1 11 B3			
Canal Wlk N1 5 B1			
Canning Pl W8 8 E5			
Cannon Row SW1 11 B5			
Cannon St EC4 13 A2			
Cannon St Rd E1 14 F1			
Canon St N1 5 A1			
Canrobert St E2 6 F2			
Canterbury Pl SE17 20 F2			
Capland St NW8 1 A4			
Caradoc Clo W2 7 C1			
Cardigan St SE11 20 D3	Bd.		20p
Cardinal's Wharf SE1 13 A3			
Cardington St NW1 3 A3	Gd.	Ave.	£1 & 20p
Carey St WC2 12 D1	Ave.		£ 1
Carlisle La SE1 12 D5			
20 D1			
Carlisle Pl SW1 18 F1	Ave.		£1 & 20p
Carlos Pl W1 10 E3	Bd.		£ 1
Carlow St NW1 2 F1			
Carlton House Terr SW1 11 A4	Gd.		£1 / P & D
Carlyle Sq SW3 17 A3	Ave.	Ave.	20p
Carlyle's House SW3 17 B4			
Carmelite St EC4 12 E2	Gd.		£1 & 20p
Carnaby St W1 10 F2			
Carnegie St N1 4 D1			
Carol St NW1 2 F1			
Caroline Gdns E2 6 D3			
Caroline Pl W2 8 D2	Bd.	Gd.	£1 & 20p
Caroline Terr SW1 18 D2			
Carriage Dri East SW11 18 D5			
Carriage Dri North SW11 17 C5			
18 D4			
Carriage Dri West SW11 17 C5			
Carroun Rd SW8 20 D5			
Carter La EC4 12 F2			
Cartwright Gdns WC1	Gd.		£1 & 20p
3 B3			
Cartwright St E1 14 E2			
Casson St E1 6 E5			
Castle Baynard St EC4 12 F2			
13 A2			
Castle La SW1 10 F5			
Castletown Rd W14 15 A3			
Cathcart Rd SW10 16 E4	Gd.	Bd.	20p
Cathedral St SE1 13 B3			
Catherine St WC2 11 C2	Ave.		£1 / P & D
Catton St WC1 11 C1	Bd.		£1 & 20p
Causton St SW1 19 B2	Gd.	Bd.	£1 & 20p
Cavendish Ave NW8 1 A2	Ave.	Gd.	£1 & 20p
Cavendish Pl W1 10 E1			
Cavendish Sq W1 10 E1			
Cavendish St N1 5 B2			
Caversham St SW3 17 C4	Bd.	Gd.	20p
Caxton St SW1 11 A5	Gd.		£ 1
Cedarne Rd SW6 16 D5			
Cenotaph SW1 11 B4			
Central Criminal Court EC4 12 F1			
Central Mkt WC2 11 C2			
Central St EC1 5 A3	Gd.	Ave.	£1 & 20p
Chadwell St EC1 4 E3	Gd.		£1 & 20p
Chadwick St SW1 19 A1	Gd.		£1 & 20p
Chagford St NW1 1 C4			
Chaldon Rd SW6 15 A5			
Challoner St W14 15 B3			
Chalton St NW1 3 A2	Gd.	Ave.	£1 & 20p
Chamber St E1 14 E2			
Chambers St SE16 14 F5			
Chambord St E2 6 E3			
Chance St E1 E2 6 D4			
Chancel St SE1 12 F4			
Chancery La WC2 12 D1	Ave.		£1 & 20p
Chandos Pl WC2 11 B3	Bd.		£ 1
Chandos St W1 10 E1	Gd.		£ 1
Chapel Mkt N1 4 E2			
Chapel Side W2 8 D2			
Chapel St NW1 1 B5	Gd.		£1 & 20p/£1/P&D
Chapel St SW1 10 D5			
Chapter Rd SE17 20 F3			
Chapter St SW1 19 A2	Ave.		£1 & 20p
Charing Cross Pier WC2 11 C3			
Charing Cross Rd WC2 11 B1			
Charlbert St NW8 1 A2	Gd.	Bd.	£1 & 20p
Charles La NW8 1 A2			
Charles Sq N1 5 C3			
Charles St W1 10 E3	Ave.		£ 1
Charles II St SW1 11 A3	Gd.		£ 1
Charleville Rd W14 15 A3			
Charlotte Rd EC2 5 C3			
Charlotte St W1 2 F5	Gd.		£1 & 20p
3 A5			
11 A1			
Charlotte Terr N1 4 D1			
Charlton Pl N1 4 F1			
Charlwood Pl SW1 19 A2	Ave.	Gd.	£1 & 20p
Charlwood St SW1 18 F3	Gd.	Gd.	£1 & 20p
Charrington St NW1 3 A2	Gd.	Bd.	£1 & 20p
Chart St N1 5 C3			
Charterhouse Sq EC1 4 F5	Bd.		£1 & 20p
Charterhouse St EC1 4 F5	Gd.	Bd.	£1 & 20p
Cheapside EC2 13 A1			
Chelsea Bridge SW1 18 E4			
Chelsea Bridge Rd SW1 SW8 18 D3			
Chelsea Embankment SW3 17 B4	Bd.	Gd.	20p
Chelsea Manor St SW3 17 B3	Ave.	Bd.	£1 & 20p
Chelsea Old Church SW3 17 A4			
Chelsea Physic Garden SW3 17 C4			
Chelsea Pk Gdns SW3 16 F4	Ave.		20p
Chelsea Royal Hospital SW3 18 D3			
Chelsea Sq SW3 17 A3	Gd.	Bd.	20p
Cheltenham Terr SW3 17 C3	Ave.	Gd.	£1 & 20p
Chenies Ms WC1 3 A4			
Chenies St WC1 3 A5	Gd.		£1 & 20p
Cheniston Gdns W8 16 D1	Ave.	Gd.	£1 & 20p
Chepstow Cres W11 7 C2	Bd.		20p
Chepstow Pl W2 7 C2	Ave.		20p
Chepstow Rd W2 7 C1	Ave.		£1 & 20p
Chepstow Vlls W11 7 C2	Gd.	Bd.	20p
Chequer St EC1 5 B4	Bd.		£1 & 20p
Cherbury St N1 5 C2			
Chesham Pl SW1 18 D1	Bd.		£1 & 20p
Chesham St SW1 18 D1			
Cheshire St E2 6 E4			
Chesson Rd W14 15 B4			
Chester Gate NW1 2 E3			
Chester Ms SW1 10 E5	Bd.		£1 & 20p
Chester Rd NW1 2 D3			
Chester Row SW1 18 D2	Ave.		£1 & 20p
Chester Sq SW1 18 E1	Gd.	Bd.	£1 & 20p
Chester St SW1 10 E5	Gd.	Bd.	£1 & 20p
Chester Terr NW1 2 E3			
Chester Way SE11 20 E2	Bd.		20p
Cheval Pl SW7 17 B1	Bd.		£1 & 20p

Each place name is followed by its postal district its atlas reference, 2 hour meters , 4 hour meters and then by the coins accepted

Street Name		2hrs	4hrs	Coins
Cheyne Gdns SW3	17 B4	Ave.	Ave.	20p
Cheyne Wlk SW3 SW10	17 A5	Ave.	Ave.	20p
Chicheley St SE1	12 D4			
Chichester St SW1	19 A3	Gd.	Gd.	£1 & 20p
Chicksand St E1	6 E5			
Chiltern St W1	2 D5	Bd.		£1
	10 D1			
Chilton St E2	6 E4			
Chilworth Ms W2	8 F1			
Chilworth St W2	8 F2	Ave.		£1 & 20p
Chiswell St EC1	5 B5	Ave.		£1 & 20p
Christ Church Spitalfields E1	6 E5			
Christchurch St SW3	17 C4	Gd.	Ave.	20p
Christian St E1	14 F1			
Christopher St EC2	5 C5	Ave.	Bd.	£1 & 20p
Chryssell Rd SW9	20 E5			
Church St NW8	1 A5	Bd.		£1 & 20p
Churchill Gardens SW1	18 F3			
Churchill Gardens Rd SW1	18 F3			
Churchway NW1	3 A3	Bd.		£1 & 20p
Churchyard Row SE11	20 F2			
Churton St SW1	18 F2	Gd.		£1 & 20p
City Garden Row N1	4 F2	Ave.		£1 & 20p
	5 A2			
City Rd EC1	4 F2	Ave.		£1 & 20p
	5 B3			
City Rd Basin N1	5 A2			
Clabon Ms SW1	17 C1	Ave.		£1 & 20p
Clanricarde Gdns W2	8 D3	Gd.	Bd.	20p
Clapham Rd SW9	20 D5			
Claredale St E2	6 F2			
Claremont Clo N1	4 E2	Bd.		£1 & 20p
Claremont Sq N1	4 E2			
Clarence Gdns NW1	2 F3			
Clarence House SW1	10 F4			
Clarendon Pl W2	9 A2			
Clarendon Rd W11	7 A2	Gd.		20p
Clarendon St SW1	18 F3	Gd.		£1 & 20p
Clareville Gro SW7	16 F2	Bd.		20p
Clareville St SW7	16 F2	Ave.	Gd.	20p
Clarges St W1	10 E3	Gd.		£1
Clarissa St E8	6 D1			
Claverton St SW1	19 A3	Gd.	Gd.	£1 & 20p
Claylands Rd SW8	20 D4			
Clayton St SE11	20 E4			
Cleaver Sq SE11	20 E3			
Cleaver St SE11	20 E3			
Clem Attlee Ct SW6	15 B4			
Clement's La EC4	13 C2			
Cleopatra's Needle WC2	11 C3			
Clere St EC2	5 C4			
Clerkenwell Green EC1	4 E4	Gd.		£1 & 20p
Clerkenwell Rd EC1	4 E5			
Cleveland Gdns W2	8 E2	Gd.	Gd.	£1 & 20p / P & D
Cleveland Sq W2	8 E2	Ave.		£1 & 20p
Cleveland St W1	2 F5	Ave.		£1 & 20p
Cleveland Terr W2	8 F1			
Clifford St W1	10 F2.	Ave.		£1
Clifton St EC2	5 C4			
Clink Exhibition SE1	13 B3			
Clink St EC1	13 B3			
Clipstone St W1	2 F5	Ave.		£1
Cliveden Pl SW1	18 D2			
Cloth Fair EC1	4 F5	Bd.		£1 & 20p
Cloudesley Pl N1	4 E1			
Cloudesley Rd N1	4 E1			
Cloudesley Sq N1	4 E1			
Cloudesley St N1	4 E1			
Club Row E1 E2	6 D4			
Cluny Ms SW5	15 C2			
Coate St E2	6 F2			
Cochrane St NW8	1 A2	Ave.		£1 & 20p
Cock La EC1	12 F1			
Cockspur St SW1	11 B3			
Coin St SE1	12 E3	Bd.	Gd.	20p
Colbeck Ms SW7	16 E2			
Cole St SE1	13 B5	Ave.		£1, 50p & 20p / 20p
Colebrooke Row N1	4 F2	Gd.		£1 & 20p
Coleherne Ct SW5	16 E3			
Coleherne Rd SW10	16 D3	Gd.	Bd.	20p
Coleman Fields N1	5 A1			
Coleman St EC2	13 B1	Gd.		£1 & 20p
Coley St WC1	4 D4	Ave.		£1 & 20p
College Pl NW1	3 A1			
College St EC4	13 B2	Ave.		£1 & 20p
Collier St N1	3 C2	Gd.		£1 & 20p
	4 D2			
Collingham Gdns SW5	16 E2	Ave.	Gd.	20p
Collingham Pl SW5	16 D2	Ave.	Bd.	20p
Collingham Rd SW5	16 E2	Ave.	Ave.	20p
Colnbrook St SE1	20 F1	Ave.	Bd.	£1, 50p & 20p / 20p
Colonnade WC1	3 C4	Bd.		£1 & 20p
Columbia Rd E2	6 D3			
Colville Gdns W11	7 B2	Gd.	Gd.	20p
Colville Ms W11	7 B2			
Colville Rd W11	7 B2	Ave.	Gd.	20p
Colville Terr W11	7 B2	Ave.	Ave.	20p
Comeragh Rd W14	15 A3			
Commercial Rd E1	14 E1			
Commercial St E1	6 D5			
Commonwealth Institute W8	7 C5			
Compton St EC1	4 F4	Gd.		£1 & 20p
Concert Hall Approach SE1	12 D4	Gd.	Bd.	20p
Conduit Ms W2	8 F2			
Conduit St W1	10 F2	Gd.		£1
Connaught Pl W2	9 C2	Gd.		£1 & 20p / P & D
Connaught Sq W2	9 B2	Ave.		£1 & 20p / P & D
Connaught St W2	9 B2	Gd.		£1 & 20p / P & D
Constitution Hill SW1	10 E5			
Cook's Rd SE17	20 F4			
Coomer Pl SW6	15 C4			
Coopers La NW1	3 B2			
Cooper's Row EC3	14 D2	Ave.		£1 & 20p
Cope Pl W8	15 C1	Ave.	Bd.	£1 & 20p
Copenhagen St N1	3 C1			
Copenhagen St N1	4 D1			
Copperfield St SE1	12 F4			
	13 A4			
Copthall Ave EC2	13 B1	Bd.		£1 & 20p
Coptic St WC1	11 B1			
Coral St SE1	12 E5			20p
Coram Foundation WC1	3 C4			
Corams' Fields WC1	3 C4			
Cork St W1	10 F3	Gd.		£1
Cornhill EC3	13 C2			
Cornwall Cres W11	7 A2			20p
Cornwall Gdns SW7	16 E1	Gd.	Bd.	£1 & 20p
Cornwall Rd SE1	12 E4	Gd.	Ave.	20p
Cornwall Terr NW1	1 C4			
Coronet St N1	5 C3			
Corporation Row EC1	4 E4			
Corsham St N1	5 B3			
Cosmo Pl WC1	3 C5			
Cosser St SE1	20 D1	Ave.		20p
Cosway St NW1	1 B5	Bd.		£1 & 20p
Cottage Pl SW3	17 A1			
Cottesmore Gdns W8	16 E1	Bd.		£1 & 20p
Cottington Clo SE11	20 F2			
Cottington St SE11	20 E2			
Coulson St SW3	17 C2	Ave.	Bd.	£1 & 20p
Counter St SE1	13 C4			
County Hall SE1	11 C4			
Courtauld Institute Galleries WC2	12 D2			
Courtenay Sq SE11	20 D3			
Courtfield Gdns SW5	16 E2	Gd.	Bd.	20p
Courtfield Rd SW7	16 E2	Ave.	Bd.	20p
Courtnell St W2	7 C1	Ave.		£1 & 20p
Cousin La EC4	13 B3			
Covent Garden WC2	11 C2			
Coventry St WC1	11 A3			
Cowcross St EC1	4 F5	Gd.	Gd.	£1 & 20p
Cowper St EC2	5 B4	Ave.	Ave.	£1 & 20p
Cramer St W1	2 D5	Bd.		£1
Cranleigh St NW1	3 A2	Ave.		£1 & 20p
Cranley Gdns SW7	16 F3	Gd.	Bd.	20p
Cranley Ms SW7	16 F3			
Cranley Pl SW7	16 F2			

Street Name	2hrs	4hrs	Coins
Cranmer Rd SW9	20 E5		
Cranwood St EC1	5 B3		
Craven Hill W2	8 F2			£1 & 20p
Craven Hill Gdns W2	8 E2	Gd.	Gd.	£1 & 20p
Craven Rd W2	8 F2			
Craven St WC2	11 B3			
Craven Terr W2	8 F2	Ave.		£1 & 20p
Crawford Pas EC1	4 E4			
Crawford Pl W1	9 B1	Ave.		£ 1
Crawford St W1	1 C5	Gd.		£ 1
Creechurch La EC3	14 D1	Ave.		£1 & 20p
Creed St EC4	12 F2			
Cremer St E2	6 D2			
Cremorne Rd SW10	16 F5			
Cresswell Gdns SW5	16 E3	Ave.	Bd.	20p
Cresswell Pl SW10	16 E3	Bd.		20p
Crestfield St WC1	3 C3	Ave.		£1 & 20p
Crewdson Rd SW9	20 D5			
Crimsworth Rd SW8	19 B5			
Crinan St N1	3 C2			
Cringle St SW8	18 F5			
Crispin St E1	6 D5			
Cromer St WC1	3 C3	Gd.		£1 & 20p
Cromwell Cres SW5	15 C2			
Cromwell Gdns SW7	17 A1			
Cromwell Pl SW7	17 A1	Bd.		£1 & 20p
Cromwell Rd SW5	16 D2			
SW7	16 F1			
Crondall St N1	5 C2			
Cropley St N1	5 B2			
Crosby Row SE1	13 B5			
Croston St E8	6 F1			
Crown Office Row EC4	12 E2			
Crowndale Rd NW1	2 F2 / 3 A1			
Crucifix La SE1	13 C4			
Cruden St N1	4 F1			
Crutched Friars EC3	14 D2	Gd.		£1 & 20p
Cubitt St WC1	4 D3			
Culford Gdns SW3	17 C2	Gd.	Bd.	£1 & 20p
Culross St W1	10 D3	Ave.		£ 1
Culworth St NW8	1 B2	Ave.		£1 & 20p
Cumberland Cres W14	15 A2			
Cumberland Gate W1	9 C2			
Cumberland Mkt NW1	2 F3			
Cumberland Place NW1	9 C2			
Cumberland St SW1	18 F3			
Cumberland Terr NW1	2 E2			
Cumberland Terr Ms NW1	2 E2			
Cumming St N1	4 D2			
Cundy St SW1	18 D2			
Cureton St SW1	19 B2			
Curlew St SE1	14 E4			
Cursitor St EC4	12 E1	Ave.		£1 & 20p
Curtain Rd EC2	5 C3			
Curzon St W1	10 D4	Gd.		£ 1
Cut The SE1	12 E4	Gd.	Bd.	20p
Cutlers Gdns E1	14 D1			
Cynthia St N1	4 D2			
Cyrus St EC1	4 F4			
D				
D'Arblay St W1	11 A2			
Dacre St SW1	11 A5			
Dallington St EC1	4 F4			
Dame St N1	5 A2	Bd.		£1 & 20p
Danbury St N1	4 F2			
Dante Rd SE11	20 F2			
Danube St SW3	17 B3			
Danvers St SW3	17 A4	Ave.	Gd.	20p
Dartmouth Clo W11	7 C1			
Dartmouth St SW1	11 A5	Bd.		£ 1
Davidson Gdns SW8	19 B5			
Davies St W1	10 E2	Gd.		£ 1
Dawes Rd SW6	15 A5			
Dawson Pl W2	7 C2			
Dawson St E2	6 E2			
De Beauvoir Cres N1	5 C1			
De Laune St SE17	20 F3			
De Vere Gdns W8	8 E5	Gd.	Bd.	£1 & 20p
Deal St E1	6 5F			

Street Name	2hrs	4hrs	Coins
Dean Ryle St SW1	19 B1			
Dean St W1	11 A1	Gd.		£ 1
Dean's Yd SW1	11 B5			
Dean Trench St SW1	21 B1	Ave.	Gd.	£1 & 20p
Decima St SE1	13 C5	Ave.	Bd.	£1, 50p & 20p / 20p
Delaford St SW6	15 A5			
Delancey St NW1	2 E1			
Delverton Rd SE17	20 F3			
Denbigh Pl SW1	18 F3	Ave.		£1 & 20p
Denbigh Rd W11	7 B2	Ave.	Bd.	20p
Denbigh St SW1	18 F2	Gd.	Bd.	£1 & 20p
Denbigh Terr W11	7 B2	Ave.	Ave.	20p
Denman St W1	11 A2			
Dennis Severs House E1	6 D5			
Denny St SE11	20 E2			
Denyer St SW3	17 B2	Ave.	Gd.	£1 & 20p
Derbyshire St E2	6 F3			
Dereham Pl EC2	6 D4			
Dericote St E8	6 F1			
Derry St W8	8 D5	Gd.		£1 & 20p
Design Centre SW1	11 A3			
Design Museum SE1	14 E4			
Devonshire Clo W1	2 E5			
Devonshire Pl W1	2 D5	Gd.	Gd.	£1 / P & D
Devonshire Sq EC2	14 D1	Gd.		£1 & 20p
Devonshire St W1	2 E5	Gd.	Bd.	£ 1
Devonshire Terr W2	8 F2	Ave.		£1 & 20p
Dewey Rd N1	4 E1			
Dickens House Museum WC1	4 D4			
Dilke St SW3	17 C4	Ave.	Bd.	20p
Dingley Rd EC1	5 A3	Gd.		£1 & 20p
Disbrowe Rd W6	15 A4			
Disney Pl SE1	13 A4			
Diss St E2	6 E2			
Dock St E1	14 E2			
Dockhead SE1	14 E5			
Dr Johnson's House EC4	12 E1			
Doddington Gro SE17	20 F3			
Doddington Pl SE17	20 F4			
Dodson St SE1	12 E5	Gd.		£1, 50p & 20p / 20p
Dolben St SE1	12 F4	Ave.		£1, 50p & 20p / 20p
Dolphin Sq SW1	19 A3			
Dombey St WC1	3 C5	Ave.		£1 & 20p
Dominion St EC2	5 B5	Gd.		£1 & 20p
Donegal St N1	4 D2	Gd.		£1 & 20p
Donne Pl SW3	17 B2			
Doon St SE1	12 E3			
Doric Way NW1	3 A3	Gd.		£1 & 20p
Dorset Rd SW8	19 C5 / 20 D5			
Dorset St NW1	1 C5			
W1	1 C5	Gd.		£1 / P & D
Doughty Ms WC1	4 D4			
Doughty St WC1	4 D4	Gd.		£1 & 20p
Douglas St SW1	19 A2	Ave.	Ave.	£1 & 20p
Douro Pl W8	8 E5			
Dove House St SW3	17 A3	Ave.	Gd.	20p
Dove Row E2	6 F1			
Dover St W1	10 F3	Gd.		£ 1
Down St W1	10 E4	Bd.		£ 1
Downing St SW1	11 B4			
Draycott Ave SW3	17 B2	Gd.	Gd.	£1 & 20p
Draycott Pl SW3	17 C2	Gd.	Gd.	£1 & 20p
Draycott Terr SW3	17 C2	Ave.	Ave.	£1 & 20p
Drayton Gdns SW10	16 F3	Bd.	Gd.	20p
Druid St SE1	14 D4			
Drummond Cres NW1	3 A3	Bd.		£1 & 20p
Drummond Gate SW1	19 B3			
Drummond St NW1	2 F4 / 3 A3	Gd.		£1 & 20p
Drury La WC2	11 C1	Gd.		£1 / £1 & 20p
Drysdale St N1	6 D3			
Duchess of Bedford's Wlk W8	7 C5	Bd.		£1 & 20p
Duchess St W1	2 E5	Gd.		£ 1
Duchy St SE1	12 E3	Ave.		20p
Dufferin St EC1	5 B4	Gd.		£1 & 20p
Duke of Wellington Pl SW1	10 D5			

Each place name is followed by its postal district, its atlas reference, 2 hour meters, 4 hour meters and then by the coins accepted

Street Name		2hrs	4hrs	Coins
Duke of York St SW1	11 A3			
Duke St SW1	10 F3	Ave		£ 1
Duke St W1	10 D2	Gd.		£ 1
Duke St Hill SE1	13 B3			
Duke's La W8	8 D4			
Duke's Rd WC1	3 B3	Ave.		£1 & 20p
Duke's Pl EC3	14 D1			
Dunbridge St E2	6 F4			
Duncan Rd E8	6 F1			
Duncan St N1	4 F2	Bd.		£1 & 20p
Duncan Terr N1	4 F2	Gd.		£1 & 20p
Dunloe St E2	6 E2			
Dunraven St W1	9 C2	Gd.		£ 1
Dunston Rd E8	6 D1			
Dunston St E8	6 D1			
Durant St E2	6 F2			
Durham St SE11	20 D3			
Durham Terr W2	8 D1	Bd.		£1 & 20p
Durward St E1	6 F5			
Dyott St WC1	11 B1	Ave.		£1 & 20p
E				
Eagle Ct EC1	4 F5			
Eagle St WC1	11 C1	Ave.		£1 & 20p
Eagle Wharf Rd N1	5 A2			
Eamont St NW8	1 B2	Gd.		£1 & 20p / P &D
Eardley Cres SW5	16D1	Ave.	Gd.	20p
Earl St EC2	5 C5			
Earlham St WC2	11 B2	Gd.		£1 & 20p
Earl's Court Exhibition				
Earl's Court Gdns SW5	16 D2	Ave.	Gd.	20p
Earl's Court Rd SW5	16 D2			
W8	15 C1	Ave.		£1 & 20p
Earl's Court Sq SW5	16 D3	Gd.	Gd.	20p
Earl's Terr W8	15 B1			
Earl's Wlk W8	15 C1			
Earsby St W14	15 A2			
East Pier E1	14 F4			
East Rd N1	5 B3			
East Smithfield E1	14 E3			
East Tenter St E1	14 E2			
Eastbourne Ms W2	8 F1			
Eastbourne Terr W2	8 F1	Gd.	Bd.	£1 & 20p / P & D
Eastcastle St W1	10 F1			
	11 A1	Gd.		£ 1
Eastcheap EC3	13 C2	Gd.		£1 & 20p
Eaton Gate SW1	18 D2			
Eaton La SW1	18 E1	Ave.	Gd.	£1 & 20p
Eaton Ms SW1	18 D1			
	18 E1			
Eaton Ms North SW1	18 D1			
Eaton Ms West SW1	18 D2			
Eaton Pl SW1	18 D1	Bd.		£1 & 20p
Eaton Sq SW1	18 D1	Gd.	Bd.	£1 & 20p / P & D
Eaton Terr SW1	18 D2	Gd.		£1 & 20p
Ebbisham Dri SW8	20 D4			
Ebor St E1	6 D4			
Ebury Bridge SW1	18 E2	Gd.		£1 & 20p
Ebury Bridge Rd SW1	18 E3			
Ebury Ms SW1	18 E1			
Ebury Sq SW1	18 E2	Gd.	Bd.	£1 & 20p / P & D
Ebury St SW1	18 E2	Gd.	Bd.	£1 & 20p
Eccleston Bridge SW1	18 E2			
Eccleston Ms SW1	18 D1			
Eccleston Pl SW1	18 E2	Gd.		£1 & 20p / P & D
Eccleston Sq SW1	18 F2	Gd.	Bd.	£1 & 20p / P & D
Eccleston St SW1	18 E1	Gd.		£1 & 20p
Edge St W8	7 C4	Gd.	Bd.	20p
Edgware Rd W2	1 A5			
	9 B1			
Edith Gro SW10	16 E4	Ave.		20p
Edith Rd W14	15 A2			
Edith Terr SW10	16 E5			
Edith Vlls W14	15 B2			
Edwardes Sq W8	15 C1	Gd.	Gd.	20p
Effie Rd SW6	15 C5			
Egerton Cres SW3	17 B1	Ave.	Ave.	£1 & 20p
Egerton Gdns SW3	17 B1	Gd.	Bd.	£1 & 20p
Egerton Pl SW3	17 B1	Ave.	Ave.	£1 & 20p
Egerton Terr SW3	17 B1	Gd.	Gd.	£1 & 20p
Elcho St SW11	17 B5			
Elder St E1	6 D5			
Eldon Rd W8	16 E1	Bd.		£1 & 20p
Eldon St EC2	5 C5			
Elgin Cres W11	7 A2	Gd.		20p
Elia St N1	4 F2	Bd.		£1 & 20p
Elizabeth Bridge SW1	18 E2			
Elizabeth St SW1	18 E2	Gd.	Bd.	£1 & 20p
Ellen St E1	14 F2			
Elliott's Row SE11	20 F1	Bd.		£1, 50p & 20p / 20p
Elm Pk Gdns SW10	16 F3	Gd.	Ave.	20p
	17 A3			
Elm Pk Rd SW3	16 F4	Ave.	Bd.	20p
	17 A3			
Elm Pl SW7	16 F3	Ave.		20p
Elm St WC1	4 D4	Ave.		£1 & 20p
Elsham Rd W14	7 A5	Gd.	Gd.	20p
Elvaston Pl SW7	16 E1	Gd.	Bd.	£1 & 20p
Elverton St SW1	19 A1	Ave.	Gd.	£1 & 20p
Elwin St E2	6 E3			
Elystan Pl SW3	17 B2	Ave.	Ave.	£1 & 20p
Elystan St SW3	17 B2	Gd.	Bd.	£1 & 20p
Emba St SE16	14 F5			
Embankment Gdns SW3	17 C4	Ave.	Gd.	20p
Emerald St WC1	4 D5	Ave.		£1 & 20p
Emerson St SE1	13 A3	Gd.	Gd.	£1, 50p & 20p / P
Emma St E2	6 F2			
Emperor's Gate SW7	16 E1	Gd.		£1 & 20p
Endell St WC2	11 B1	Gd.		£1 & 20p
Endsleigh Gdns WC1	3 A4	Gd.		£1 & 20p
Endsleigh St WC1	3 A4	Gd.		£1 & 20p
Enford St W1	1 B5			
English Grounds SE1	13 C4			
Enid St SE16	14 E5			
Ennismore Gdns SW7	9 A5	Gd.		£ 1
Ennismore Gdns Ms SW7	9 A5			
Ensign St E1	14 F2			
Epirus Rd SW6	15 C5			
Epworth St EC2	5 C4	Ave.	Bd.	£1 & 20p
Erasmus St SW1	19 B2			
Errol St EC1	5 B4	Ave.	Gd.	£1 & 20p
Essex Rd N1	4 F1			
Essex St WC2	12 D2	Gd.		£1
Essex Vlls W8	7 C5	Ave.	Bd.	£1 & 20p
Estcourt Rd SW6	15 B5			
Esterbrooke St SW1	19 A2	Bd.		£1 & 20p
Eustace Rd SW6	15 C5			
Euston Rd NW1	2 F4			
	3 A4			
Euston Sq NW1	3 A3			
Euston St NW1	3 A4	Ave.		£1 & 20p
Evelyn Gdns SW7	16 F3	Gd.	Gd.	20p
Evelyn Wlk N1	5 B2			
Eversholt St NW1	2 F2			
Eversholt St NW1	3 A3			
Ewer St SE1	13 A4	Ave.		£1, 50p & 20p / 20p
Exeter St WC2	11 C2	Bd.		£ 1
Exhibition Rd SW7	9 A5	Gd.	Bd.	£1 & 20p / £1 / P & D
	17 A1			
Exton St SE1	12 E4			
Eyre St Hill EC1	4 E4			
Ezra St E2	6 E3			
F				
Fabian Rd SW6	15 B5			
Fair St SE1	14 D4			
Fairclough St E1	14 F1			
Fairholme Rd W14	15 A3			
Fakruddin St E1	6 F4			
Falkirk St N1	6 D2			
Fane St W14	15 B4			
Fann St EC1	5 A5	Ave.		£1 & 20p
Fanshaw St N1	5 C3			
Faraday Museum W1	10 F3			
Farm La SW6	15 C5			
Farm St W1	10 E3	Ave.		£ 1
Farmer's Rd SE5	20 F5			
Farncombe St SE16	14 F5			
Farnham Royal SE11	20 D3			
Farringdon La EC1	4 E4	Gd.	Bd.	£1 & 20p
Farringdon Rd EC1	4 E4	Ave.	Gd.	£1 & 20p
Farringdon St EC4	12 F1	Gd.		£1 & 20p
Fashion St E1	6 E5			
Faunce St SE17	20 F3			

Street Name		2hrs	4hrs	Coins
Fawcett St SW10	16 E4	Ave.	Bd.	20p
Featherstone St EC1	5 B4	Ave.		£1 & 20p
Felton St N1	5 B1			
Fenchurch Ave EC3	13 C2			
Fenchurch Bldgs EC3	14 D2			
Fenchurch St EC3	13 C2			
	14 D2			
Fentiman Rd SW8	19 C4			
	20 D5			
Fernshaw Rd SW10	16 E4	Ave.		20p
Festival/South Bank Pier SE1	12 D3			
Fetter La EC4	12 E1	Ave.		£1 & 20p
Field Rd W6	15 A4			
Fieldgate St E1	14 F1			
Filmer Rd SW6	15 B5			
Finborough Rd SW10	16 E4	Gd.	Ave.	20p
Finsbury Circus EC2	5 B5	Gd.		£1 & 20p
	13 B1			
Finsbury Mkt EC2	5 C5			
Finsbury Pavement EC2	5 B5			
Finsbury Sq EC2	5 B5	Gd.		£1 & 20p
Finsbury St EC2	5 B5	Gd.		£1 & 20p
First St SW3	17 B1	Ave.	Gd.	£1 & 20p
Fisherton St NW8	1 A4			
Fishmongers' Hall EC3	13 B2			
Fitzalan St SE11	20 D2			
Fitzgeorge Ave W14	15 A2			
Fitzjames Ave W14	15 A2			
Fitzroy Sq W1	2 F4			
Fitzroy St W1	2 F5	Ave.		£1 & 20p
Flaxman Terr WC1	3 B3	Ave.		£1 & 20p
Fleet St EC4	12 E1			
Fleming Rd SE17	20 F4			
Fleur de Lis St E1	6 D5			
Flitcroft St WC2	11 B1	Bd.		£1 & 20p
Flood St SW3	17 B3	Gd.	Bd.	20p
Flood Wlk SW3	17 B3	Ave.	Ave.	£1 & 20p
Floral St WC2	11 C2	Bd.		£ 1
Florence Nightingale Museum SE1	12 D5			
Florida St E2	6 F3			
Flower Wlk The SW7	8 F5			
Foley St W1	2 F5	Gd.		£ 1
Folgate St E1	6 D5			
Forbes St E1	14 F2			
Fordham St E1	14 F1			
Fore St EC2	5 B5	Gd.		£1 & 20p
Foreign & Commonwealth Office SW1	11 B4			
Forset St W1	9 B1			
Forston St N1	5 B2			
Forsyth Gdns SE17	20 F4			
Fortune St EC1	5 A4	Bd.	Gd.	£1 & 20p
Foster La EC2	13 A1	Bd.		£1 & 20p
Foubert's Pl W1	10 F2			
Foulis Terr SW7	17 A2	Gd.	Bd.	£1 & 20p
Fount St SW8	19 B5			
Fountains The W2	8 F3			
Fournier St E1	6 E5			
Foxley Rd SW9	20 E5			
Frampton St NW8	1 A4	Gd.	Gd.	£1 & 20p / P & D
Francis St SW1	18 F1	Gd.		£1 & 20p
	19 A1			
Franklins Row SW3	17 C3	Gd.	Ave.	£1 & 20p
Frazier St SE1	12 E5			
Frederick St WC1	4 D3	Ave.		£1 & 20p
Friend St EC1	4 F3	Bd.		£1 & 20p
Frith St W1	11 A2	Gd.		£ 1
Frome St N1	5 A2			
Fulham Broadway SW6	15 C5			
Fulham Rd SW6	15 C5	Gd.	Bd.	£1 & 20p / 20p
Fulham Rd SW10	16 F4			
Fulham Rd SW3	17 A2			
Fulwood Pl WC1	4 D5			
Furnival St EC4	12 E1	Ave.		£1 & 20p
G				
Gabriel's Wharf SE1	12 E3			
Gainsford St SE1	14 D4			
Galway St EC1	5 A3			
Gambia St SE1	12 F4	Gd.		£1, 50p & 20p / 20p
Ganton St W1	10 F2			
Garden History Museum of SE1	19 C1			
Garden Ms W2	9 A2			
Garden Row SE1	20 F1	Bd.		£1, 50p & 20p / 20p
Garden Wlk EC2	5 C4			
Gardners La EC4	13 A2			
Garlick Hill EC4	13 A2			
Garrett St EC1	5 A4	Bd.	Gd.	£1 & 20p
Garrick St WC2	11 B2	Ave.		£ 1
Garway Rd W2	8 D2	Ave.		£1 & 20p
Gascoigne Pl E2	6 D3			
Gasholder Pl SE11	20 D3			
Gaskin St N1	4 F1			
Gatliff Rd SW1	18 E3			
Gayfere St SW1	19 B1			
Gaza St SE17	20 F3			
Gee St EC1	5 A4	Ave.		£1 & 20p
Geffrye Museum E2	6 D2			
Geffrye St E2	6 D2			
George Row SE16	14 E5			
George St W1	10 D1	Gd.		£1 / P & D
Gerald Rd SW1	18 D2			
Geraldine Mary Harmsworth Park SE11	20 E1			
Geraldine St SE11	20 F1			
Gerrard Pl WC2	11 B2			
Gerrard Rd N1	4 F2	Ave.		£1 & 20p
Gerrard St W1	11 A2			
Gerridge St SE1	12 E5	Ave.		£1, 50p & 20p / 20p
Gertrude St SW10	16 F4			
Gibbs Grn W14	15 B3			
Gibson Rd SE11	20 D2			
Gibson Sq N1	4 E1			
Gilbert Rd SE11	20 E2			
Gilbert St W1	10 D2	Ave.		£ 1
Gillingham St SW1	18 F2	Gd.	Bd.	£1 & 20p
Gilston Rd SW10	16 F3	Gd.	Ave.	20p
Giltspur St EC1	12 F1			
Gladstone St SE1	20 F1	Bd.		£1, 50p & 20p / 20p
Glasgow Terr SW1	18 F3			
Glasshill St SE1	12 F4	Gd.	Gd.	£1, 50p & 20p / 20p
Glasshouse St W1	11 A3	Ave.		£ 1
Glasshouse Wlk SE11	19 C3			
Glaz'bury Rd W14	15 A2			
Glebe Pl SW3	17 B4	Gd.	Bd.	20p
Gledhow Gdns SW5	16 E2	Ave.	Ave.	20p
Gledstanes Rd W14	15 A3			
Glentworth St NW1	1 C4	Gd.		£1 & 20p
Gliddon Rd W14	15 A2			
Globe St SE1	13 B5	Bd.		£1, 50p & 20p / 20p
Gloucester Ave NW1	2 D1			
Gloucester Cres NW1	2 E1			
Gloucester Gate NW1	2 E2			
Gloucester Ms W2	8 F2			
Gloucester Ms West W2	8 E1			
Gloucester Pl NW1	1 C4	Gd.		£1/£1&20p
Gloucester Pl W1	9 C1			
Gloucester Pl Ms W1	9 C1			
Gloucester Rd SW7	16 E1	Gd.	Bd.	£1 & 20p
Gloucester Sq W2	9 A2	Ave.		£1 & 20p
Gloucester St SW1	18 F3	Ave.	Gd.	£1 & 20p
Gloucester Terr W2	8 E1	Gd.	Bd.	£1 & 20p / P & D
Gloucester Way EC1	4 E3	Gd.	Gd.	£1 & 20p / 20p
Gloucester Wlk W8	7 C4			
Godfrey St SW3	17 B3	Bd.	Gd.	£1 & 20p
Goding St SE11	19 C3			
Godson St N1	4 E2			
Golden La EC1	5 A4	Gd.		£1 & 20p
Golden Sq W1	10 F2	Gd.		£ 1
	11 A2			
Goldington Cres NW1	3 A1	Gd.		£1 & 20p
Goldington St NW1	3 A2	Ave.	Bd.	£1 & 20p
Goldsmith's Row E2	6 F2			
Goldsmith's Sq E2	6 F2			
Goodge Pl W1	3 A5	Ave.		£1 & 20p
Goodge St W1	3 A5			
Goodmans Yd E1	14 E2			
Goods Way NW1	3 B2	Gd.	Gd.	£1 & 20p
Gopsall St N1	5 B1			
Gordon Sq WC1	3 A4	Gd.		£1 & 20p
Gordon St WC1	3 A4	Gd.		£1 & 20p
Gorleston St W14	15 A2			
Gorsuch St E2	6 D2			

Each place name is followed by its postal district, its atlas reference, 2 hour meters, 4 hour meters and then by the coins accepted

Street Name		2hrs	4hrs	Coins
Harrington Gdns SW7	16 E2	Gd.	Ave.	20p
Harrington Rd SW7	16 F2	Ave.	Bd.	£1 & 20p
	17 A2			
Harrington Sq NW1	2 F2			
Harrington St NW1	2 F3			
Harrison St WC1	3 C3	Gd.		£1 & 20p
Harrow Rd W2	1 A5	Bd.		£1 & 20p
Harrowby St W1	9 B1	Gd.		£1
Hart St EC3	14 D2			
Hartington Rd SW8	19 B5			
Hartismere Rd SW6	15 B5			
Harvey St N1	5 C1			
Harwood Rd SW6	16 D5			
Hasker St SW3	17 B1	Ave.	Ave.	£1 & 20p
Hastings St WC1	3 B3	Gd.		£1 & 20p
Hatfields SE1	12 E3	Gd.	Bd.	£1, 50p & 20p / 20p
Hatton Pl EC1	4 E5			
Havelock St N1	3 C1			
Hay Hill W1	10 F3			
Hay St E2	6 F1			
Haydon St EC3	14 D2			
Hayles St SE11	20 F1	Bd.		£1, 50p & 20p / 20p
Haymarket SW1	11 A3			
Hay's Galleria SE1	13 C3			
Hay's La SE1	13 C3			
Hay's Ms W1	10 E3	Ave.		£1
Hayward Gallery SE1	12 D3			
Hazlitt Rd W14	15 A1			
Headfort Pl SW1	10 D5			
Hearn St EC2	5 C4			
Heathcote St WC1	3 C4	Ave.		£1 & 20p
Heddon St W1	10 F2			
Helmet Row EC1	5 A4			
Hemans St SW8	19 B5			
Hemingford Rd N1	4 D1			
Hemming St E1	6 F4			
Hemsworth St N1	5 C2			
Heneage St E1	6 E5			
Henrietta Pl W1	10 E1	Ave.		£1
Henrietta St WC2	11 C2	Gd.		£1
Henriques St E1	14 F1			
Herbal Hill EC1	4 E5			
Herbert Cres SW1	17 C1	Bd.	Gd.	£1 & 20p
Herbrand St WC1	3 B4	Gd.		£1 & 20p
Hercules Rd SE1	12 D5	Gd.		20p
Hercules Rd SE1	20 D1			
Hereford Rd W2	7 C1	Gd.	Bd.	£1 & 20p
	8 D2			
Hereford St E2	6 F4			
Hermit St EC1	4 F3			
Herrick St SW1	19 B2	Gd.		£1 & 20p / P & D
Hertford St W1	10 E4	Gd.		£1
Hesper Ms SW5	16 D2	Bd.		20p
Hessel St E1	14 F1			
Hester Rd SW11	17 B5			
Hewett St EC2	6 D4			
Heyford Ave SW8	19 C5			
Hide Pl SW1	19 A2	Ave.		£1 & 20p
High Holborn WC1	4 D5	Bd.		£1 & 20p
	11 B1			
	12 D1			
High Timber St EC4	13 A2	Ave.		£1 & 20p
Highway The E1	14 F2			
Hilary Clo SW6	16 D5			
Hill St W1	10 E3	Gd.		£1
Hillgate Pl W8	7 C3			
Hillgate St W8	7 C3	Gd.	Bd.	20p
Hillingdon St SE5	20 F5			
Hillsleigh Rd W8	7 B4			
Hindmarsh Clo E1	14 F2			
HMS Belfast SE1	14 D3			
Hobart Pl SW1	18 E1			
Hobury St SW10	16 F4	Ave.	Gd.	20p
Hogarth Rd SW5	16 D2	Gd.	Gd.	20p
Holbein Pl SW1	18 D2	Gd.		£1 & 20p / P & D
Holborn EC1	12 E1	Bd.		£1 & 20p
Holborn Circus E4	12 E1			
Holburn Viaduct EC1	12 F1			
Holford St WC1	4 D3			
Holland Gdns W14	15 A1	Bd.	Gd.	20p
Holland Gro SW9	20 E5			
Holland House W8	7 B5			
Holland Park W8	7 B4	Gd.	Bd.	20p
Holland Pk W11	7 A4			
Holland Pk Ave W11	7 A4			
Holland Pk Gdns W14	7 A4	Ave.		20p
Holland Pk Ms W11	7 B4			
Holland Pk Rd W14	15 B1	Ave.	Ave.	20p
Holland Rd W14	7 A5	Ave.	Ave.	20p
	15 A1			
Holland St SE1	12 F3	Ave.	Gd.	£1, 50p & 20p / 20p
Holland St W8	8 D5	Ave.		£1 & 20p
Holland Vlls Rd W14	7 A5	Ave.	Gd.	20p
Holland Wlk W8	7 B4			
Holles St W1	10 E1			
Hollywood Rd SW10	16 E4	Gd.	Bd.	20p
Holmead Rd SW6	16 E5			
Holwell La EC2	6 D4			
Holyoak Rd SE11	20 F2			
Holyrood St SE1	13 C4			
Homer Row W1	9 B1			
Homestead Rd SW6	15 B5			
Hooper St E1	14 E2			
Hop Exchange EC1	13 B4			
Hopetown St E1	6 E5			
Hopton St SE1	12 F3	Gd.	Bd.	£1, 50p & 20p / 20p
Horatio St E2	6 E2			
Horbury Cres W11	7 C3			
Hornton St W8	8 D5			
Horse Guards SW1	11 B4			
Horse Guards Rd SW1	11 B4			
Horseferry Rd SW1	19 B1	Gd.	Bd.	£1 & 20p
Horseguards Ave SW1	11 B4			
Hortensia Rd SW10	16 E5	Ave.	Bd.	20p
Hosier La EC1	12 F1	Gd.		£1 & 20p
Houghton St WC2	12 D2	Bd.		£1
Houndsditch EC3	14 D1	Gd.		£1 & 20p
Houses of Parliament SW1	11 C5			
Howick Pl SW1	19 A1	Gd.		£1 & 20p / P & D
Howie St SW11	17 B5			
Howland St W1	2 F5			
Hows St E2	6 D2			
Hoxton Sq N1	5 C3			
Hoxton St N1	5 C1			
Hugh St SW1	18 E2	Ave.		£1 & 20p
Humbolt Rd W6	15 A4			
Hungerford Foot Bridge SE1	11 C3			
Hunter St WC1	3 C4			
Huntley St WC1	3 A4	Gd.		£1 & 20p
Hunton St E1	6 E5			
Hyde Park W2	9 B3			
Hyde Pk Corner W1	10 D4			
Hyde Pk Cres W2	9 A1	Gd.	Bd.	£1 & 20p
Hyde Pk Gate SW7	8 E5	Bd.		£1 & 20p
Hyde Pk Gdns W2	9 A2	Ave.	Gd.	£1 & 20p
Hyde Pk Sq W2	9 A2	Gd.	Gd.	£1 & 20p / P & D
Hyde Pk St W2	9 B2	Gd.		£1 & 20p
Hyde Rd N1	5 C1			
I				
Ifield Rd SW10	16 E4	Gd.	Ave.	20p
Ilchester Gdns W2	8 D2	Bd.		£1 & 20p
Ilchester Pl W14	7 B5	Ave.	Ave.	20p
Imperial College Rd SW7	16 F1			
Imperial War Museum SE11	20 E1			
Inglebert St EC1	4 E3	Ave.	Ave.	£1 & 20p
Inner Circle NW1	2 D3			
Inner Temple Gdns EC4	12 E2			
Institute of Contemporary Arts SW1	11 B3			
Instruments Museum of SW7	8 F5			
Inverness Ms W2	8 E2			
Inverness Pl W2	8 E2	Bd.		£1 & 20p
Inverness Terr W2	8 E2	Gd.	Gd.	£1 & 20p / P & D
Ironmonger La EC2	13 B1			
Ironmonger Row EC1	5 A3	Gd.	Bd.	20p
Islington Grn Gdns N1	4 F1			
Islington High St N1	4 E2			
Iverna Ct W8	8 D5	Ave.	Bd.	£1 & 20p
Iverna Gdns W8	16 D1	Gd.		£1 & 20p

Each place name is followed by its postal district, its atlas reference, 2 hour meters, 4 hour meters and then by the coins accepted

Street Name	2hrs	4hrs	Coins
Ives St SW3	17 B2			
Ivor Pl NW1	1 B4	Gd.	Bd.	£1 & 20p
Ivy St N1	5 C2			
Ixworth Pl SW3	17 B2	Gd.	Bd.	£1 & 20p
J				
Jackman St E8	6 F1			
Jacob St SE1	14 E5			
Jamaica Rd SE1	14 E5			
Jamaica Rd SE16	14 F5			
James St W1	10 D1	Ave.		£1
James St WC2	11 C2			
Jameson St W8	7 C3			
Jamme Masjid E1	6 E5			
Janeway St SE16	14 F5			
Jay Ms SW7	8 F5			
Jermyn St SW1	12 F3			
	11 A3	Gd.		£1
Jewel Tower SW1	11 B5			
Jewish Museum WC1	3 B4			
Jewry St EC3	14 D2	Gd.		£1 & 20p
Joan St SE1	12 F4	Ave.		£1, 50p & 20p / 20p
Jockey's Fields WC1	4 D5	Ave.		£1 & 20p
John Adam St WC2	11 C3	Gd.		£1
John Carpenter St EC4	12 E2	Gd.		£1 & 20p
John Fisher St E1	14 E2			
John Islip St SW1	19 B2	Gd.	Gd.	£1 & 20p
John Ruskin St SE5	20 F5			
John's Ms WC1	4 D5	Bd.		£1 & 20p
John's St WC1	4 D5			
Johnson's Pl SW1	18 F3			
Jonathan St SE11	20 D2			
Jubilee Gardens SE1	12 D4			
Jubilee Pl SW3	17 B3	Ave.		£1 & 20p
Judd St WC1	3 B3			
Juer St SW11	17 B5			
Juxon St SE11	20 D1			
K				
Kathleen & May SE1	13 B4			
Kay St E2	6 F2			
Kean St WC2	11 C2	Gd.		£1
Keeton's Rd SE16	14 F5			
Kelsey St E2	6 F4			
Kelso Pl W8	16 D1			
Kemble St WC2	11 C2	Gd.		£1 / £1 & 20p
Kempsford Gdns SW5	16 D3	Ave.	Gd.	20p
Kempsford Rd SE11	20 E2	Bd.		20p
Kenchester Clo SW8	19 C5			
Kendal Clo SW9	20 F5			
Kendal St W2	9 B2	Gd.		£1 & 20p / P & D
Kenley Wlk W11	7 A3			
Kennet St E1	14 F3			
Kennington Gro SE11	20 D4			
Kennington La SE11	20 D3			
Kennington Oval SE11	20 D4			
Kennington Park SE11	20 E4			
Kennington Pk Gdns SE11	20 F4			
Kennington Pk Rd SE11	20 E4			
Kennington Rd SE1	20 E1			
Kensington Church St W8	8 D4	Ave.		20p
Kensington Ct Pl W8	8 E5			
Kensington Ct W8	8 E5	Gd.	Bd.	£1 & 20p
Kensington Gardens W2	8 E4	Gd.	Bd.	£1 & 20p / P & D
Kensington Gdns Sq W2	8 D2			
Kensington Gate W8	8 E5	Gd.		£1 & 20p
Kensington Gore SW7	8 F5	Gd.	Gd.	£1 / P & D
Kensington High St W8	7 C5			
	8 D5			
Kensington High St W14	15 B1			
Kensington Palace				
W8	8 D4			
Kensington Palace Gdns W8	8 D3			
Kensington Pk Gdns W11	7 B3	Gd.		20p
Kensington Pk Rd W11	7 B2	Gd.	Gd.	20p
Kensington Pl W8	7 C4	Ave.		20p
Kensington Rd W7 W8	8 E5			
Kensington Rd SW7	9 A5			
Kensington Sq W8	8 D5	Bd.	Gd.	£1 & 20p
Kent Pas NW1	1 B4			
Kent St E2	6 E2			
Kentish Bldgs SE1	13 B4			
Kenton St WC1	3 B4			
Kenway Rd SW5	16 D2	Gd.	Gd.	20p
Keyworth St SE1	12 F5	Gd.	Bd.	£1, 50p & 20p / 20p
Kildare Gdns W2	8 D1			
Kildare Terr W2	8 D1	Bd.		£1 & 20p
Killick St N1	3 C2	Gd.		£1 & 20p
King St EC2	13 B1			
King St SW1	10 F4			
	11 A3			
King St WC2	11 B2	Gd.		£1 / P & D
King Charles St SW1	11 B5			
King Edward St EC1	13 A1			
King Edward Wlk SE1	20 E1	Bd.	Gd.	20p
King James St SE1	12 F5	Ave.		£1, 50p & 20p / 20p
King William St EC4	13 B2			
Kingly St W1	10 F2			
King's Bench Wlk EC4	12 E2			
King's Head Yd SE1	13 B4			
Kings Rd SW3	17 A4	Gd.	Bd.	£1 & 20p / 20p
King's Rd SW6 SW10	16 E5			
King's Scholars Pas SW1	18 F1			
King's Terr NW1	2 F1			
King's Cross Rd WC1	3 C2			
	4 D3			
Kingsland Basin N1	6 D1			
Kingsland Rd E2	6 D1			
Kingsmill Ter NW8	1 A2			
Kingstown St NW1	2 D1			
Kingsway WC2	11 C1			
Kinnerton St SW1	9 C5	Bd.		£1 & 20p
Kinnoul Rd W6	15 A4			
Kipling St SE1	13 C5			
Kirby Gro SE1	13 C4			
Kirby St EC1	4 E5	Bd.		£1 & 20p
Kirtling St SW8	18 F4			
Kirton Gdns E2	6 E3			
Knaresborough Pl SW5	16 D2	Ave.	Ave.	20p
Knighten St E1	14 F4			
Knightrider St EC4	12 F2			
Knightsbridge SW1	10 D5			
Knivet Rd SW6	15 C4			
Knox St W1	1 C5	Bd.		£1
Kynance Pl SW7	16 E1	Ave.	Bd.	£1 & 20p
L				
Laburnum St E2	6 D1			
Lackington St EC2	5 B5	Bd.		£1 & 20p
Ladbroke Cres W11	7 A1			
Ladbroke Gdns W11	7 B2	Bd.		20p
Ladbroke Gro W11	7 A1	Gd.	Ave.	20p
Ladbroke Rd W11	7 B3	Gd.	Bd.	20p
Ladbroke Sq W1	17 B3	Gd.	Ave.	20p
Ladbroke Terr W11	7 B3	Bd.		20p
Ladbroke Wlk W11	7 B3			
Lafone St SE1	14 D4			
Lamb St E1	6 D5			
Lamb Wlk SE1	13 C5			
Lamb's Conduit St WC1	3 C4			
Lamb's Pas EC1	5 B5			
Lambeth Bridge SE1	19 C1			
Lambeth High St SE1	19 C2	Gd.		20p
Lambeth Palace Rd SE1	12 D5			
	19 C1			

Street Name		2hrs	4hrs	Coins
Lambeth Palace SE1	19 C1			
Lambeth Rd SE1	20 D1	Gd.	Gd.	£1, 50p & 20p / 20p
Lambeth Wlk SE11	20 D1	Gd.		20p
Lamlash St SE11	20 F1			
Lamont Rd SW10	16 F4			
Lancaster Ct SW6	15 C5			
Lancaster Gate W2	8 F2	Gd.	Gd.	£1 & 20p / P & D
Lancaster House SW1	10 F4			
Lancaster Ms W2	8 F2	Bd.		£1 & 20p
Lancaster Pl WC2	11 C2			
Lancaster Rd W11	7 A1	Gd.	Bd.	20p
Lancaster St SE1	12 F5	Ave.		£1, 50p & 20p / 20p
Lancaster Terr W2	8 F2			
Lancaster Wlk W2	8 F3			
Lancelot Pl SW7	9 B5	Ave.		£ 1
Langham Hilton Hotel W1	10 E1			
Langham Pl W1	10 E1			
Langham St W1	10 F1	Gd.		£ 1
Langley La SW8	19 C4			
Langley St WC2	11 B2			
Langton Rd SW9	20 F5			
Langton St SW10	16 F4	Gd.	Bd.	20p
Lansdowne Cres W11	7 A3	Ave.		20p
Lansdowne Rd W11	7 A2	Gd.	Bd.	20p
Lansdowne Rise W11	7 A3	Gd.	Bd.	20p
Lansdowne Terr WC1	3 C4			
Lansdowne Wlk W11	7 B3	Gd.	Gd.	20p
Lant St SE1	13 A5			
Launceston Pl W8	16 E1	Gd.	Ave.	£1 & 20p
Laundry Rd W6	15 A4			
Laurence Poutney La EC4	13 B2			
Laverton Pl SW5	16 D2			
Lavington St SE1	12 F4	Gd.	Ave.	£1, 50p & 20p / 20p
Lawn La SW8	19 C4			
Lawrence St SW3	17 A4	Gd.	Ave.	20p
Laystall St EC1	4 D4	Bd.		£1 & 20p
Leadenhall Mkt EC3	13 C2			
Leadenhall St EC3	13 C2			
	14 D2			
Leake St SE1	14 D4			
Leamington Rd Vlls W11	7 B1	Ave.	Gd.	£1 & 20p
Leather La EC1	4 E5			
Leathermarket St SE1	13 C5			
Ledbury Rd W11	7 C2	Gd.	Bd.	20p / £1 & 20p
Leeke St WC1	3 C3			
Lees Pl W1	10 D2	Ave.		£ 1
Leicester Pl WC2	11 B2			
Leicester Sq WC2	11 B3			
Leicester St WC2	11 A2			
Leigh St WC1	3 B4	Ave.		£1 & 20p
Leighton House W14	15 B1			
Leinster Gdns W2	8 E2	Gd.	Gd.	£1 & 20p
Leinster Pl W2	8 E2			
Leinster Sq W2	8 D2	Gd.	Ave.	£1 & 20p / P & D
Leinster Terr W2	8 E2	Gd.		£1 & 20p
Leman St E1	14 E1			
Lennox Gdns Ms SW1	17 B1			
Lennox Gdns SW1	17 C1	Gd.	Bd.	£1 & 20p / P & D
Leonard St EC2	5 C4	Ave.	Bd.	£1 & 20p
Letterstone Rd SW6	15 B5			
Lever St EC1	5 A3	Gd.	Bd.	£1 & 20p
Lexham Gdns W8	16 D1	Gd.	Bd.	£1 & 20p
Lexington St W1	11 A2			
Leyden St E1	14 D1			
Library St SE1	12 F5	Ave.		£1, 50p & 20p / 20p
Lidlington Pl NW1	2 F2			
Lilestone St NW8	1 B4			
Lillie Rd SW6	15 A5			
Lime St EC3	13 C2	Bd.		£1 & 20p
Limerston St SW10	16 F4	Gd.	Gd.	20p
Lincoln's Inn Fields WC2	12 D1	Gd.		£1 / £1 & 20p
Lincoln's Inn WC2	12 D1			
Linden Gdns W2	7 C3	Gd.	Bd.	20p
Linhope St NW1	1 B4			
Linley Sambourne House W8	7 C5			
Linton St N1	5 A1			
Lisgar Terr W14	15 B2			
Lisle St WC2	11 A2	Ave.		£ 1
Lisson Gro NW1	1 B5	Gd.	Bd.	£1 & 20p / P & D

Street Name		2hrs	4hrs	Coins
Lisson Gro NW8	1 A4			
Lisson St NW1	1 A5	Ave.		£1 & 20p
Little Boltons The SW10	16 E3	Ave.	Bd.	20p
Little Britain EC1	13 A1			
Little Chester St SW1	10 E5			
Little College St SW1	19 B1	Gd.		£1 & 20p
Little Dorrit Ct SE1	13 A4			
Little Portland St W1	10 F1			
Liverpool Rd N1	4 E1			
Liverpool St EC2	13 C1	Gd.		£1 & 20p
Lizard St EC1	5 A3			
Lloyd Baker St WC1	4 D3	Ave.		£1 & 20p
Lloyd St WC1	4 D3	Ave.	Gd.	£1 & 20p
Lloyd's of London EC3	13 C2			
Lloyd's Ave EC3	14 D2	Gd.		£1 & 20p
Lloyd's Row EC1	4 E3	Ave.		£1 & 20p
Lodge Rd NW8	1 A3	Gd.	Bd.	£1 & 20p
Logan Ms W8	15 C2			
Logan Pl W8	15 C2	Ave.		20p
Lollard St SE11	20 D2			
Loman St SE1	12 F4	Gd.	Gd.	£1, 50p & 20p / 20p
Lombard St EC3	13 B2			
London Bridge SE1	13 B3			
London Bridge City Pier SE1	13 C3			
London Bridge St EC1	13 B4			
London Central Mosque NW1	1 B3			
London Coliseum WC2	11 B3			
London Dungeon SE1	13 C3			
London Rd SE1	12 F5			
	20 F1			
London St W2	8 F1			
	9 A1	Gd.	Bd.	£1 & 20p
London Toy & Model Museum WC2	11 C2			
London Transport Museum WC2	13 A1			
London Wall EC2	2 D2			
London Zoo NW1	13 A1			
London Museum of EC2	11 B2	Gd.		£ 1
Long Acre WC1	4 F5			
Long La EC1	5 A5	Gd.		£1 & 20p
Long La SE1	13 B5			
Long St E2	6 D3			
Longford St NW1	2 E4	Bd.		£1 & 20p
Longmoore St SW1	18 F2	Ave.	Gd.	£1 & 20p
Longridge Rd SW5	15 C2	Gd.	Gd.	20p
Longville Rd SE11	20 F2			
Lonsdale Rd W11	7 B2	Gd.	Gd.	20p/ P&D all coins
Lord Hill Bridge W2	8 D1			
Lord's Cricket Ground NW8	1 A3			
Lorrimore Rd SE17	20 F4			
Lorrimore Sq SE17	20 F4			
Lot's Rd SW10	16 E5	Gd.	Gd.	20p
Lothbury EC2	13 B1			
Loughborough St SE11	20 D3	Ave.		20p
Lovat La EC3	13 C2			
Love La EC2	13 A1			
Lower Addison Gdns W14	7 A5	Ave.	Bd.	20p
Lower Belgrave St SW1	18 E1	Gd.	Ave.	£1 & 20p / P & D
Lower Grosvenor Pl SW1	18 E1			
Lower Marsh SE1	12 D5			
Lower Sloane St SW1	18 D3			
Lower Thames St EC3	13 C3			
	14 D3			
Lowndes Pl SW1	18 D1	Gd.		£1 & 20p / P & D
Lowndes Sq SW1	9 C5	Gd.		P & D
Lowndes St SW1	18 D1	Gd.	Bd.	£1 & 20p
Lucan Pl SW3	17 B2	Gd.	Bd.	£1 & 20p
Ludgate Circus EC4	12 F1			
Ludgate Hill EC4	12 F1			
Luke St EC2	5 C4			

Each place name is followed by its postal district, its atlas reference, 2 hour meters, 4 hour meters and then by the coins accepted

Street Name		2hrs	4hrs	Coins
Lupus St SW1	18 F3	Gd.	Bd.	£1 & 20p / P & D
	19 A3			
Luscombe Way SW8	19 B5			
Luton St NW8	1 A4			
Luxborough St W1	2 D5	Ave.		£1
Lyall St SW1	18 D1	Gd.	Bd.	£1 & 20p
M				
Mabledon Pl WC1	3 B3	Ave.		£1 & 20p
Mablethorpe Rd SW6	15 A5			
Macclesfield Rd EC1	5 A3	Ave.		£1 & 20p
McGregor Rd W11	7 B1			
Mackennal St NW8	1 B2	Ave.		£1 & 20p
Macklin St WC2	11 C1			
Mackworth St NW1	2 F3			
McLeod's Ms SW7	16 E1			
Maclise Rd W14	15 A1			
Madame Tussauds' NW1	2 D5			
Maddox St W1	10 F2	Gd.		£1
Maiden La WC2	11 C2	Bd.		£1
Malet St WC1	3 A5	Gd.		£1 & 20p
Mall The SW1	10 F4			
	11 A4			
Mallord St SW3	17 A4	Ave.	Bd.	20p
Mallow St EC1	5 B4			
Malta St EC1	4 F4	Bd.		£1 & 20p
Maltby St SE1	14 D5			
Malton Rd W10	7 A1			
Manchester Sq W1	10 D1	Gd.		£1 / P & D
Manchester St W1	10 D1	Gd.		£1 / P & D
Manciple St SE1	13 B5	Bd.		£1, 50p & 20p / 20p
Mandela St NW1	2 F1			
Mandela St SW9	20 E5			
Mandeville Pl W1	10 D1	Ave.		£1
Manette St W1	11 B1	Ave.		£1
Mankind Museum of W1	10 F3			
Manor Pl SE17	20 F3			
Manresa Rd SW3	17 A3	Gd.	Gd.	20p
Mansell St E1	14 E2			
Mansfield St W1	8 E1	Gd.		£1
	2 E5			
Mansford St E2	6 F2			
Mansion House EC4	13 B2			
Manson Pl SW7	16 F2			
Maple St E2	6 F4			
Maple St W1	2 F5			
Marble Arch W1	9 C2			
Marchbank Rd W14	15 B4			
Marchmont St WC1	3 B4	Ave.		£1 & 20p
Margaret St W1	10 F1	Gd.		£1
Margaretta Terr SW3	17 B4	Bd.	Gd.	20p
Margery St WC1	4 D3	Bd.	Gd.	£1 & 20p
Marigold St SE16	14 F5			
Marine St SE16	14 E5			
Mark St EC2	5 C4			
Market Entrance SW8	19 A5			
Market Ms W1	10 E4			
Markham Sq SW3	17 B3	Gd.		£1 & 20p
Markham St SW3	17 B3	Gd.	Bd.	£1 & 20p
Marlborough Bldgs SW3	17 B2			
Marlborough House SW1	11 A4			
Marlborough Rd SW1	11 A4			
Marlborough St SW3	17 B2	Ave.	Bd.	£1 & 20p
Marloes Rd W8	16 D1	Gd.	Bd.	£1 & 20p
Marshall St W1	10 F2			
Marshalsea Rd SE1	13 A4	Ave.		£1, 50p & 20p / 20p
Marsham St SW1	19 B1	Gd.		£1 & 20p
Mary Pl W11	7 A3			
Mary St N1	5 A1			
Marylebone High St W1	2 D5	Gd.		£1
Marylebone La W1	10 E1	Gd.		£1
Marylebone Rd NW1	1 B5			
	2 D5			
Marylebone St W1	2 D5	Ave.		£1
Marylee Way SE11	20 D2			
Mason's Pl EC1	5 A3			
Matheson Rd W14	15 B2			
Matilda St N1	4 D1			
Maunsel St SW1	19 A1	Bd.		£1 & 20p
Mawbey St SW8	19 B5			

Street Name		2hrs	4hrs	Coins
Maxwell Rd SW6	16 D5			
Maygood St N1	4 D2			
Meadow Rd SW8	19 C5			
	20 D4			
Mecklenburgh Gardens WC1	3 C4			
Medway St SW1	19 A1	Gd.		£1 & 20p
Melbury Rd W14	15 B1	Gd.	Bd.	20p
Mendora Rd SW6	15 A5			
Mercer St WC2	11 B2	Ave.		£1 & 20p
Meredith St EC1	4 F3	Ave.		£1 & 20p
Mermaid Ct SE1	13 B4			
Methley St SE11	20 E3			
Mews St E1	14 E3			
Meymott St SE1	12 E4	Ave.		£1, 50p & 20p / 20p
Micawber St N1	5 A3			
Middle St EC1	5 A5			
Middle Temple La EC4	12 E2			
Middlesex St E1	14 D1	Gd.		£1 & 20p
Midland Rd NW1	3 B2	Gd.	Ave.	£1 & 20p
Milborne Gro SW10	16 F3	Ave.	Bd.	20p
Miles St SW8	19 B4			
Milford La WC2	12 D2			
Milk St EC2	13 A1			
Mill Row N1	6 D1			
Mill St SE1	14 E5			
Millbank SW1	19 B1	Gd.		£1 & 20p / P & D
Millman St WC1	3 C4	Gd.		£1 & 20p
Milmans St SW10	17 A4			
Milner St SW3	17 C1	Ave.		£1 & 20p
Milson Rd W14	15 A1			
Milton St EC2	5 B5	Gd.	Ave.	£1 & 20p
Milverton St SE11	20 E3			
Mincing La EC3	13 C2	Gd.		£1 & 20p
Minera Ms SW1	18 D2			
Ministry of Defence SW1	11 C4			
Minories EC3	14 D2	Gd.		£1 & 20p
Minories Hill EC3	14 D2			
Mint St SE1	13 A4			
Mintern St N1	5 C2			
Mirabel Rd SW6	15 B5			
Mitchell St EC1	5 A4			
Mitre Rd SE1	12 E4			
Mitre St EC3	14 D2	Ave.		£1 & 20p
Molyneux St W1	9 B1	Ave.		£1
Monck St SW1	19 B1			
Monkton St SE11	20 E2	Bd.		20p
Monmouth Rd W2	8 D2	Ave.		£1 & 20p
Monmouth St WC2	11 B2			
Montpelier St SW7	9 B1			
Montagu Mansions W1	1 C5			
Montagu Pl W1	2 D5	Gd.		£1
	9 C1			
Montagu Sq W1	9 C1	Gd.		£1 / P & D
Montagu St W1	9 C1	Bd.		£1
Montague Pl WC1	3 B5	Gd.		£1 & 20p
Montague St WC1	3 B5	Ave.		£1 & 20p
Montclare St E2	6 D4			
Montford Pl SE11	20 D3			
Montpelier Pl SW7	9 B5	Bd.		£1
Montpelier Sq SW7	9 B5	Gd.	Bd.	£1
Montpelier Wlk SW7	9 B5	Ave.		£1
Montrose Ct SW7	9 A5			
Montrose Pl SW1	10 D5	Ave.	Gd.	£1 & 20p
Monument EC3	13 C2			
Monument St EC3	13 C2	Gd.		£1 & 20p
Moorhouse Rd W2	7 C1			
Moor La EC2	5 B5	Gd.		£1 & 20p
Moore Pk Rd SW6	16 D5			
Moore St SW3	17 C2	Ave.	Bd.	£1 & 20p
Moorfields EC2	5 B5	Gd.		£1 & 20p
Moorgate EC2	5 B5			
	13 B1			
Mora St EC1	5 A3	Ave.	Bd.	£1 & 20p
Moravian Pl SW10	17 A4			
Moreland St EC1	4 F3			
	5 A3			
Moreton Pl SW1	19 A3			
Moreton St SW1	19 A3	Gd.		£1 & 20p
Morgan's La SE1	13 C4			
Morley St SE1	12 E5	Bd.		£1, 50p & 20p / 20p
Mornington Ave W14	15 B2			
Mornington Cres NW1	2 F2			
Mornington St NW1	2 F2			

Street Name	2hrs	4hrs	Coins
Mornington Terr NW1	2 E1		
Morocco St SE1	13 C5		
Morpeth Terr SW1	18 F1	Ave.	Gd.	£1 & 20p
Mortimer St W1	10 F1		
Morwell St WC1	11 A1	Ave.		£1 & 20p
Moscow Rd W2	8 D2	Gd.	Bd.	£1 & 20p / 20p
Mossop St SW3	17 B2		
Motcomb St SW1	10 D5	Bd.		£1 & 20p
Mount Pleasant WC1	4 D4	Gd		£1 & 20p
Mount Row W1	10 E3	Bd.		£ 1
Mount St W1	10 D3	Gd.		£1 / P & D
Moving Image Museum of the SE1	12 D3		
Mowll St SW9	20 D5		
Moylan Rd W6	15 A4		
Mulberry St E1	14 F1		
Mulberry Wlk SW3	17 A4	Ave.	Ave.	20p
Mulgrave Rd SW6	15 B4	Bd.		£1 & 20p
Mulvaney Way SE1	13 C5	Bd.		£1 & 20p
Mund St W14	15 B3		
Munden St W14	15 A2		
Munster Rd SW6	15 A5		
Munster Sq NW1	2 F4		
Muriel St N1	4 D1		
Murphy St SE1	12 E5		
Murray Gro N1	5 B2		
Musard Rd W6	15 A4		
Museum St WC1	11 B1	Bd.		£1 & 20p
Myddelton Pas EC1	4 E3		
Myddelton Sq EC1	4 E3		
Myddelton St EC1	4 E4	Bd.		£1 & 20p
Myrdle St E1	14 F1		
N			
Napier Gro N1	5 B2		
Napier Pl W14	15 B1		
Napier Rd W14	15 A1	Ave.	Ave.	20p
Nash St NW1	2 E3		
National Army Museum SW3	17 C4		
National Film Theatre SE1	12 D3		
National Gallery WC2	11 B3		
National Portrait Gallery WC2	11 B3		
National Postal Museum EC1	13 A1		
National Sound Archive SW7	9 A5		
National Theatre SE1	12 D3		
Natural History Museum SW7	16 F1 17 A1		
Navarre St E2	6 D4		
Nazrul St E2	6 D2		
Neal St WC2	11 B1		
Neal's Yd WC2	11 B1		
Neckinger St SE1	14 E5		
Needham Rd W11	7 C2	Ave.		£1 & 20p
Nelson Gdns E2	6 F3		
Nelson Pl N1	4 F2		
Nelson Sq SE1	12 F4	Bd.		£1, 50p & 20p / 20p
Nelson's Column WC2	11 B3		
Nesham St E1	14 F3		
Netherton Gro SW10	16 F4	Gd.	Gd.	20p
Nevern Pl SW5	15 C2	Gd.	Gd.	20p
Nevern Rd SW5	15 C2	Ave.	Gd.	20p
Nevern Sq SW5	15 C2	Gd.	Gd.	20p
Neville St SW7	17 A3	Ave.	Ave.	£1 & 20p
New Bond St W1	10 E2	Gd.		£ 1
New Bridge St EC4	12 F2		
New British Library NW1	3 B3		
New Broad St EC2	13 C1		
New Cavendish St W1	2 E5	Gd.		£ 1
New Change EC4	13 A2		
New Compton St WC2	11 B1	Gd.		£1 & 20p
New Covent Garden Mkt SW8	19 A5		
New Fetter La EC4	12 E1	Ave.		£1 & 20p
New Inn Yd EC2	6 D4		
New North Rd N1	5 B1		

Street Name	2hrs	4hrs	Coins
New North St WC1	3 C5	Ave.		£1 & 20p
New Oxford St WC1	11 B1	Ave.		£1 & 20p
New Palace Yd SW1	11 B5		
New Rd E1	6 F5 14 F1		
New Row WC2	11 B2		
New Scotland Yd SW1	11 A5		
New Sq WC2	12 D1		
New St EC2	14 D1	Bd.		£1 & 20p
New Wharf Rd N1	3 C2		
New Zealand House SW1	11 A3		
Newburn St SE11	20 D3	Gd.		20p
Newcomen St SE1	13 B4		
Newcourt St NW8	1 A2	Bd.		£1 & 20p
Newgate St EC1	12 F1 13 A1		
Newington Butts SE11	20 F2		
Newington Causeway SE1	13 A5		
Newman St W1	11 A1	Gd.		£1 / P & D
Newport St SE11	20 D2		
Newton Rd W2	8 D1	Ave.	Ave.	£1 & 20p
Newton St WC2	11 C1	Ave.		£1 & 20p
Nicholas La EC4	13 B2	Bd.		£1 & 20p
Nile St N1	5 B3		
Nine Elms La SW8	19 A4		
Noble St EC2	13 A1	Gd.		£1 & 20p
Noel Rd N1	4 F2 5 A2	Bd.		£1 & 20p
Noel St W1	11 A1	Ave.		£ 1
Norfolk Cres W2	9 B1	Gd.		£1 / P & D
Norfolk Pl W2	9 A1	Ave.	Gd.	£1 & 20p
Norfolk Rd NW8	1 A1		
Norfolk Sq W2	9 A1	Gd.	Gd.	£1 & 20p / P & D
Norland Sq W11	7 A4	Ave.		20p
Norman St EC1	5 A4	Ave.	Gd.	£1 & 20p
Normand Rd W14	15 B4		
North Audley St W1	10 D2	Gd.		£1 / P & D
North East Pier E1	14 F4		
North End Rd SW6	15 C3		
North End Rd W14	15 A2		
North Gower St NW1	2 F3	Gd.		£1 & 20p
North Row W1	9 C2	Ave.		£ 1
North Tenter St E1	14 E2		
North Terr SW3	17 A1		
North West Pier E1	14 F4		
North Wharf Rd W2	8 F1	Gd.	Bd.	£1 & 20p
Northampton Rd EC1	4 E4	Bd.	Bd.	£1 & 20p
Northampton Sq EC1	4 F3	Ave.		£1 & 20p
Northburgh St EC1	4 F4		
Northdown St N1	3 C2	Ave.		£1 & 20p
Northington St WC1	4 D5	Ave.		£1 & 20p
Northumberland Ave WC2	11 B3	Gd.		£1 / P & D
Northumberland Pl W2	7 C1	Ave.	Gd.	£1 & 20p
Norton Folgate E1	6 D5		
Notting Hill Gate W11	7 C3 8 D3		
Nottingham Pl W1	2 D5	Gd.		£ 1
Nottingham St W1	2 D5	Gd.		£1 / P & D
Nutford Pl W1	9 B1		
Nuttall St N1	5 C1 6 D1		
O			
Oak Tree Rd NW8	1 A3	Ave.		£1 & 20p
Oakden St SE11	20 E2	Bd.	Gd.	20p
Oakfield St SW10	16 E4	Bd.	Ave.	20p
Oakley Gdns SW3	17 B4	Ave.	Ave.	20p
Oakley Sq NW1	3 A2		
Oakley St SW3	17 B4	Ave.	Ave.	20p
Oakwood Ct W14	7 B5	Gd.	Ave.	20p
Oat La EC2	13 A1	Bd.		£1 & 20p
Observatory Gdns W8	7 C4	Bd.		£1 & 20p
Offley Rd SW9	20 E5		
Old Bailey EC4	12 F1		
Old Bethnal Grn Rd E2	6 F3		
Old Bond St W1	10 F3	Ave.		£ 1

Each place name is followed by its postal district, its atlas reference, 2 hour meters, 4 hour meters and then by the coins accepted

Street Name		2hrs	4hrs	Coins
Old Broad St EC2	13 C1	Bd.		£1 & 20p
Old Brompton Rd SW5	16 D3	Gd.	Bd.	£1 & 20p / 20p
Old Brompton Rd SW7	17 A2			
Old Castle St E1	14 D1			
Old Cavendish St W1	10 E1			
Old Church St SW3	17 A3	Gd.	Gd.	20p
Old Compton St W1	11 A2			
Old Ct Pl W8	8 D5			
Old Gloucester St WC1	3 C5	Ave.		£1 & 20p
Old Jamaica Rd SE16	14 E5			
Old Jewry EC2	13 B1	Ave.		£1 & 20p
Old Marylebone Rd NW1	1 B5			
	9 B1			
Old Montague St E1	6 E5			
Old Nichol St E2	6 D4			
Old Palace Yd SW1	11 B5			
Old Paradise St SE11	20 D2			
Old Pk La W1	10 E4			
Old Pye St SW1	19 A1	Ave.		£1 & 20p
Old Quebec St W1	9 C2	Ave.		£1
Old Queen St SW1	11 B5	Gd.		£1
Old St EC1	5 A4			
Old St Thomas's Operating Theatre EC1	13 B4			
Old Vic SE1	12 E5			
Olympia W14	15 A1			
Olympia Way W14	15 A1			
Ongar Rd SW6	15 C4			
Onslow Gdns SW7	16 F2	Gd.	Bd.	£1 & 20p / 20p
Onslow Sq SW7	17 A2	Gd.	Bd.	£1 & 20p
Ontario St SE1	20 F1	Ave.		£1, 50p & 20p / 20p
Opal St SE11	20 F2			
Orange St WC2	11 B3			
Orbain Rd SW6	15 A5			
Orchard St W1	10 D2			
Orchardson St NW8	1 A4			
Orde Hall St WC1	3 C5	Ave.		£1 & 20p
Ordnance Hill NW8	1 A1			
Orme Ct W2	8 D3			
Orme La W2	8 D3	Ave.		£1 & 20p
Ormonde Gate SW3	17 C3	Gd.	Gd.	20p
Ormonde Terr NW8	1 C1			
Ormsby St E2	6 D2			
Orsett St SE11	20 D3			
Orsett Terr W2	8 E1	Ave.	Gd.	£1 & 20p
Orsman Rd N1	5 C1			
	6 D1			
Osborn St E1	14 E1			
Osnaburgh St NW1	2 E4	Gd.	Bd.	£1 & 20p
Ossington St W2	8 D3			
Ossulston St NW1	3 A2	Gd.	Gd.	£1 & 20p
Oswin St SE11	20 F1	Bd.		£1, 50p & 20p / 20p
Otto St SE17	20 F4			
Outer Circle NW1	1 B2			
	2 D2			
Oval Pl SW8	20 D5			
Oval Rd NW1	2 E1			
Oval The SE11	20 D4			
Oval Way SE11	20 D3			
Ovington Gdns SW3	17 B1	Ave.	Bd.	£1 & 20p
Ovington Sq SW3	17 B1	Gd.	Ave.	£1 & 20p
Ovington St SW3	17 B1	Ave.	Gd.	£1 & 20p
Owen St EC1	4 E2			
Oxford Gdns W10	7 A1			
Oxford Sq W2	9 B1			
Oxford St W1	10 D2			
	11 A1			
P				
Pakenham St WC1	4 D4			
Packington Sq N1	5 A1			
Packington St N1	4 F1			
	5 A1			
Paddington Basin W2	9 A1			

Street Name		2hrs	4hrs	Coins
Paddington Garden W2	1 A5			
Paddington St W1	2 D5			
Page St SW1	19 B2	Gd.	Gd.	£1 & 20p / P & D
Paget St EC1	4 F3			
Palace Ave W8	8 D4			
Palace Ct W2	8 D3	Ave.		£1 & 20p
Palace Gate W8	8 E5			
Palace Gdns Ms W8	8 D3			
Palace Gdns Terr W8	8 D3	Gd.	Bd.	20p
Palace Grn W8	8 D4			
Palace St SW1	10 F5	Gd.		£1
Palace Theatre WC2	11 B2			
Palfrey Pl SW8	20 D5			
Pall Mall SW1	11 A3	Gd.		£1
Pall Mall East SW1	11 B3			
Palliser Rd W14	15 A3			
Palmer St SW1	11 A5			
Pancras Rd NW1	3 B2	Bd.		£1 & 20p
Panton St SW1	11 A3			
Parade The SW11	17 C5			
Paradise Wlk SW3	17 C4			
Pardoner St SE1	13 B5	Bd.	Gd.	£1, 50p & 20p / 20p
Paris Garden SE1	12 E3	Ave.		£1, 50p & 20p / 20p
Park Cres W1	2 E5	Gd.		£1 / P & D
Park La W1	9 C2	Gd.		£1 / P & D
	10 D3			
Park Pl SW1	10 F4	Ave.		£1
Park Rd NW1 NW8	1 B3	Ave.		£1 & 20p
Park Sq East NW1	2 E4			
Park Sq Gdns NW1	2 E4			
Park Sq West NW1	2 E4			
Park St SE1	13 A3	Gd.		£1, 50p & 20p / 20p
Park St W1	10 D2	Gd.		£1
Park Village East NW1	2 E2	Gd.	Bd.	£1 & 20p
Park West Pl W2	9 B1	Gd.	Gd.	£1 & 20p
Park Wlk SW10	16 F4	Gd.	Bd.	20p
Parker St WC2	11 C1			
Parkfield St N1	4 E2			
Parkgate Rd SW11	17 B5			
Parkville Rd SW6	15 B5			
Parkway NW1	2 E1			
Parliament Sq SW1	11 B5			
Parliament St SW1	11 B4			
Parr St N1	5 B2			
Parry St SW8	19 C4			
Pascal St SW8	19 B5			
Pater St W8	15 C1	Bd.		£1 & 20p
Paul St EC2	5 C4			
Paultons Sq SW3	17 A4	Gd.	Gd.	20p
Paultons St SW3	17 A4	Bd.		20p
Paveley Dri SW11	17 A5			
Paveley St NW8	1 B4			
Pavilion Rd SW1	9 C5	Gd.	Bd.	£1 & 20p
	17 C1			
Pavilion St SW1	17 C1	Ave.	Gd.	£1 & 20p
Peabody Ave SW1	18 E3			
Peace Pagoda SW11	17 C5			
Pear Tree St EC1	5 A4			
Pearman St SE1	12 E5			
Pearson St E2	6 D2			
Pedley St E1	6 E4			
Peel St W8	7 C4	Ave.	Bd.	20p
Peerless St EC1	5 B3	Bd.	Bd.	£1 & 20p
Pelham Cres SW7	17 A2	Ave.	Bd.	£1 & 20p
Pelham Pl SW7	17 A2			
Pelham St SW7	17 A2	Ave.	Bd.	£1 & 20p
Pellant Rd SW6	15 A5			
Pelter St E2	6 D3			
Pembridge Cres W11	7 C2	Ave.	Bd.	20p
Pembridge Gdns W2	7 C3	Gd.		20p
Pembridge Pl W2	7 C2	Ave.	Bd.	20p
Pembridge Rd W11	7 C3			
Pembridge Sq W2	7 C3	Gd.	Ave.	20p
Pembridge Vlls W11	7 C2	Gd.		20p
Pembroke Gdns W8	15 C1	Ave.		20p
Pembroke Gdns Clo W8	15 C1			
Pembroke Rd W8	15 C1	Gd.	Bd.	20p
Pembroke Sq W8	15 C1	Gd.	Gd.	20p
Pembroke Vlls W8	15 C1	Ave.	Gd.	20p
Penfold St NW8	1 A4	Ave.		£1 & 20p
Penn St N1	5 B1			
Pennant Ms W8	16 D1			

Each place name is followed by its postal district, its atlas reference, 2 hour meters, 4 hour meters and then by the coins accepted

Street Name	2hrs	4hrs	Coins
SW7	16 F1		
Queen's Gate Terr			
SW7	16 E1	Gd.	Bd.	£1 & 20p
Queen's Gro NW8	1 A1	Ave.		£1 & 20p
Queen's Wlk SW1	10 F4		
Queenhithe EC4	13 A2		
Queensberry Pl SW7	16 F1	Gd.	Ave.	£1 & 20p
Queensborough Ms			
W2	8 E2		
Queensborough			
Terr W2	8 E2	Gd.	Gd.	£1 & 20p / P & D
Queensbridge Rd			
E2 E8	6 E1		
Queensdale Rd W11	7 A4	Ave.	Gd.	20p
Queenstown Rd SW8	18 E4		
Queensway W2	8 D2	Gd.		£1 & 20p / P & D
Quilter St E2	6 E3		
R			
Racton Rd SW6	15 C4		
Radnor Ms W2	9 A2		
Radnor Pl W2	9 A1	Ave.		£1 & 20p
Radnor St EC1	5 A3	Gd.	Bd.	£1 & 20p
Radnor Terr W14	15 B1	Ave.	Ave.	20p
Radnor Wlk SW3	17 B3	Bd.	Gd.	£1 & 20p
Radstock St SW11	17 B5		
Railway Approach			
SE1	13 B3		
Railway St N1	3 C2	Gd.		£1 & 20p
Raleigh St N1	4 F1		
Rampayne St SW1	19 A3		
Randall Rd SE11	19 C2		
Ranelagh Gardens			
SW3	18 D3		
Ranelagh Gro SW1	18 D3	Bd.		£1 & 20p
Raphael St SW7	9 B5	Bd.		£ 1
Rathbone Pl W1	11 A1		
Rathbone St W1	11 A1	Ave.		£ 1
Ravenscroft St E2	6 E2		
Ravensdon St SE11	20 E3		
Ravent Rd SE11	20 D2		
Rawlings St SW3	17 B2	Ave.	Bd.	£1 & 20p
Rawstorne St EC1	4 F3	Ave.		£1 & 20p
Ray St EC1	4 E4	Ave.		£1 & 20p
Raymond Bldgs WC1	4 D5		
Rector St N1	5 A1		
Red Lion Sq WC1	3 C5	Gd.		£1 & 20p
Red Lion St WC1	4 D5	Gd.		£1 & 20p
Redan Pl W2	8 D2		
Redburn St SW3	17 B4	Ave.	Bd.	20p
Redchurch St E2	6 D4		
Redcliffe Gdns SW10	16 E3	Gd.	Bd.	20p
Redcliffe Ms SW10	16 E3		
Redcliffe Pl SW10	16 E4	Ave.		20p
Redcliffe Rd SW10	16 4F	Ave.	Ave.	20p
Redcliffe Sq SW10	16 D3		
Redcross Way SE1	13 A4	Bd.		£1, 50p & 20p / 20p
Redesdale St SW3	17 B3	Ave.	Ave.	£1 & 20p
Redfield La SW5	16 D2		
Redhill St NW1	2 E3	Gd.		£1 & 20p
Redvers St N1	6 D2		
Reedworth St SE11	20 E2		
Rees St N1	5 B1		
Reeves Ms W1	10 D3	Bd.		£ 1
Regan Way N1	5 C2		
Regency Pl SW1	19 A1	Ave.	Gd.	£1 & 20p
Regency St SW1	19 A2		
Regent Sq WC1	3 C3	Bd.		£1 & 20p
Regent St W1 SW1	10 F1	Bd.		£ 1
	11 A3		
Regent's Park NW1	3 C2		
	2 D2		
Regent's Pk Terr			
NW1	2 E1		
Regent's Pk Rd NW1	1 C1		
	2 D1		
Regent's Row E8	6 E1		
Renfrew Rd SE11	20 F2	Ave.		20p
Rennie St SE1	12 F3	Ave.		£1, 50p & 20p / 20p
Rheidol Terr N1	5 A1		
Richard's Pl SW3	17 B2		
Richborne Terr SW8	20 D5		
Richmond Terr SW1	11 B4		
Rick La SW5	16 D3		
Rickett St SW6	15 C4		

Street Name	2hrs	4hrs	Coins
Ridgmount Gdns			
WC1	3 A5	Ave.		£1 & 20p
Ridgmount St WC1	3 A5	Gd.		£1 & 20p
Riding House St W1	10 F1	Ave.		£ 1
Riley Rd SE1	14 D5		
Ring The W2	9 A3		
Risinghill St N1	4 D2		
Rita Rd SW8	19 C5		
Ritz Hotel SW1	10 F3		
River St EC1	4 E3	Bd.		£1 & 20p
Rivington St EC2	5 C3		
Robert St NW1	2 F3	Gd.	Bd.	£1 & 20p
Robert Adam St W1	10 D1	Gd.		£ 1
Roberta St E2	6 F3		
Rochester Row SW1	19 A2	Gd.		£1 & 20p
Rodmarton St W1	9 C1	Gd.		£ 1
Rodney St N1	4 D2	Bd.		£1 & 20p
Roger St WC1	4 D4	Ave.		£1 & 20p
Roland Gdns SW7	16 F3	Gd.	Bd.	20p
Roland Way SW7	16 F3		
Romilly St W1	11 A2	Bd.		£ 1
Romney St SW1	19 B1	Ave.	Gd.	£1 & 20p
Rood La EC3	13 C2	Bd.		£1 & 20p
Ropemaker St EC2	5 B5	Ave.		£1 & 20p
Roper's Garden SW3	17 A4		
Rosaline Rd SW6	15 A5		
Rosary Gdns SW7	16 E2	Ave.	Bd.	20p
Rosaville Rd SW6	15 B5		
Rose Alley SE1	13 A3		
Rose St WC2	11 B2		
Rosebery Ave EC1	4 E4	Ave.		£1 & 20p
Rosemoor St SW3	17 B2	Ave.	Ave.	£1 & 20p
Rosmead Rd W11	7 A2	Gd.	Bd.	20p
Rossmore Rd NW1	1 B4	Bd.	Bd.	£1 & 20p / P & D
Rotary St SE1	12 F5	Ave.	Ave.	£1, 50p & 20p / 20p
Rotten Row SW7	9 A4		
Roupell St SE1	12 E4	Ave.	Gd.	20p
Rowallan Rd SW6	15 A5		
Royal Academy of			
Arts W1	10 F3		
Royal Academy of			
Music NW1	2 D4		
Royal Albert Hall			
SW7	8 F5		
Royal Ave SW3	17 C3	Ave.		£1 & 20p
Royal College of			
Art SW7	8 F5		
Royal College of			
Music SW7	8 F5		
Royal College St			
NW1	3 A1	Gd.	Bd.	£1 & 20p
Royal Courts of			
Justice WC2	12 D2		
Royal Exchange EC4	13 C2		
Royal Festival Hall			
SE1	12 D4		
Royal Hospital Rd			
SW3	17 C3	Ave.	Ave.	20p
Royal Hospital Rd			
SW3	18 D3		
Royal Mint St E1	14 E2		
Royal Ms SW1	10 E5		
Royal Opera House			
Royal Rd SE17	20 F4		
Royal St SE1	12 D5	Gd.		20p
Rumbold Rd SW6	16 E5		
Rupert St W1	11 A2		
Rushton St N1	5 B2		
Rushworth St SE1	12 F4		
Russell Gdns W14	7 A5	Gd.	Gd.	20p
Russell Gdns Ms W14	7 A5		
Russell Rd W14	15 A1	Gd.	Gd.	20p
Russell Sq WC1	3 B5	Gd.		£1 & 20p
Russell St WC2	11 C2	Gd.		£ 1
Ruston Ms W11	7 A1		
Rutherford St SW1	19 A2	Ave.		£1 & 20p
Rutland Gdns SW7	9 B5		
Rutland Gate SW7	9 B5	Gd.	Ave.	£1 / P & D
Ryder St SW1	10 F4	Ave.		£ 1
Rylston Rd SW6	15 B4		
S			
St Agnes Pl SE11	20 E4		
St Alban's St SW1	11 A3		
St Andrew's EC4	12 E1		

Street Name		2hrs	4hrs	Coins
St Andrew's Gdns WC1	4 D4			
St Andrew's Pl NW1	2 E4			
St Andrews St EC4	12 E1	Ave.		£1 & 20p
St Ann's St SW1	19 B1	Ave.		£1 & 20p / P & D
St Ann's Terr NW8	1 A2	Bd.		£1 & 20p
St Barnabas St SW1	18 D2	Ave.		£1 & 20p
St Bartholomew's Hospital EC1	12 F1			
St Bartholomews-the-Great EC1	4 F5			
St Botolph Church EC1	13 A1			
St Botolph St EC3	14 D1			
St Bride St EC4	12 E1	Ave.		£1 & 20p
St Bride's EC4	12 F2			
St Chad's Pl WC1	3 C3			
St Chad's St WC1	3 C3	Gd.		£1 & 20p
St Clements Danes WC2	12 D2			
St Cross St EC1	4 E5			
St Edmund's Terr NW8	1 B1	Bd.		£1 & 20p
St Ethelreda's EC1	4 E5			
St George's Blooms-bury WC1	11 B1			
St George's Cathedral SE1	12 E5			
St George's Circus SE1	12 F5			
St George's Dri SW1	18 F2	Gd.	Ave.	£1 & 20p
St George's Fields W2	9 B2			
St George's Gdn W1	10 D3			
St George's Gdns WC1	3 C4			
St George's Rd SE1	20 F1			
St George's Sq SW1	19 A3	Gd.	Gd.	£1 & 20p
St Giles EC2	5 A5			
St Giles Cripplegate High St WC2	11 B1			
St Helen's Bishops-gate EC3	13 C1			
St James's Church SW1	11 A3			
St James's Palace SW1	10 F4			
St James's Park SW1	11 A4			
St James's Pk Lake SW1	11 A4			
St James's Pl SW1	10 F4	Bd.		£ 1
St James's Rd SE16	14 F5			
St James's Sq SW1	11 A3	Gd.		£1 / P & D
St James's St SW1	10 F3	Gd.		£ 1
St John St EC1	4 E2			
St John's SE1	12 E4			
St John's Gdns SW1	19 B1			
St John's Gdns W11	7 A3	Ave.		20p
St John's High St NW8	1 A2			
St John's La EC1	4 F5	Gd.	Bd.	£1 & 20p
St John's Smith Sq SW1	19 B1			
St John's Sq EC1	4 F4			
St John's Wood Church Gdns NW8	1 A3			
St John's Wood High St NW8	1 A2	Gd.		£1 & 20p
St John's Wood Rd NW8	1 A3	Gd.	Gd.	£1 & 20p
St John's Wood Terr NW8	1 A2	Gd.	Ave.	£1 & 20p
St Katherines Dock E1	14 E3			
St Katherines Pier E1	14 E3			
St Katharine's Way E1	14 E3			
St Lawrence Terr W10	7 A1			
St Leonard's Terr SW3	17 C3	Gd.	Ave.	£1 & 20p
St Loo Ave SW3	17 B4	Ave.	Bd.	20p
St Luke's Ms W11	7 B1			
St Luke's Rd W11	7 B1			
St Luke's St SW3	17 B3	Bd.	Gd.	£1 & 20p
St Magnus the Martyr EC3	13 C3			
St Margaret Pattens EC3	13 C2			
St Margaret's Church SW1	11 B5			
St Margaret St SW1	11 B5			
St Mark St E1	14 E2			
St Mark's Cres NW1	2 D1			
St Mark's Rd W11	7 A2	Gd.	Ave.	20p
St Martin's La WC2	11 B2	Gd.		£ 1
St Martin's Le Grand EC1	13 A1			
St Martin's Pl WC2	11 B3			
St Martin's St WC2	11 B3			
St Martin-in-the-Fields WC2	11 B3			
St Mary Abbots Terr W14	15 B1			
St Mary at Hill EC3	13 C2	Bd.		£1 & 20p
St Mary Axe EC3	15 C1	Ave.		£1 & 20p
St Mary's Hospital W2	9 A1			
St Mary Le Strand WC2	12 D2			
St Mary's Path N1	4 F1			
St Mary's Wlk SE11	20 E2			
St Mary-le-Bow EC4	13 A2			
St Marylebone Parish				
St Matthew's Row E2	6 E4			
St Michael's St W2	9 A1			
St Olaf's House SE1	13 C3			
St Olaf's Rd SW6	15 A5			
St Oswald's Pl SE11	20 D3			
St Pancras Church WC1	3 B3			
St Pancras Way NW1	3 A1	Gd.	Ave.	£1 & 20p
St Paul St N1	5 A1			
St Paul's Cathedral EC4	13 A2			
St Paul's Church WC2	11 C2			
St Paul's Churchyard EC4	13 A1			
St Peter's Clo E2	6 F2			
St Peter's St N1	4 F1			
	5 A2			
St Petersburgh Pl W2	8 D3	Bd.		£1 & 20p
St Stephen Walbrook EC4	13 B2			
St Stephen's Gdns W2	7 C1	Gd.		£1 & 20p
St Stephen's Terr SW8	19 C5			
St Swithin's La EC4	13 B2			
St Thomas St SE1	13 B4			
St Thomas' Hospital SE1	11 C5			
St Thomas' Way SW6	15 B5			
Sackville St W1	10 F3	Gd.		£ 1
Saffron Hill EC1	4 E5	Ave.		£1 & 20p
Sail St SE11	20 D1			
Salamanca St SE11	19 C2			
Sale Pl W2	9 A1	Ave.	Gd.	£1 & 20p
Salem Rd W2	8 D2	Ave.	Gd.	£1 & 20p
Salisbury Ct EC4	12 E2			
Salisbury St NW8	1 A4	Gd.		£1 & 20p
Sampson St E1	14 F4			
Sancroft St SE11	20 D2	Gd.	Bd.	20p
Sandwich St WC1	3 B3	Ave.		£1 & 20p
Sandys Row E1	6 D5			
Sans Wlk EC1	4 E4			
Savile Row W1	10 F2	Gd.		£ 1
Savona St SW8	18 F5			
Savoy Chapel WC2	11 C2			
Savoy Hill WC2	11 C3	Ave.		£ 1
Savoy Pl WC2	11 C3	Gd.		£ 1
Savoy Row WC2	11 C3			
Savoy St WC2	11 C2	Ave.		£ 1
Savoy The WC2	11 C2			
Scala St W1	3 A5			
Scarborough St E1	14 E2			
Scarsdale Vlls W8	15 C1			
Science Museum	16 D1	Gd.	Bd.	£1 & 20p
	17 A1			
Sclater St E1	6 E4			
Scott Lidgett Cres SE16	14 F5			
Scott St E1	6 F4			

Each place name is followed by its postal district, its atlas reference, 2 hour meters, 4 hour meters and then by the coins accepted

Street Name		2hrs	4hrs	Coins
Scovell Cresent SE1	13 A5			
Scrutton St EC2	5 C4			
Seagrave Rd SW6	15 C4			
	16 D4			
Sebastian St EC1	4 F3	Gd.		£1 & 20p
Sedlescombe Rd SW6	15 C4			
Seething La EC3	14 D2	Ave.		£1 & 20p
Sekforde St EC1	4 F4	Gd.		£1 & 20p
Selby St E1	6 F4			
Selfridge's W1	10 D2			
Selwood Pl SW7	16 F3	Ave.	Ave.	20p
Selwood Terr SW7	16 F3			
Semley Pl SW1	18 E2	Bd.		£1 & 20p
Serle St WC2	12 D1	Gd.		£1 & 20p / £1
Serpentine Gallery W2	9 A4			
Serpentine Rd W2	9 C4			
	10 D4			
Serpentine The W2	9 B4			
Settles St E1	14 F1			
Seven Dials WC2	11 B2			
Seville St SW1	9 C5	Ave.	Gd.	£1 & 20p
Seward St EC1	5 A4	Bd.		£1 & 20p
Seymour Ms W1	10 D1			
Seymour Pl W1	1 B5			
	9 B1	Gd.		£1 & 20p
Seymour St W1 W2	9 C2	Gd.		£1 & 20p / P & D
Seymour Wlk SW10	16 E4	Ave.	Ave.	20p
Shad Thames SE1	14 E4			
Shaftesbury Ave W1	11 A2	Gd.		£1 & 20p
Shaftesbury Ave WC2	11 B1			
Shaftesbury St N1	5 B2			
Shafto Ms SW1	17 C1			
Shafts Ct EC3	13 C1			
Shakespeare's Globe Museum SE1	13 A3			
Shalcomb St SW10	16 F4	Gd.	Ave.	20p
Sharsted St SE17	20 F3			
Shawfield St SW3	17 B3	Bd.		£1 & 20p
Sheffield Ter W8	7 C4	Ave.	Ave.	20p
Sheldrake Pl W8	7 C5			
Shelton St WC2	11 B2			
Shenfield St N1	6 D2			
Shepherd Mkt W1	10 E4	Bd.		£1
Shepherd St W1	10 E4	Bd.		£1
Shepherdess Wlk N1	5 A2			
Shepperton Rd N1	5 B1			
Sherbourne La EC4	13 B2			
Sherbrooke Rd SW6	16 D5			
Sherlock Holmes Museum W1	1 C5			
Sherwood St W1	11 A2			
Shipton St E2	6 E2			
Shoe La EC4	12 E1	Gd.		£1 & 20p
Shoreditch High St EC2 SE3	6 D3			
Shoreditch Park E2	5 B1			
Shorrold's Rd SW6	15 C5			
Short St SE1	12 E4	Bd.		£1, 50p & 20p / 20p
Shouldham St W1	9 B1	Gd.		£1
Shroton St NW1	1 B5	Bd.		£1 & 20p
Sidmouth St WC1	3 C3	Ave.		£1 & 20p
Silk St EC2	5 B5			
Sinclair Rd W14	15 A1			
Singer St EC2	5 C4			
Sir John Soane's Museum WC2	12 D1			
Skinner St EC1	4 E4	Bd.		£1 & 20p
Slaidburn St SW10	16 F4			
Sleaford St SW8	18 F5			
Sloane Ave SW3	17 B2	Gd.	Bd.	£1 & 20p
Sloane Ct East SW3	18 D3			
Sloane Gdns SW1	18 D2	Gd.	Ave.	£1 & 20p
Sloane Sq SW1	17 C2			
	18 D2			
Sloane St SW1	9 C5			
	17 C1			
Smith Sq SW1	19 B1	Gd.		£1 & 20p
Smith St SW3	17 C3	Gd.	Bd.	£1 & 20p / 20p
Smith Terr SW3	17 C3	Bd.		£1 & 20p
Smithfield Mkt EC1	4 F5			
Snow Hill EC1	12 F1	Gd.		£1 & 20p
Snowfields SE1	13 B4			
Soho Sq W1	11 A1	Gd.		£1 / P & D
Soho St W1	11 A1			
Somers Cres W2	9 A1			
South Audley St W1	10 D3	Gd.		£1
South Crescent WC1	3 A5	Gd.		£1 & 20p
South Eaton Pl SW1	18 D2	Ave.		£1 & 20p
South Edwardes Sq W8	15 C1			
South Island Pl SW9	20 D5			
South Lambeth Pl SW8	19 C4			
South Lambeth Rd SW8	19 C4			
South Molton La W1	10 E2			
South Molton St W1	10 E2			
South Parade SW3	17 A3	Gd.	Bd.	20p
South Pl EC2	5 B5	Ave.		£1 & 20p
South St W1	10 D3	Gd.		£1
South Tenter St E1	14 E2			
South Terr SW7	17 A2			
South Wharf Rd W2	9 A1	Gd.	Bd.	£1 & 20p / P & D
Southampton Pl WC1	11 C1	Gd.		£1 & 20p
Southampton Row WC1	3 C5			
Southampton St WC2	11 C2	Gd.		£1
Southern St N1	3 C2	Bd.		£1 & 20p
Southwark Bridge SE1	13 A3			
Southwark Bridge Rd SE1	13 A4	Gd.		£1, 50p & 20p / 20p
Southwark Cathedral EC1	13 B3			
Southwark St SE1	12 F3			
	13 A4	Gd.		£1, 50p & 20p / 20p
Southwell Gdns SW7	16 E1	Ave.	Bd.	£1 & 20p
Southwick St W2	9 A1	Ave.	Gd.	£1 & 20p
Spa Fields EC1	4 E4			
Speakers' Corner W2	9 C2			
Spelman St E1	6 E5			
Spencer House SW1	10 F4			
Spencer St EC1	4 F3	Gd.	Gd.	£1 & 20p / £1
Spenser St SW1	18 F1			
Spital Sq E1	6 D5			
Spital St E1	6 E5			
Spitalfields Heritage Centre E1	6 E5			
Spring St W2	8 F2	Ave.		£1 & 20p
Spur Rd SW1	10 F5			
Squirries St E2	6 F3			
Stable Yd Rd SW1	10 F4			
Stafford Terr W8	7 C5	Ave.	Bd.	£1 & 20p
Stag Pl SW1	18 F1			
Stamford St SE1	12 E3			
Stanford Rd W8	16 E1	Gd.	Gd.	£1 & 20p
Stanhope Gdns SW7	16 F2	Gd.	Ave.	20p
Stanhope Gate W1	10 D4	Gd.		£1
Stanhope Ms East SW7	16 F2			
Stanhope Ms West SW7	16 F2			
Stanhope Pl W2	9 B2			
Stanhope St NW1	2 F3	Ave.		£1 & 20p
Stanhope Terr W2	9 A2			
Stanley Cres W11	7 B2	Gd.	Ave.	20p
Stanley Gdns W11	7 B2			
Stannary St SE11	20 E3			
Stanway St N1	6 D2			
Stanwick Rd W14	15 B2			
Staple Inn WC1	12 E1			
Staple St SE1	13 B5	Bd.		£1, 50p & 20p / 20p
Star Rd W14	15 B4			
Star St W2	9 A1	Gd.		£1 & 20p / P & D
Starcross St NW1	2 F3	Bd.		£1 & 20p
Stean St E8	6 D1			
Stephen St W1	11 A1	Gd.		£1 & 20p
Stephenson Way NW1	3 A4	Gd.	Ave.	£1 & 20p
Steward St E1	6 D5			
Stewart's Rd SW8	18 F5			
Stock Exchange EC2	13 B1			
Stone Bldgs WC2	12 D1			
Stonefield St N1	4 E1			
Stones End St SE1	13 A5	Bd.		£1, 50p & 20p / 20p
Stoney La E1	14 D1	Ave.		£1 & 20p
Stoney St SE1	13 B3			
Stonor Rd W14	15 B2			
Store St WC1	3 A5	Gd.		£1 & 20p
Storey's Gate SW1	11 B5			

Street Name		2hrs	4hrs	Coins
Strand WC2	11 B3	Gd.		£1
Strand La WC2	12 D2			
Stratford Rd W8	16 D1	Gd.	Bd.	£1 & 20p
Stratton St W1	10 E3	Ave.		£1
Streatham St WC1	11 B1	Bd.		£1 & 20p
Strode Rd SW6	15 A5			
Strutton Ground SW1	19 A1			
Sturt St N1	5 A2			
Stutfield St E1	14 F2			
Sudeley St N1	4 F2	Ave.		£1 & 20p
Suffolk La EC4	13 B2			
Suffolk Pl SW1	11 A3	Gd.		£1
Suffolk St WC1	11 B3	Gd.		£1
Sumner Pl SW7	17 A2	Gd.	Bd.	£1 & 20p
Sumner St SE1	13 A3	Ave.		£1, 50p & 20p / 20p
Sun Rd W14	15 B3			
Sun St EC2	5 C5			
Sunderland Terr W2	8 D1			
Surrey Row SE1	12 F4	Bd.		£1, 50p & 20p / 20p
Surrey St WC2	12 D2	Gd.		£1 / P & D
Sussex Gdns W2	9 A1			
Sussex Pl NW1	1 C4			
Sussex Pl W2	9 A2	Gd.	Bd.	£1
Sussex Sq W2	9 A2	Gd.		£1 & 20p / P & D
Sussex St SW1	18 F3	Ave.		£1 & 20p
Sutherland Pl W2	7 C1	Ave.		£1 & 20p
Sutherland St SW1	18 E3	Ave.		£1 & 20p
Sutton Row W1	11 A1	Ave.		£1
Swallow St W1	10 F3			
Swan La EC4	13 B3			
Swan La Pier SE1	13 B3			
Swan St SE1	13 A5	Gd.		£1, 50p & 20p / 20p
Swan Wlk SW3	17 C4	Ave.	Bd.	20p
Swanfield St E2	6 E3			
Swinton St WC1	3 C3	Ave.		£1 & 20p
Sydney Pl SW3	17 A2			
Sydney St SW3	17 A3	Ave.	Gd.	£1 & 20p
Symons St SW3	17 C2	Gd.	Bd.	£1 & 20p
T				
Tabard St SE1	13 B5	Ave.		£1, 50p & 20p / 20p
Tabernacle St EC2	5 C4	Bd.		£1 & 20p
Tachbrook St SW1	19 A2	Ave.		£1 & 20p
Tadema Rd SW10	16 F5	Bd.	Gd.	20p
Talbot Rd W2 W11	7 C1	Gd.	Ave.	£1 & 20p / 20p
Talbot Sq W2	9 A2	Gd.	Gd.	£1 & 20p / P & D
Talgarth Rd W6 W14	15 A3			
Tallis St EC4	12 E2	Ave.		£1 & 20p
Tanner St SE1	14 D5			
Tamworth St SW6	15 C4			
Taplow St N1	5 A2			
Tasso Rd W6	15 A4			
Tate Gallery SW1	19 B2			
Tavistock Cres W11	7 B1	Gd.	Bd.	20p
Tavistock Pl WC1	3 B4	Bd.		£1 & 20p
Tavistock Rd W11	7 B1	Gd.	Gd.	£1 & 20p / 20p
Tavistock Sq WC1	3 B4	Ave.		£1 & 20p
Tavistock St WC2	11 C2	Gd.		£1 / P & D
Taviton St WC1	3 A4	Gd.		£1 & 20p
Teale St E2	6 F2			
Tedworth Sq SW3	17 C3	Gd.	Ave.	£1 & 20p / 20p
Teesdale Clo E2	6 F2			
Teesdale St E2	6 F2			
Telegraph St EC2	13 B1			
Temple EC4	12 E2			
Temple Ave EC4	12 E2	Ave.		£1 & 20p
Temple Bar Memorial WC2	12 D2			
Temple La EC4	12 E2			
Temple Pl WC2	12 D2	Gd.		£1 / P & D
Temple St E2	6 F2			
Templeton Pl SW5	15 C2	Ave.	Gd.	20p
Tent St E1	6 F4			
Tenterden St W1	10 E2	Ave.		£1
Terminus Pl SW1	18 F1			
Tetcott Rd SW10	16 E5	Gd.	Gd.	20p
Thanet St WC1	3 B3	Ave.		£1 & 20p
Thaxton Rd W14	15 B4			
Thayer St W1	10 D1			
Theatre Museum WC2	11 C2			
Theatre Royal WC2	11 C2			
Theberton St N1	4 E1			
Theed St SE1	12 E4			
Theobald's Rd WC1	3 C5			

Street Name		2hrs	4hrs	Coins
	4 D5			
Thessaly Rd SW8	18 F5			
Thirleby Rd SW1	18 F1			
Thistle Gro SW7	16 F3			
Thomas More St E1	14 E3			
Thoresby St N1	5 A3			
Thorncroft St SW8	19 B5			
Thorney St SW1	19 B1			
Thornhaugh St WC1	3 B5			
Thrale St SE1	13 A4			
Thrawl St E1	6 E5			
Threadneedle St EC4	13 B2			
Throgmorton Ave EC2	13 C1			
Throgmorton St EC2	13 B1			
Thurloe Pl SW7	17 A1	Ave.	Gd.	£1 & 20p
Thurloe Sq SW7	17 A1	Gd.	Bd.	£1 & 20p
Thurloe St SW7	17 A2	Ave.	Gd.	£1 & 20p
Tiber Gdns N1	3 C1			
Tilney St W1	10 D3			
Tilton St SW6	15 B4			
Tinworth St SE11	19 C3			
Titchborne Row W2	9 B2			
Titchfield Rd NW8	1 B1	Ave.		£1 & 20p
Tite St SW3	17 C4	Bd.		20p
Tolmers Sq NW1	2 F4	Ave.	Ave.	£1 & 20p
Tolpuddle St N1	4 E2			
Tomlinson Clo E2	6 E3			
Tompion St EC1	4 F3			
Tonbridge St WC1	3 B3	Bd.		£1 & 20p
Tooley St EC1	13 B3			
Tooley St SE1	14 D4			
Tor Gdns W8	7 C4	Bd.		20p
Torrington Pl WC1	3 A5	Ave.		£1 & 20p
Torrington Sq WC1	3 A4			
Tothill St SW1	11 B5	Gd.		£1 / P & D
Tottenham Ct Rd W1	2 F4	Ave.		£1 & 20p
	3 A5			
	11 A1			
Tottenham St W1	3 A5	Ave.		£1 & 20p
Toulmin St SE1	13 A5			
Tournay Rd SW6	15 C5			
Tower Bridge E1	14 D3			
Tower Bridge SE1	14 D4			
Tower Bridge Approach E1	14 E3			
Tower Bridge Rd SE1	14 D4			
Tower Hill EC3	14 D2			
Tower of London EC3	14 D3			
Townshend Rd NW8	1 B1	Gd.	Bd.	£1 & 20p / P & D
Toynbee St E1	14 D1			
Tradescant Rd SW8	19 C5			
Trafalgar Sq SW1	11 B3			
Trafalgar Sq WC2	11 B3			
Treasury The SW1	11 B5			
Treaty St N1	3 C1			
Trebovir Rd SW5	15 C3	Gd.	Gd.	20p
Tregunter Rd SW10	16 E4	Ave.	Bd.	20p
Trevanion Rd W14	15 A2			
Trevor Pl SW7	9 B5	Ave.		£1
Trevor Sq SW7	9 B5	Gd.	Ave.	£1
Trevor St SW7	9 B5			
Trinity Church Sq SE1	13 A5	Ave.		£1, 50p & 20p / 20p
Trinity Sq EC3	14 D2			
Trinity St SE1	13 A5	Gd.		£1, 50p & 20p / 20p
Triton Sq NW1	2 F4			
Trocadero Centre W1	11 A2			
Tudor St EC4	12 E2	Gd.		£1 & 20p
Tufton St SW1	19 B1			
Turin St E2	6 E3			
Turk's Row SW3	17 C3			
	18 D3	Gd.	Bd.	£1 & 20p
Turneville Rd W14	15 B4			
Turnmill St EC1	4 E5	Gd.	Ave.	£1 & 20p
Turpentine La SW1	18 E3			
Thurtle Rd E2	6 E1			
Twyford St N1	3 C1			
Tyers Gate SE1	13 C5			
Tyers St SE11	20 D2			
Tyers Terr SE11	20 D3			
U				

Each place name is followed by its postal district, its atlas reference, 2 hour meters, 4 hour meters and then by the coins accepted

Street Name		2hrs	4hrs	Coins
Ufford St SE1	12 E4	Ave.		£1, 50p & 20p / 20p
Underwood Rd E1	6 F5			
Underwood St N1	5 B3			
Unicorn Pass SE1	14 D3			
Union Sq N1	5 A1			
Union St SE1	12 F4			
	13 A4	Gd.		£1, 50p & 20p / 20p
Union Wlk E2	6 D3			
University St WC1	3 A4	Gd.		£1 & 20p
University College WC1	3 A4			
University College Hospital WC1	3 A4			
Upcerne Rd SW10	16 E5	Gd.	Gd.	20p
Upper St N1	4 F1			
Upper Belgrave Street SW1	18 E1	Gd.	Bd.	£1 & 20p
Upper Berkeley St W1	9 C1	Gd.		£1 / P & D
Upper Brook St W1	10 D2	Gd.		£1 / P & D
Upper Cheyne Row SW3	17 B4			
Upper Grosvenor St W1	10 D3	Gd.		£1 / P & D
Upper Ground SE1	12 E3	Gd.		20p
Upper Marsh SE1	12 D5	Ave.	Bd.	20p
Upper Montagu St W1	1 C5	Gd.		£ 1
Upper Phillimore Gdns W8	7 C5	Ave.		£1 & 20p
Upper St Martin's La WC2	11 B2			
Upper Tachbrook St SW1	18 F2	Gd.		£1 & 20p / P & D
Upper Thames St EC4	13 A2			
Upper Wimpole St W1	2 D5	Gd.	Bd.	£1 / P & D
Upper Woburn Pl WC1	3 B4	Ave.		£1 & 20p
US Embassy W1	10 D2			
Uverdale Rd SW10	16 F5	Ave.	Gd.	20p
Uxbridge St W8	7 C3	Gd.	Bd.	20p
V				
Vale The SW3	17 A4	Gd.	Bd.	20p
Valentine Pl SE1	12 F5	Bd.		£1, 50p & 20p / 20p
Vallance Rd E1 E2	6 F4			
Vanston Pl SW6	15 C5			
Varndell St NW1	2 F3	Ave.		£1 & 20p
Vassall Rd SW9	20 E5			
Vaughan Way E1	14 F3			
Vauxhall Bridge SW1	19 B3			
Vauxhall Bridge Rd SW1 SE1	18 F1			
	19 A2			
Vauxhall Gro SW8	19 C4			
Vauxhall Park SW8	19 C4			
Vauxhall St SE11	20 D3			
Vauxhall Wlk SE11	19 C3			
Vere St W1	10 E1			
Vereker Rd W14	15 A3			
Vernon Rise WC1	4 D3	Ave.		£1 & 20p
Vernon St W14	15 A2			
Vestry St N1	5 B3			
Vicarage Gate W8	8 D4	Gd.	Bd.	20p
Victoria & Albert Museum SW7	17 A1			
Victoria Embankment EC4	12 E2			
Victoria Embankment SW1	11 C4			
Victoria Embankment WC2	11 C3	Gd.		£1 / P & D / £1 & 20p
Victoria Gro W8	16 E1			
Victoria Rd W8	8 E5			
	16 E1	Gd.	Bd.	£1 & 20p
Victoria Sq SW1	18 E1	Ave.	Gd.	£1 & 20p
Victoria St SW1	11 B5			
	18 F1			
	19 A1			
Victoria Tower Gardens SW1	19 C1			
Villiers St WC2	11 C3			
Vince St EC1	5 C3			
Vincent Sq SW1	19 A2	Gd.	Bd.	£1 & 20p / P & D
Vincent St SW1	19 A2	Ave.		£1 & 20p
Vincent Terr N1	4 F2	Gd.		£1 & 20p
Vine La SE1	14 D4			
Vine St EC3	14 D2	Ave.		£1 & 20p
Vintner's Pl EC4	13 A2			
Virginia Rd E2	6 D3			
Voss St E2	6 F3			
W				
Wakefield St WC1	3 C4	Bd.		£1 & 20p
Wakley St EC1	4 F3			
Walbrook EC4	13 B2	Ave.		£1 & 20p
Walcot Sq SE11	20 E1	Gd.	Bd.	20p
Waldorf Hotel WC2	11 C2			
Walham Gro SW6	15 C5			
Wallace Collection W1	10 D1			
Walmer Rd W11	7 A3	Gd.	Gd.	20p
Walnut Tree Wlk SE11	20 D1	Ave.		20p
Walpole St SW3	17 C3	Gd.	Bd.	£1 & 20p
Walton Pl SW3	17 C1	Ave.	Ave.	£1 & 20p
Walton St SW3	17 B2	Ave.	Gd.	£1 & 20p
Wandon Rd SW6	16 E5			
Wandsworth Rd SW8	19 B5			
Wansdown Pl SW6	16 D5			
Wapping High St E1	14 F4			
Wardour St W1	11 A2	Gd.		£ 1
Warham St SE5	20 F5			
Warner Pl E2	6 F2			
Warner St EC1	4 E4	Gd.		£1 & 20p
Warren St W1	2 F4	Gd.		£1 & 20p
Warwick Gdns W14	15 B1	Gd.	Ave.	20p
Warwick La EC4	12 F1			
Warwick Rd SW5	16 D3	Gd.	Gd.	20p
Warwick Rd W14	15 B1			
Warwick Sq SW1	18 F2	Gd.		£1 & 20p / P & D
Warwick St W1	10 F2	Gd.		£ 1
Warwick Way SW1	18 F2	Bd.		£1 & 20p
Waterford Rd SW6	16 D5			
Watergate EC4	12 F2	Ave.		£1 & 20p
Waterloo Bridge SE1 WC2	12 D3	Gd.		20p
Waterloo Pl SW1	11 A3	Gd.		£1 / P & D
Waterloo Rd SE1	12 E4	Ave.		20p
Waterson St E2	6 D3			
Watling St EC4	13 A2	Gd.		£1 & 20p
Weaver St E1	6 E4			
Weavers La SE1	14 D4			
Webber Row SE1	12 E5	Gd.		£1, 50p & 20p / 20p
Webber St SE1	12 E4			
	13 A5	Gd.		£1, 50p & 20p / 20p
Weighouse St W1	10 D2			
Welbeck St W1	10 D1	Gd.		£ 1
Weller St SE1	13 A5			
Wellesley Terr N1	5 A3			
Wellington Arch W1	10 D4			
Wellington Bldgs SW1	18 E3			
Wellington Pl NW8	1 A3	Gd.	Gd.	£1 & 20p
Wellington Rd NW8	1 A2			
Wellington Row E2	6 E3			
Wellington Sq SW3	17 C3			
Wellington St WC2	11 C2	Gd.		£ 1
Wells Rise NW8	1 C1			
Wells St W1	10 F1	Gd.		£ 1
Wenlock Basin N1	5 A2			
Wenlock Rd N1	5 A2			
Wenlock St N1	5 B2			
Wentworth St E1	14 D1			
Werrington St NW1	3 A2	Ave.		£1 & 20p
Wesley's House & Chapel EC1	5 B4			
West Sq SE11	20 F1			
West St WC2	11 B2			
West Cromwell Rd SW5 W14	15 B3	Bd.	Gd.	20p
West Eaton Pl SW1	18 D1			
West Harding St EC4	12 E1			
West Pier E1	14 F4			
West Smithfield EC1	12 F1	Gd.		£1 & 20p
West Tenter St E1	14 E2			
Westbourne Cres W2	8 F2			
Westbourne Gdns W2	8 D1	Gd.	Gd.	£1 & 20p

Street Name		2hrs	4hrs	Coins
Westbourne Gro W2	8 D2	Gd.	Ave.	20p / £1 & 20p / P & D
Westbourne Gro W11	7 B2	Bd.		£1 & 20p
Westbourne Grove Terr W2	8 D1	Bd.		£1 & 20p
Westbourne Pk Rd W2	8 D1			
Westbourne Pk Rd W11	7 B1	Gd.	Bd.	20p / £1 & 20p
Westbourne Pk Vlls W2	8 D1	Ave.		£1 & 20p
Westbourne St W2	9 A2			
Westbourne Terr W2	8 E1			
Westcott Rd SE17	20 F4			
Westgate Terr SW10	16 D3	Bd.		20p
Westland Pl N1	5 B3			
Westminster Abbey SW1	11 B5			
Westminster Bridge SE1 SW1	11 C5			
Westminster Bridge Rd SE1	12 D5	Ave.		£1, 50p & 20p / 20p
Westminster Cathedral SW1	18 F1			
Westminster Hospital SW1	19 B1			
Westminster School Playing Fields SW1	19 A2			
Westmoreland Pl SW1	18 E3			
Westmoreland St W1	2 D5	Gd.		£ 1
Westminster Terr SW1	18 E3	Ave.	Gd.	£1 & 20p
Weston Rise WC1	4 D3	Ave.		£1 & 20p
Weston St SE1	13 C4	Ave.		£1, 50p & 20p / 20p
Westway A40(M) W10	7 A1			
Wetherby Gdns SW5	16 E2	Gd.	Ave.	20p
Wetherby Pl SW7	16 E2			
Weymouth Ms W1	2 E5			
Weymouth St W1	2 E5	Gd.		£ 1
Weymouth Terr E2	6 E2			
Wharf Pl E2	6 F1			
Wharf Rd N1	5 A2			
Wharfedale St SW10	16 D1	Ave.	Gd.	20p
Wharfdale Rd N1	3 C2			
Wharton St WC1	4 D3	Ave.		£1 & 20p
Wheatsheaf La SW8	19 C5			
Wheler St E1	6 D4			
Whetstone Pk WC2	12 D1	Bd.		£1 & 20p
Whiston Rd E2	6 D1			
Whitbread Brewery EC2	5 B5			
Whitcomb St WC2	11 A3	Bd.		£ 1
White Lion St N1	4 E2	Gd.		£1 & 20p
White's Row E1	6 D5			
Whitechapel Art Gallery E1	14 E1			
Whitechapel High St E1	14 E1			
Whitechapel Rd E1	6 F5 / 14 E1			
Whitechurch La E1	14 E1			
Whitecross St EC1 EC2	5 A4	Ave.	Bd.	£1 & 20p
Whitfield St W1	2 F4	Gd.		£1 & 20p
Whitefriars St EC4	12 E2			
Whitehall SW1	11 B3			
Whitehall Ct SW1	11 C4			
Whitehall Pl SW1	11 B4			
Whitehall Theatre SW1	11 B3			
Whitehead's Gro SW3	17 B2	Gd.	Ave.	£1 & 20p
White's Grounds SE1	14 D4			
Whitfield St W1	3 A5			
Whitgift St SE11	19 C2			
Whitmore Rd N1	5 C1			
Whittaker St SW1	18 D2		Gd.	£1 & 20p
Whittlesey St SE1	12 E4	Ave.		20p
Wicker St E1	14 F2			
Wickham St SE11	20 D3			
Wicklow St WC1	3 C3	Bd.		£1 & 20p
Wigmore Hall W1	10 E1			
Wigmore St W1	10 D1	Ave.		£ 1
Wilcox Rd SW8	19 B5			
Wild Ct WC2	11 C1			
Wild St WC2	11 C1			
Wild's Rents SE1	13 C5	Ave.		£1, 50p & 20p / 20p
Wilfred St SW1	10 F5	Ave.		£ 1
Wilkinson St SW8	19 C5			
William St SW1	9 C5	Ave.		£1 & 20p
William IV St WC2	11 B3	Gd.		£ 1
William Rd NW1	2 F3	Ave.		£1 & 20p
Willow Pl SW1	18 F2	Ave.		£1 & 20p
Willow St EC2	5 C4			
Wilmer Gdns N1	5 C1			
Wilmer Gdns N1	6 D1			
Wilmington Ms SW1	9 C5			
Wilmington Sq WC1	4 E3	Bd.		£1 & 20p
Wilsham St W11	7 A3			
Wilkes St E1	6 E5			
Wilson Gro SE16	14 F5			
Wilson St EC2	5 C5			
Wilton Cres SW1	10 D5	Gd.		£1 & 20p / P & D
Wilton Pl SW1	10 D5	Ave.	Gd.	£1 & 20p
Wilton Rd SW1	18 F1	Bd.		£1 & 20p
Wilton Row SW1	10 D5			
Wilton Sq N1	5 B1			
Wilton St SW1	18 E1	Gd.	Bd.	£1 & 20p
Wiltshire Row N1	5 B1			
Wimborne St N1	5 B2			
Wimpole Ms W1	2 E5			
Wimpole St W1	2 E5 / 10 E1	Gd.		£1 / P & D
Winchester Clo SE17	20 F2			
Winchester St SW1	18 E3	Ave.	Gd.	£1 & 20p
Wincott St SE11	20 E2	Bd.		20p
Windmill Wlk SE1	12 E4	Bd.		20p
Windsor Terr N1	5 A3			
Winfield House NW1	1 B3			
Winsland St W2	8 F1 / 9 A1			
Woburn Pl WC1	3 B4	Ave.		£1 & 20p
Woburn Sq WC1	3 B4			
Woburn Wlk WC1	3 B4			
Wolseley St SE1	14 E5			
Wood Clo E2	6 F4			
Wood St EC2	13 A1	Gd.		£1 & 20p
Woodbridge St EC1	4 F4	Ave.		£1 & 20p
Woods Ms W1	10 D2	Bd.		£ 1
Woodseer St E1	6 E5			
Woodsford Sq W14	7 A4			
Woodstock St W1	10 E2	Ave.		£ 1
Wootton St SE1	12 E4			
Worfield St SW11	17 B5			
World's End Pas SW10	16 F5			
Wormwood St EC2	13 C1			
Woronzow Rd NW8	1 A1	Bd.		£1 & 20p
Worship St EC2	5 C4	Ave.	Bd.	£1 & 20p
Wren St WC1	4 D4	Gd.		£1 & 20p
Wright's La W8	8 D5		Gd.	£1 & 20p
Wyclif St EC1	4 F3	Bd.		£1 & 20p
Wyndham Rd SE5	20 F5			
Wyndham St W1	1 C5	Gd.		£ 1
Wynford Rd N1	4 D2			
Wynyatt St EC1	4 F3			
Wyvil Rd SW8	19 B5			
Y				
Yardley St WC1	4 E4	Ave.	Bd.	£1 &
Yeoman's Row SW3	17 B1	Bd.	Gd.	£1 &
York Gate NW1	2 D4			
York House Pl W8	8 D4			
York Rd SE1	12 D4			
York St W1	1 B5	Gd.		
York Ter East NW1	2 D4			
York Ter West NW1	2 D4			
York Way N1	3 C1			
Yorkton St E2	6 E2			
Young St W8	8 D5			

0p
20p

1 / P & D

eters and then by the coins accepted